THE NEXT 4 BILLION

MARKET SIZE AND BUSINESS STRATEGY AT THE BASE OF THE PYRAMID

THE NEXT 4 BILLION

MARKET SIZE AND BUSINESS STRATEGY AT THE BASE OF THE PYRAMID

Four billion low-income consumers, a majority of the world's population, constitute the base of the economic pyramid. New empirical measures of their aggregate purchasing power and their behavior as consumers suggest significant opportunities for market-based approaches to better meet their needs, increase their productivity and incomes, and empower their entry into the formal economy.

Allen L. Hammond, William J. Kramer,
Robert S. Katz, Julia T. Tran, Courtland Walker

World Resources Institute
International Finance Corporation

A co-publication of World Resources Institute and International Finance Corporation

World Resources Institute
10 G Street NE, Suite 800
Washington DC 20002

International Finance Corporation
2121 Pennsylvania Avenue NW
Washington DC 20433

ISBN 1-56973-625-1 (soft cover)
Library of Congress Control Number 2007923530

Order Information:
Western Hemisphere and Japan
Hopkins Fulfillment Service
P.O. Box 50370
Baltimore, MD 21211-4370
Phone: (410) 516-6956 or (1-800) 537-5487
Fax: (410) 516-6998
Email: hfscustserv@press.jhu.edu
Visit WRI's online bookstore: www.wristore.com

U.K, Europe, Middle East, Africa, Asia
Eurospan Group, c/o Turpin Distribution
Phone: +44 (0) 1767 604972
Fax: +44 (0)1767 601640
Email: eurospan@turpin-distribution.com
Visit Eurospan's online bookstore: www.eurospangroup.com/bookstore

Sponsors and underwriters

Principal underwriting for *The Next 4 Billion* has been provided by the International Finance Corporation and the Inter-American Development Bank.

IFC
International Finance Corporation
World Bank Group

Inter-American Development Bank

Additional financial support has been provided by Intel, Microsoft, the Shell Foundation, and Visa International.

intel

Microsoft

Shell Foundation

VISA

Acknowledgments

This report owes its existence to many people and institutions, but the underlying research project would not have happened without the early, enthusiastic, and sustained support of Donald F. Terry, manager of the Multilateral Investment Fund of the Inter-American Development Bank (IDB). Don understood early on how important the markets formed by low-income communities are to the fund's investment strategy, and he has been an unflagging source of advice and assistance throughout the research. Through Don and other IDB colleagues, the IDB made a substantive contribution to the development of this report.

Luis Alberto Moreno, president of the IDB, provided important leadership. Under his guidance the IDB, through its Opportunity for the Majority initiative, became the first major international financial institution to incorporate a focus on the base of the economic pyramid (BOP) into new program strategies. We gratefully acknowledge the IDB for making this research a cornerstone of its "Building Opportunity for the Majority" conference in June 2006, where preliminary research results for Latin America and the Caribbean were first publicly presented.

The International Finance Corporation (IFC) stepped in to provide the major funding and to collaborate in the research. Michael Klein, vice president for financial and private sector development jointly for the World Bank and IFC as well as chief economist, IFC, immediately recognized its potential, agreed to a partnership, and became the project's chief advocate. We are grateful to IFC not only for its financial support but also for its substantive engagement with the project, including access to data, help with developing the methodology, and thoughtful advice in shaping the editorial content. Penelope Brook and Facundo Martin have been our caring and efficient task managers at IFC, making the partnership a uniquely effective one.

The research data structures are derived from the work of Branko Milanovic, lead economist with the World Bank's Research Department, and Olivier Dupriez, senior statistician and economist with the World Bank's Development Data Group. We are indebted to both for their gracious permission to use their research, much of which has not been previously published. They provided keen insights into the data and guidance on how best to understand and present them.

Research
We would also like to thank the following people for their research assistance:
IFC: Tefera Bekele and Gouthami Padam
IDB: Julio Guzman, Pavel Luengas-Sierra, Jose Antonia Mejia, Karen Mokate, and Jorge Ugaz

Content advice and review
We appreciate and acknowledge the advice of the following reviewers:
WRI: Alex Acs, Jennie Hommel, David Jhirad, Christian Layke, Smita Nakhooda, Daniel Prager, Clayton Rigdon, and Fred Wellington
IFC/World Bank: Alex Preker, Christine Zhen-Wei Quiang, Dilip Ratha, and Mark Williams

Content advice and review
External: Robert Annibale (Citigroup)
Louis Boorstin (Bill and Melinda Gates Foundation)
Christine Eibs Singer (E+Co)
Jeffery Galinovsky (Intel)
Kurt Hoffman (Shell Foundation)
Beth Jenkins (John F. Kennedy School of Government)
Christopher Jennings (IDB)
Alain Mathys (Suez)
Dominic Montagu (University of California, Berkeley)
Jane Nelson (John F. Kennedy School of Government),
C. K. Prahalad (University of Michigan)
James Wells (Wellspring Consulting)
Christopher West (Shell Foundation)
David Wheeler (York University)

General advice
For general advice we would like to thank:
IDB: Ana-Mita Betancourt, Suzanne Duryea, Nohra Rey de Marulanda, and Daniel Shepherd

IFC/World Bank: Doug Barnes, Kathleen Beegle, Paolo Belli, Robert Buckley, Marinela Dado, Vivien Foster, Jed Friedman, Elena Gagieva-Petrova, Matthew Gamser, Nadine Shamounki Ghannam, Iva Ilieva Hamel, April Harding, Martin Holtmann, Ada Karina Izaguirre, R. Mukami Kariuki, Elizabeth Littlefield, Alain Locussol, Emmett Moriarty, Vincent Palmade, Andrea Ryan-Rizvi, Prem Sangraula, Katherine Scott, Suzanne Smith, Kees van der Meer, and Patricia Veevers-Carter.

External: Brian Richardson (Wizzit)

WRI project manager
Allen L. Hammond

Book design
Design: Lloyd Greenberg Design, LLC
Information Graphics: Gerald Quinn / G.Quinn Information Design

Copyediting
Alison Strong

Photo credits
Cover photo: ©Julie Houck/Corbis
Health ©Karen Kasmauski/Corbis
ITC ©Anatoliy Rakhimbayev/World Bank
Water ©Benjamin Lowy/Corbis
Transportation courtesy of EMBARQ World Resources Institute
Housing ©Gideon Mendell/Corbis
Energy ©Rupak De Chowdhuri/Reuters/Corbis
Food ©Jehad Nga/ActionAid/Corbis
Finance ©Gideon Mendell/Corbis

CONTENTS

Data Guide

International dollars (purchasing power parity exchange rates) are used throughout this report unless otherwise specified. Market figures and household income and expenditure measured by household surveys are given in 2005 international dollars.

Current US dollars means 2005 dollars.

For convenience, however, BOP income figures used to describe BOP income segments or the BOP and mid-market income cut-offs are measured in 2002 international dollars (purchasing power parity dollars or PPP), since 2002 is the reference year to which the surveys used in this analysis were normalized. The BOP population segment is defined as those with annual incomes up to and including $3000 per capita per year (2002 PPP). The mid-market population segment is defined as those with annual incomes above $3,000 and up to and including $20,000 PPP. The high income segment includes annual incomes above $20,000 PPP. The report and accompanying country tables use annual income increments of $500 PPP within the BOP to distinguish six BOP income segments, denoted as BOP500, BOP1000, BOP1500, etc.

In 2005 international dollars, the cutoff for the BOP and the mid-market population segments are $3,260 and $21,731.

Regional aggregates

Aggregate data are presented for four developing regions—Africa, Asia (including the Middle East), Eastern Europe, and Latin America and the Caribbean as well as for the world as a whole. The report refers to surveyed countries, which includes 110 countries for which household survey data were available. (See Appendix A for a list of countries by developing region and for additional countries.) The report also refers to measured countries as those for which standardized survey data on household expenditures were available. (See Appendix B for a list of countries by region.)

Market Composition

The report analyzes market composition in terms of total annual income or expenditures by BOP income segments. The graphics representing the data, in 2005 PPP dollars, are scaled to produce figures of workable size, but show accurately the relative total household spending by income segment.

Household Expenditures

The report also analyzes household spending in terms of average annual per household expenditures. Again, the graphics representing the data are scaled, but show accurately the relative household spending for each BOP income segment.

Urban/Rural Analysis

The report illustrates the market composition by urban and rural locations, both for the total BOP market and by BOP income segment. The graphics representing the data are scaled, but show accurately the relative urban and rural spending.

EXECUTIVE SUMMARY

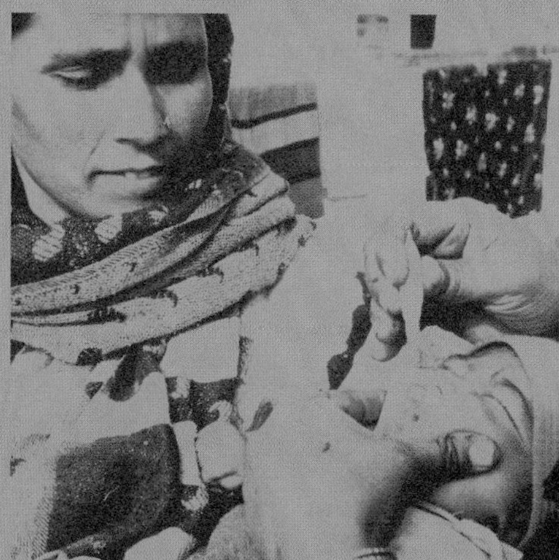

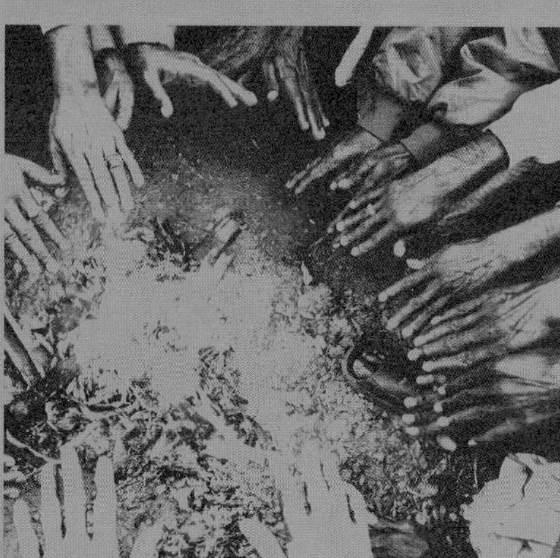

Four billion low-income people, a majority of the world's population, constitute the base of the economic pyramid. New empirical measures of their behavior as consumers and their aggregate purchasing power suggest significant opportunities for market-based approaches to better meet their needs, increase their productivity and incomes, and empower their entry into the formal economy.

The 4 billion people at the base of the economic pyramid (BOP)—all those with incomes below $3,000 in local purchasing power—live in relative poverty. Their incomes in current U.S. dollars are less than $3.35 a day in Brazil, $2.11 in China, $1.89 in Ghana, and $1.56 in India.[1] Yet together they have substantial purchasing power: the BOP constitutes a $5 trillion global consumer market.

The wealthier mid-market population segment, the 1.4 billion people with per capita incomes between $3,000 and $20,000, represents a $12.5 trillion market globally. This market is largely urban, already relatively well served, and extremely competitive.

In contrast, BOP markets are often rural—especially in rapidly growing Asia—very poorly served, dominated by the informal economy, and, as a result, relatively inefficient and uncompetitive. Yet these markets represent a substantial share of the world's population. Data from national household surveys in 110 countries show that the BOP makes up 72% of the 5,575 million people recorded by the surveys and an overwhelming majority of the population in Africa, Asia, Eastern Europe, and Latin America and the Caribbean—home to nearly all the BOP.

Analysis of the survey data—the latest available on incomes, expenditures, and access to services—shows marked differences across countries in the composition of these BOP markets. Some, like Nigeria's, are concentrated in the lowest income segments of the BOP; others, like those in Ukraine, are concentrated in the upper income segments. Regional differences are also apparent. Rural areas dominate most BOP markets in

Africa and Asia; urban areas dominate most in Eastern Europe and Latin America.

Striking patterns also emerge in spending. Not surprisingly, food dominates BOP household budgets. As incomes rise, however, the share spent on food declines, while the share for housing remains relatively constant—and the shares for transportation and telecommunications grow rapidly. In all regions half of BOP household spending on health goes to pharmaceuticals. And in all except Eastern Europe the lower income segments of the BOP depend mainly on firewood as a cooking fuel, the higher segments on propane or other modern fuels.

That these substantial markets remain underserved is to the detriment of BOP households. Business is also missing out. But there is now enough information about these markets, and enough experience with viable business strategies, to justify far closer business attention to the opportunities they represent. Market-based approaches also warrant far more attention in the development community, for the potential benefits they offer in bringing more of the BOP into the formal economy and in improving the delivery of essential services to this large population segment.

A BOP Portrait

The development community has tended to focus on meeting the needs of the poorest of the poor—the 1 billion people with incomes below $1 a day in local purchasing power. But a much larger segment of the low-income population—the 4 billion people of the BOP, all with incomes well below any Western poverty line—both deserves attention and is the appropriate focus of a market-oriented approach.

The starting point for this argument is not the BOP's poverty. Instead, it is the fact that BOP population segments for the most part are not integrated into the global market economy and do not benefit from it. They also share other characteristics:

- **Significant unmet needs.** Most people in the BOP have no bank account and no access to modern financial services. Most do not own a phone. Many live in informal settlements, with no formal title to their dwelling. And many lack access to water and sanitation services, electricity, and basic health care.
- **Dependence on informal or subsistence livelihoods.** Most in the BOP lack good access to markets to sell their labor, handi-

crafts, or crops and have no choice but to sell to local employers or to middlemen who exploit them. As subsistence and small-scale farmers and fishermen, they are uniquely vulnerable to destruction of the natural resources they depend on but are powerless to protect (World Resources Institute and others 2005). In effect, informality and subsistence are poverty traps.

- **Impacted by a BOP penalty.** Many in the BOP, and perhaps most, pay higher prices for basic goods and services than do wealthier consumers—either in cash or in the effort they must expend to obtain them—and they often receive lower quality as well. This high cost of being poor is widely shared: it is not just the very poor who often pay more for the transportation to reach a distant hospital or clinic than for the treatment, or who face exorbitant fees for loans or for transfers of remittances from relatives abroad.

Addressing the unmet needs of the BOP is essential to raising welfare, productivity, and income—to enabling BOP households to find their own route out of poverty. Engaging the BOP in the formal economy must be a critical part of any wealth-generating and inclusive growth strategy. And eliminating BOP penalties will increase effective income for the BOP. Moreover, to the extent that unmet needs, informality traps, and BOP penalties arise from inefficient or monopolistic markets or lack of attention and investment, addressing these barriers may also create significant market opportunities for businesses.

Perhaps most important, it is the entire BOP and not just the very poor who constitute the low-income market—and it is the entire market that must be analyzed and addressed for private sector strategies to be effective, even if there are segments of that market for which market-based solutions are not available or not sufficient.

Taking a market-based approach to poverty reduction

Analysis of BOP markets can help businesses and governments think more creatively about new products and services that meet BOP needs and about opportunities for market-based solutions to achieve them. For businesses, it is an important first step toward identifying business opportunities, considering business models, developing products, and expanding investment in BOP markets. For governments, it can help focus attention on reforms needed in the business environment to allow a larger role for the private sector.

BOP market analysis, and the market-based approach to poverty reduction on which it is based, are equally important for the development community. This approach can help frame the debate on poverty reduction more in terms of enabling opportunity and less in terms of aid. A successful market-based approach would bring significant new private sector resources into play, allowing development assistance to be more targeted to the segments and sectors for which no viable market solutions can presently be found.

There are distinct differences between a market-based approach to poverty reduction and more traditional approaches. Traditional approaches often focus on the very poor, proceeding from the assumption that they are unable to help themselves and thus need charity or public assistance. A market-based approach starts from the recognition that being poor does not eliminate commerce and market processes: virtually all poor households trade cash or labor to meet much of their basic needs. A market-based approach thus focuses on people as consumers and producers and on solutions that can make markets more efficient, competitive, and inclusive—so that the BOP can benefit from them.

Traditional approaches tend to address unmet needs for health care, clean water, or other basic necessities by setting targets for meeting those needs through direct public investments, subsidies, or other handouts. The goals may be worthy, but the results have not been strikingly successful. A market-based approach recognizes that it is not just the very poor who have unmet needs—and asks about willingness to pay across market segments. It looks for solutions in the form of new products and new business models that can provide goods and services at affordable prices.

Those solutions may involve market development efforts with elements similar to traditional development tools—hybrid business strategies that incorporate consumer education; microloans, consumer finance, or cross-subsidies among different income groups; franchise or retail agent strategies that create jobs and raise incomes; partnerships with the public sector or with nongovernmental organizations (NGOs). Yet the solutions are ultimately market oriented and demand driven—and many successful companies are adopting such strategies.

Perhaps most important, traditional approaches do not point toward sustainable solutions—while a market-oriented approach recognizes that only sustainable solutions can scale to meet the needs of 4 billion people.

Growing interest, growing success in BOP markets

Business interest in BOP markets is rising. Multinational companies have been pioneers, especially in food and consumer products. Large national companies have proved to be among the most innovative in meeting the needs of BOP consumers and producers, especially in such sectors as housing, agriculture, consumer goods, and financial services. And small start-ups and social entrepreneurs focusing on BOP markets are rapidly growing in number. But perhaps the strongest and most dramatic BOP success story is mobile telephony.

Between 2000 and 2005 the number of mobile subscribers in developing countries grew more than fivefold—to nearly 1.4 billion. Growth was rapid in all regions, but fastest in sub-Saharan Africa—Nigeria's subscriber base grew from 370,000 to 16.8 million in just four years (World Bank 2006b). Household surveys confirm substantial and growing mobile phone use in the BOP population, which has clearly benefited from the access mobile phones provide to jobs, to medical care, to market prices, to family members working away from home and the remittances they can send, and, increasingly, to financial services (Vodafone 2005).

A strong value proposition for low-income consumers has translated into financial success for mobile companies. Celtel, an entrepreneurial company operating in some of the poorest and least stable countries in Africa, went from start-up to telecom giant in just seven years. Acquired for US$3.4 billion in 2005, the company now has operations in 15 African countries and licenses covering more than 30% of the continent.

Not all sectors have found their footing in BOP markets yet. Privatized urban water systems, for example, have encountered financial and political difficulties in developing countries, and the result has been neither better service for low-income communities nor success for the companies. The energy sector has similarly had only limited success in providing affordable off-grid electricity or clean cooking fuels to rural BOP communities. But even these sectors have seen encouraging new ventures, and further development of technology and business models may expand BOP markets.

Moving toward a more hospitable environment for business

The operating and regulatory environments in developing countries can be challenging. Micro and small businesses especially face disadvantages. If they are informal, they cannot get investment finance, participate in value chains of larger companies, or sometimes even legally receive services from utilities. Condemned to remain small, they cannot generate wealth or many jobs. Nor do they contribute to the broader economy by paying taxes.

Most face barriers to joining the formal economy in the form of antiquated regulations and prohibitive requirements—dozens of steps, delays of many months, capital requirements beyond attainment for most of the BOP. In El Salvador, for example, starting a legitimate business used to take 115 days and many separate procedures—until recent reforms reduced the effort to 26 days and allowed registration with four separate agencies in a single visit. But even for legitimate small businesses, investment capital is generally unavailable and supporting services scarce.

Fortunately, there is growing recognition of the importance of removing barriers to small and medium-size businesses and a growing toolbox for moving firms into the formal economy and creating more efficient markets. And as the World Bank and International Finance Corporation (IFC) show, in their annual Doing Business reports, there is also mounting evidence that the tools work. In El Salvador five times as many businesses register annually since its reforms. Many countries, including China, have dropped minimum capital requirements. The pace of reform is accelerating, with more than 40 countries making changes in the most recent year surveyed.[2]

Coupled with reform is growing attention to enterprise development initiatives focusing on BOP markets and investment capital for small and medium-size businesses. Several international and bilateral development agencies are launching investment funds to support the growth of small and medium-size enterprises across the developing world. These efforts, and the growing private sector interest in investing in such enterprises in developing countries, explicitly recognize that an expanded private sector role and a bottom-up market approach are essential development strategies.

What BOP markets look like

Total household income of $5 trillion a year establishes the BOP as a potentially important global market. Within that market are large variations across regions, countries, and sectors in size and other characteristics.

Asia (including the Middle East) has by far the largest BOP market: 2.86 billion people with income of $3.47 trillion. This BOP market represents 83% of the region's population and 42% of the purchasing power—a significant share of Asia's rapidly growing consumer market.

Eastern Europe's $458 billion BOP market includes 254 million people, 64% of the region's population, with 36% of the income.

In Latin America the BOP market of $509 billion includes 360 million people, representing 70% of the region's population but only 28% of total household income, a smaller share than in other developing regions.

Africa has a slightly smaller BOP market, at $429 billion. But the BOP is by far the region's dominant consumer market, with 71% of purchasing power. It includes 486 million people—95% of the surveyed population.

Sector markets for the 4 billion BOP consumers range widely in size. Some are relatively small, such as water ($20 billion) and information and communication technology, or ICT ($51 billion as measured, but probably twice that now as a result of rapid growth). Some are medium scale, such as health ($158 billion), transportation ($179 billion), housing ($332 billion), and energy ($433 billion). And some are truly large, such as food ($2,895 billion).[3]

Evidence of BOP penalties emerges in several sectors. Wealthier mid-market households are seven times as likely as BOP households to have access to piped water. Some 24% of BOP households lack access to electricity, while only 1% of mid-market households do. Rural BOP households have significantly lower ICT spending and are significantly less likely to own a phone than rural mid-market households or even urban BOP households—consistent with the broad lack of access to ICT services in rural areas.

BOP business strategies that work

Why are some enterprises succeeding in meeting BOP needs, and others are not? Successful enterprises operating in these markets use four broad strategies that appear to be critical:

- **Focusing on the BOP** with unique products, unique services, or unique technologies that are appropriate to BOP needs and that require completely reimagining the business, often through significant investment of money and management talent. Examples are found in such sectors as water (point-of-use systems), food (healthier products), finance (microfinance and low-cost remittance systems), housing, and energy.
- **Localizing value creation** through franchising, through agent strategies that involve building local ecosystems of vendors or suppliers, or by treating the community as the customer, all of which usually involve substantial investment in capacity building and training. Examples can be seen in health care (franchise and agent-based direct marketing), ICT (local phone entrepreneurs and resellers), food (agent-based distribution systems), water (community-based treatment systems), and energy (mini-hydropower systems).
- **Enabling access** to goods or services—financially (through single-use or other packaging strategies that lower purchase barriers, prepaid or other innovative business models that achieve the same result, or financing approaches) or physically (through novel distribution strategies or deployment of low-cost technologies). Examples occur in food, ICT, and consumer products (in packaging goods and services in small unit sizes, or "sachets") and in health care (such as cross-subsidies and community-based health insurance). And cutting across many sectors are financing strategies that range from microloans to mortgages.
- **Unconventional partnering** with governments, NGOs, or groups of multiple stakeholders to bring the necessary capabilities to the table. Examples are found in energy, transportation, health care, financial services, and food and consumer goods.

Enterprises may—and often do—use more than one of these strategies serially or in combination.

Endnotes

1. In this report current U.S. dollars means 2005 dollars. Unless otherwise noted, however, market information is given in 2005 international dollars (adjusted for purchasing power parity); for convenience, BOP and mid-market income cutoffs are given in international dollars for 2002 (the base year to which household surveys used in the analysis for the report have been normalized). U.S. dollars are generally denoted by US$, international dollars by $.
2. The tools are available in the World Bank and IFC's annual Doing Business reports, along with country ratings of progress on reform. For the most recent results, see World Bank and IFC (2006).
3. The analysis of market size starts with household expenditure data from 36 countries for which recorded expenditures have been mapped into standard spending categories. (The underlying surveys may vary from country to country and across time, however, so that information collected may not be directly comparable.) The analysis estimates the size of sector markets in each region by extrapolating from these measured countries to a broader set of surveyed countries for which BOP income data exist. This approach assumes that the ratio of sector expenditure to total household expenditure will be similar in the two sets of countries within a region. It also assumes that total household income equals total household expenditure.

CHAPTER ONE

Introduction and Market Overview

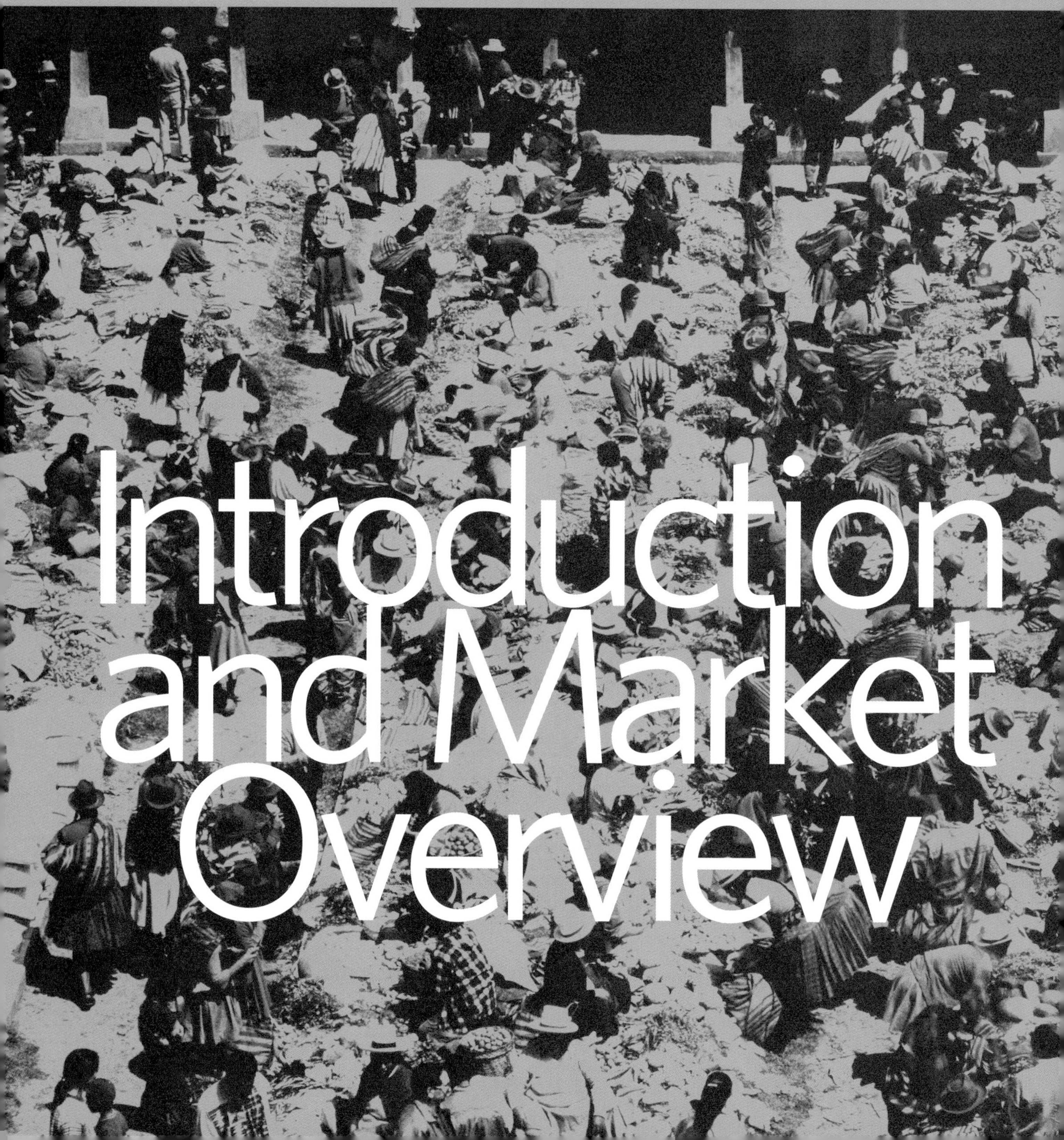

In an informal suburb of Guadalajara, Mexico, a growing family is struggling to expand their small house. Help arrives from a major industrial company in the form of construction designs, credit, and as-needed delivery of materials, enabling rapid completion of the project at less overall cost.

In rural Madhya Pradesh, an Indian farmer gains access to soil testing services, to market price trends that help him decide what to grow and when to sell, and to higher prices for his crop than he can obtain in the local auction market. The new system is an innovation of a large grain-buying corporation, which also benefits from cost saving and more direct market access.

A South African who lives in an impoverished, crime-ridden neighborhood of Johannesburg has no bank account, cannot order items from a distant store, and is sometimes robbed of her pay packet. She finds that a new financial service offered by a local start-up company allows her mobile phone to become a solution—her pay is deposited directly to her phone-based account, she can make purchases via an associated debit card, and she carries no cash to steal.

In a small community outside Tianjin, China, a small merchant whose children have been repeatedly sickened by drinking water from a heavily-polluted river is distraught. He finds help not from the overwhelmed municipal government but from a new, low-cost filtering system, developed by an entrepreneurial company, which enables his family to treat its water at the point of use.

Four billion people such as these form the base of the economic pyramid (BOP)—those with incomes below $3,000 (in local purchasing power). The BOP makes up 72% of the 5,575 million people recorded by available national household surveys worldwide and an overwhelming majority of the population in the developing countries of Africa, Asia, Eastern Europe, and Latin America and the Caribbean—home to nearly all the BOP.

BOP market—$5 trillion
TOTAL BY INCOME SEGMENT

Four billion people form the base of the economic pyramid (BOP)—those with incomes below $3,000 (in local purchasing power).

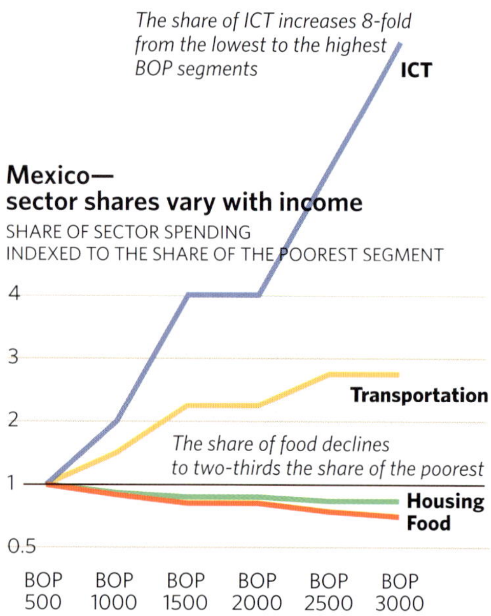

This large segment of humanity faces significant unmet needs and lives in relative poverty: in current U.S. dollars their incomes are less than $3.35 a day in Brazil, $2.11 in China, $1.89 in Ghana, and $1.56 in India. Yet together they have substantial purchasing power: the BOP constitutes a $5 trillion global consumer market.

The wealthier mid-market population segment, the 1.4 billion people with per capita incomes between $3,000 and $20,000, represents a $12.5 trillion market globally. This market is largely urban, already relatively well served, and extremely competitive.

BOP markets, in contrast, are often rural—especially in rapidly growing Asia—very poorly served, dominated by the informal economy, and as a result relatively inefficient and uncompetitive. The analysis reported here suggests significant opportunities for more inclusive market-based approaches that can better meet the needs of those in the BOP, increase their productivity and incomes, and empower their entry into the formal economy.

The analysis draws on data from national household surveys in 110 countries and an additional standardized set of surveys from 36 countries. Using these data—on incomes, expenditures, and access to services—it characterizes BOP markets regionally and nationally, in urban and rural areas, and by sector and income level. The results show striking patterns in spending. Food dominates BOP household budgets. As incomes rise, however, the share spent on food declines, while the share for housing remains relatively constant—and the share for transportation and telecommunications grows rapidly.

The composition of these BOP markets differs markedly across countries. Some, like Nigeria's, are concentrated in the lowest income segments of the BOP; others, like those in Ukraine, are concentrated in the upper income segments. Regional differences are also apparent. Rural areas dominate most BOP markets in Africa and Asia; urban areas dominate most in Eastern Europe and Latin America and the Caribbean.

Nigeria
TOTAL SPENDING BY INCOME SEGMENT

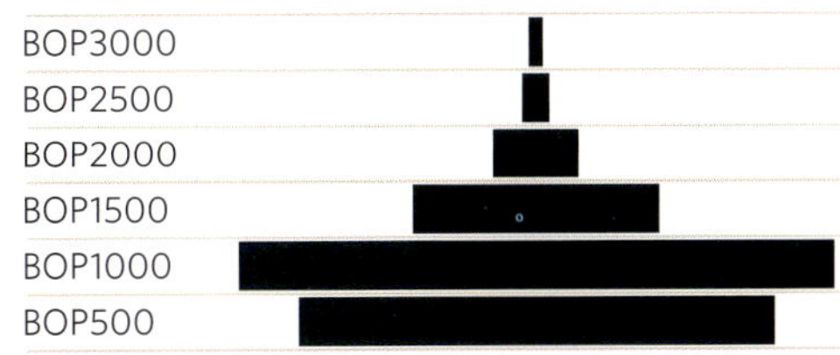

Ukraine
TOTAL SPENDING BY INCOME SEGMENT

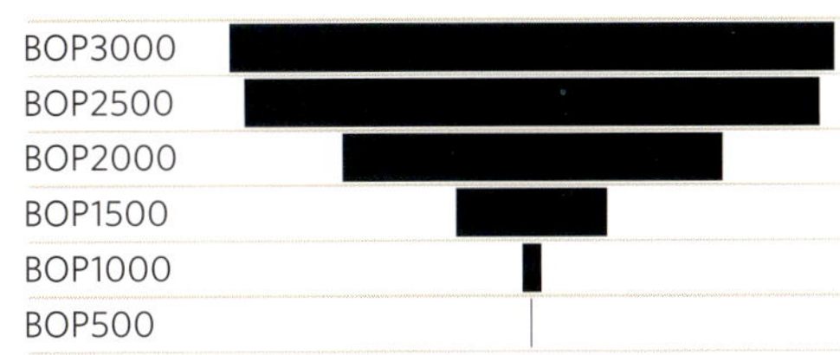

What's new in this analysis?

The underlying proposition that business activities can help reduce poverty is not new. Many books and influential reports have outlined both the need and the preconditions for a greater role for the private sector in development (see, for example, Commission on the Private Sector and Development 2004).

This report adds two important missing elements: a detailed if preliminary economic portrait of the BOP—based on recorded incomes and expenditures—and an overview of sector-specific business strategies from successful enterprises operating in BOP markets. These data and the record of experience back the calls for broader business engagement with the BOP. Moreover, a guide to BOP markets is timely because significant new investment—public and private—is being committed to serving the BOP.

This work builds on concepts introduced by Hart and Prahalad (2002), Prahalad and Hammond (2002), Prahalad (2005), and Hart (2005) and explored by a growing number of authors (Banerjee and Duflo 2006; Kahane and others 2005; Lodge and Wilson 2006; Wilson and Wilson 2006; Sullivan 2007). Based on their own definitions of the BOP, these analysts have offered preliminary estimates of the BOP population varying from 4 billion to 5 billion. Providing an empirical foundation and a consistent, worldwide set of baseline data is one motivation for the analysis reported here. The analysis, with a focus on documenting BOP income and expenditures, parallels similar efforts by Hernando De Soto to document their assets (see box 1.1).

The development community has tended to focus on meeting the needs of the poorest of the poor—the 1 billion people with incomes below $1 a day (in local purchasing power). This analysis argues that a much larger segment of the low-income population—the 4 billion people of the BOP, all with incomes well below any Western poverty line—both deserves our concern and is the appropriate focus of a market-oriented approach. The starting point for the analysis is not just the BOP's relative poverty. Instead, it is the fact that BOP populations for the most part are

Asia

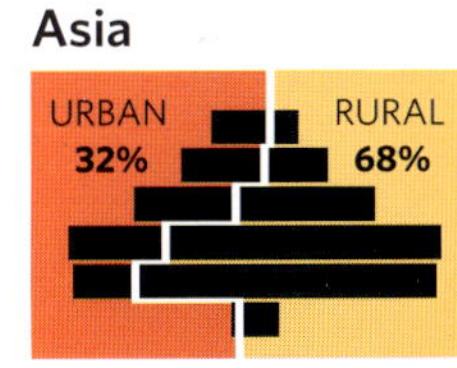

Latin America

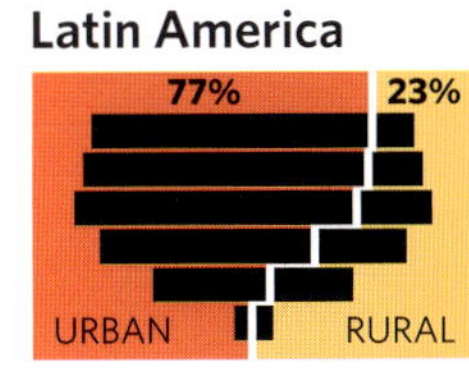

Total BOP spending by income segment, urban and rural

> BOX 1.1:
> **HIDDEN PURCHASING POWER, DEAD CAPITAL**
>
> The income and spending patterns of the BOP, made explicit in this report's analysis, have for too long been hidden from business by lack of data on the informal economy and the perception of the purchasing power of the poor as insignificant. As Hernando De Soto (2003) has pointed out, this purchasing power could be substantially increased if the BOP could leverage the wealth trapped in the assets of the informal economy. A recent study showed, for example, that the "dead capital" represented by informal properties and businesses in 12 Latin American countries is worth as much as US$1.2 trillion (ILD 2006; IDB 2006). Unlocking these assets, by providing land titles and lowering barriers to formal registration of small businesses, could greatly expand BOP markets.

not integrated into the global market economy and do not benefit from it. Those in the BOP also have significant unmet basic needs and often pay higher prices than mid-market consumers for the same service or commodity—a BOP penalty. These characteristics profile a unique market (see box 1.2).

A key issue in understanding BOP markets is informality. The International Labour Organisation (ILO 2002) estimates that more than 70% of the workforce in developing countries operates in the informal or underground economy, suggesting that most BOP livelihoods come from self-employment or from work in enterprises that are not legally organized businesses. This informal economy is a significant fraction of the size of the formal economy. According to a detailed study by economist Friedrich Schneider (2005), the informal economy averages 30% of official GDP in Asia, 40% in Eastern Europe, and 43% in both Africa and Latin America and the Caribbean. Informality is a trap for the assets and the growth potential of micro and small businesses and those who work in them.

Another important source of income for many BOP households is remittances from family members working overseas, much of which travels through informal channels. Recent work by the Inter-American Development Bank and the World Bank has documented the growing importance of remittances. In 2005 such transfers through official channels amounted to US$232 billion, of which US$167 billion went to developing countries—though actual amounts, including remittances through informal channels, may have been as much as 50% more (World Bank 2006a).[3]

These results together suggest that a significant part of BOP income comes from activities and sources that are only indirectly reflected in national economic statistics. Household surveys, in contrast, usually seek to capture all sources of income or total expenditures. Reporting of income may not be precise, but in this report the income data are buttressed by detailed, standardized expenditure data in a substantial subset of countries. Thus the BOP market analysis here, based on household surveys, provides the most direct measure of total income and expenditures and of the economic impact of informal employment and remittances.

Moreover, the surveys, despite some limitations for the purposes here,[4] provide direct information on the BOP as consumers that is not available from other sources of economic data. This report uses those data to dissect and characterize the economic behavior of the BOP in some detail—providing, for the first time, a systematic empirical characterization of BOP markets.

This work underlines the fact that the low income market includes far more people than the very poor—and the entire market must be analyzed and addressed for private sector strategies to be effective, even if there are segments of that market for which market-based solutions are not available or not sufficient.

Addressing the unmet needs of the BOP is essential to raising welfare, productivity, and income—to enabling BOP households to find their own route out of poverty. Engaging the BOP in the formal economy must be a critical part of any wealth-generating and inclusive growth strategy. And eliminating BOP penalties will increase effective income for the BOP. Moreover, to the extent that unmet needs, informality traps, and BOP penalties arise from inefficient or monopolistic markets or lack of attention and investment, addressing these barriers may also create significant market opportunities for businesses.

A key issue in understanding BOP markets is informality. The International Labour Organisation (ILO 2002) estimates that more than 70% of the workforce in developing countries operates in the informal or underground economy, suggesting that most BOP livelihoods come from self-employment or from work in enterprises that are not legally organized businesses.

BOX 1.2:

A BOP PORTRAIT

LIVING AT THE BOP

The BOP is characterized not only by low income—below $3,000 per capita per year—but also by several other shared characteristics:

- **Significant unmet needs.** Most of those in the BOP have no bank account or access to modern financial services—if they borrow, it is typically from local moneylenders at very high interest rates. Most do not own a phone. Many live in informal settlements and have no formal title to their dwelling. And many lack access to water and sanitation services, electricity, and basic health care.
- **Dependence on informal or subsistence livelihoods.** Most of those in the BOP are poorly integrated into the formal economy, which limits their economic opportunities. As producers, they often lack good access to markets to sell their labor, handicrafts, or surplus crops and have no choice but to sell to local employers or to middlemen who exploit them. As subsistence and small-scale farmers and fishermen, they are uniquely vulnerable to destruction of the natural resources they depend on but are powerless to protect (World Resources Institute and others 2005). In effect, informality and subsistence are poverty traps.
- **Impacted by a BOP penalty.** Many of those in the BOP, and perhaps most, pay higher prices for basic goods and services than do wealthier consumers—either in cash or in the effort they must expend to obtain them—and they often receive lower quality as well. For some services BOP consumers lack access altogether. The high cost of being poor is widely shared: it is not just the very poor who must walk long distances for water or firewood, or who often pay more for the transportation to reach a distant hospital or clinic than for the treatment, or who face exorbitant fees for loans or for transfers of remittances from relatives abroad.

POPULATION AND SPENDING

Low income is not no income. While the lowest BOP income segments are very poor by any standard, the economic structure of low-income populations varies from region to region and country to country. In addition, there are very large numbers of people in the mid- to high-income segments of the BOP itself, and these populations represent significant purchasing power.

Africa

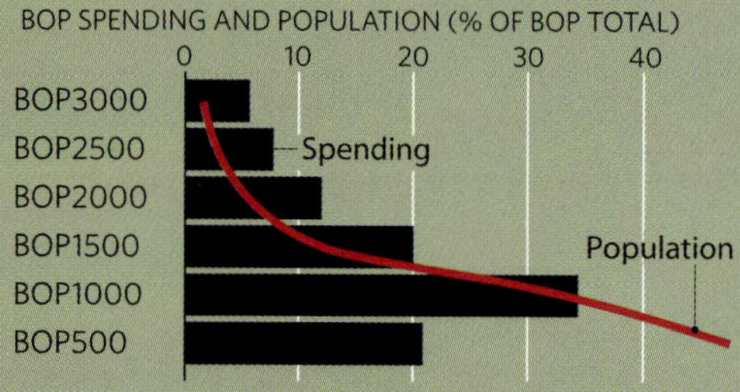

Asia

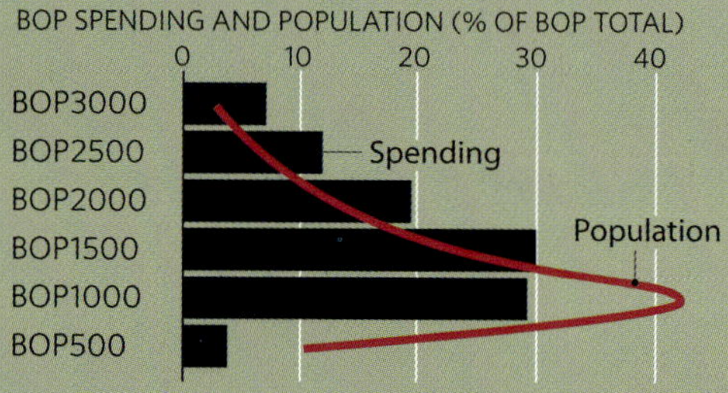

REGIONAL PROFILES

The BOP market in Asia (including the Middle East) is by far the largest: 2.86 billion people in 19 surveyed countries, with an aggregate income of $3.47 trillion (box 1.4). The BOP market in these countries represents 83% of the region's population and 42% of its aggregate purchasing power—a significant share of Asia's rapidly growing consumer market. In rural areas the BOP is the majority of the market—representing 76% of aggregate household income in rural China and effectively 100% in rural India and rural Indonesia.

The BOP market in Eastern Europe is $458 billion and includes 254 million people in 28 surveyed countries, 64% of the region's population, with 36% of the region's aggregate income. In Russia, the region's largest economy, the BOP market includes 86 million people and $164 billion in income.

In Latin America the BOP market is $509 billion and includes 360 million people, 70% of the population in the 21 countries surveyed. The BOP market accounts for 28% of the region's aggregate household income, a smaller share than in other developing regions. In both Brazil and Mexico the BOP constitutes 75% of the population, representing aggregate income of $172 billion and $105 billion.

In Africa the BOP market, $429 billion, is smaller than that of Eastern Europe or Latin America. But it is by far the region's dominant consumer market, with 71% of aggregate purchasing power. The African BOP includes 486 million people in 22 surveyed countries—95% of the population in those countries. South Africa has the region's strongest and most modern economy, yet 75% of the population remains in the BOP. The South African BOP market has an aggregate income of $44 billion. Other countries in the region offer even larger BOP market opportunities, notably Ethiopia ($84 billion) and Nigeria ($74 billion).

A new way of thinking about poverty reduction

The BOP market analysis in this report is intended to help businesses and governments think more creatively about new products and services that meet BOP needs and about opportunities for market-based solutions to achieve them. For businesses, characterizing the market in empirical terms is an important first step toward identifying business opportunities, considering business models, developing products, and expanding investment in BOP markets. Put simply, while an analysis of the depth of poverty does not generate private sector enthusiasm for investment, an analysis of BOP market size and willingness to pay might—and is thus a critical step toward market-based solutions.

For governments, such an analysis can help focus attention on reforms needed in the operating and regulatory environment to allow a larger role for the private sector.

The market-based approach to poverty reduction and empirical market data described in this report are equally important for the development community. They can help frame the debate on poverty reduction more in terms of enabling opportunity and less in terms of aid. A successful market-based approach would bring significant new private sector resources into play, allowing development assistance to be more sharply targeted to the segments and sectors for which no viable market solutions can presently be found. Market-based approaches and smart development policies are synergistic strategies.

There are distinct differences between a market-based approach to poverty reduction and more traditional approaches, and it is useful to clarify those differences. As suggested, traditional approaches often focus on the very poor, proceeding from the assumption that they are unable to help themselves and thus need charity or public assistance. In contrast, a market-based approach starts from the recognition that being poor does not eliminate commerce and market processes: virtually all poor households trade cash or labor to meet a significant part of their basic needs. A

The BOP market analysis in this report is intended to help businesses and governments think more creatively about new products and services that meet BOP needs and about opportunities for market-based solutions to achieve them.

market-based approach thus focuses on people as consumers and producers and on solutions that can make BOP markets more efficient, competitive, and inclusive—so that the BOP can benefit from them.

Traditional approaches also tend to address unmet needs for health care, clean water, or other basic necessities by setting targets for meeting those needs through direct public investments, subsidies, or other handouts. The goals may be worthy, but the results have not been strikingly successful. A market-based approach recognizes that it is not just the very poor who have unmet needs and asks about the willingness to pay of different market segments. It looks for solutions in the form of new products and new business models that can provide goods and services at affordable prices.

Those solutions may involve market development efforts that include elements similar to traditional development tools—hybrid business strategies that incorporate consumer education or other forms of capacity building; microloans, consumer finance, or cross-subsidies among different income groups; franchise or retail agent strategies that create jobs and raise incomes; and partnerships with the public sector or with nongovernmental organizations (NGOs). Many successful companies are adopting such innovative strategies, as this report illustrates, sometimes even co-creating solutions with community groups and civil society (Brugman and Prahalad 2007). But the solutions ultimately are market oriented and demand driven.

Perhaps most important, traditional approaches do not point toward sustainable solutions, while a market-oriented approach recognizes that only sustainable solutions can scale to meet the needs of 4 billion people.

Growing private sector interest

Already business interest in BOP markets is rising, both among large national companies and multinational corporations and among small entrepreneurial ventures and social entrepreneurs. One indicator is the business presence at conferences devoted to the topic[5] and the growing journalistic coverage in business publications.[6]

A stronger indicator is the number of large companies conducting pilots, launching new businesses, or extending product lines in existing businesses that serve BOP markets. Of these, multinational consumer product companies such as Unilever and Procter & Gamble have the most extensive track record, with "sachet" marketing now widely known and single-serving product sizes now dominant in many consumer markets.

Large national companies have proved to be among the most innovative and adept in meeting needs of BOP consumers and producers. Standouts include India's ITC in agriculture and ICICI Bank in financial services, Brazil's Casas Bahia in consumer goods, and Mexico's Cemex in housing (Annamalai and Rao 2003). But perhaps the strongest and most dramatic BOP success story—whether measured by market penetration, by the documented benefits to low-income customers, or by the financial success of the companies—comes from mobile telephony.

A decade ago phone service in most developing countries was poor, and few BOP communities had access to phone service or could afford it on the terms offered. The entry of mobile phone companies transformed this picture. The number of mobile subscribers in developing countries grew more than fivefold between 2000 and 2005 to reach nearly 1.4 billion. Growth was rapid in all regions, but fastest in Sub-Saharan Africa: Nigeria's subscriber base grew from 370,000 to 16.8 million in just four years. Meanwhile, the Philippines' grew sixfold to 40 million (World Bank 2006b). Wireless subscribers in China, India, and Brazil together now outnumber those in either the United States or the European Union (ITU 2006).[7]

Comparison of these numbers with the size of BOP populations suggests substantial and growing penetration of mobile phone use in the BOP, confirmed by the household surveys analyzed in this report. Industry analysts expect more than 1 billion additional mobile subscribers worldwide by 2010, with 80% of the growth in developing countries, almost entirely in BOP markets (Wireless Intelligence 2005).

Low-income populations have clearly benefited from access to mobile phones, which ease access to jobs, to medical care, to market prices, to family members working away from home and the remittances they can send, and, increasingly, to financial services (Vodafone 2005). All this depends on the affordability of mobile services, and a critical factor in this has been innovative business models such as prepaid voice and prepaid text-messaging services, available in ever-smaller units. For example, the Philippines' Smart Communications has a growing, profitable business with more than 20 million BOP customers, virtually all of whom use pre-

A decade ago phone service in most developing countries was poor, and few BOP communities had access to phone service or could afford it on the terms offered. The entry of mobile phone companies transformed this picture. The number of mobile subscribers in developing countries grew more than fivefold between 2000 and 2005 to reach nearly 1.4 billion.

paid text-messaging services bought in units as small as US$0.03 (Smith 2004b).

Another innovative business model—shared access, in which an entrepreneur with a phone provides pay-per-use access to a community—has extended the social and economic impact of mobile phones beyond the subscriber base. In South Africa more than half the traffic on Vodacom's mobile network in 2004 came not from its 8 million subscribers but from 4,400 entrepreneur-owned phone shops where customers rent access to phones by the minute. In Bangladesh, Grameen Telecom's village phone entrepreneurs now serve 80,000 rural villages, generating more than US$100 in monthly revenue per phone by aggregating the demand of (and providing service to) entire villages (Cohen 2001).

A strong value proposition for low-income consumers has translated into financial success for mobile companies. In 2006 the Kenyan mobile company Safaricom posted the biggest profit ever in East Africa—K Sh 12.77 billion (US$174 million)—edging out East African Breweries as the region's biggest profit maker.[8] Celtel, an entrepreneurial company founded by a British entrepreneur of Sudanese descent and operating in some of the poorest and least stable countries in Africa, went from start-up to telecom giant in just seven years. In 2005 the company was acquired for US$3.4 billion. It now has operations in 15 African countries and holds licenses covering more than 30% of the continent.[9]

Not all sectors have found their footing yet in BOP markets, however. Privatized urban water systems, for example, have encountered financial and political difficulties in developing countries, and the result has been neither better service for low-income communities nor success for the companies. The energy sector has similarly had only limited success in providing affordable off-grid electricity or clean cooking fuels to rural BOP communities.

Even in these sectors, however, there are encouraging entrepreneurial ventures—providing affordable water filters or home treatment systems so that households can purify water for themselves, offering low-cost solar-powered LED (light-emitting diode) lighting systems that can provide a few hours of light in the evening, or introducing efficient, multi-fuel cookstoves that can burn propane, plant oils, or gathered biomass fuels. Further development of technology and business models may expand BOP markets in these sectors.

Some observers have raised concerns about market-based approaches to reducing poverty (box 1.3). On the ground, however, BOP-oriented business activity is accelerating, in many cases generating evidence of significant benefits for BOP households and communities.

The enabling environment for business

The operating and regulatory environments in developing countries can be challenging. Micro and small businesses especially face disadvantages. If they are informal, they cannot get investment finance, participate in value chains of larger companies, or sometimes even legally receive services from utilities. Condemned to remain small, they cannot generate wealth or large numbers of jobs. Nor do they contribute to the broader economy by paying taxes.

Most face significant barriers to joining the formal economy in the form of antiquated regulations and prohibitive requirements—dozens of steps, delays of many months, capital requirements beyond attainment for most of the BOP. In El Salvador, for example, it used to take 115 days and many separate procedures to start a legitimate business—until recent reforms reduced the effort to 26 days and allowed registration with four separate agencies in a single visit (World Bank and IFC 2006). Even for legitimate small businesses investment capital is generally unavailable and supporting services scarce.

Fortunately, there is growing recognition of the importance of removing barriers to small and medium-size businesses and a growing toolbox for moving firms into the formal economy and creating more efficient markets. These tools, and country ratings of progress on reform, are available in the World Bank and International Finance Corporation's (IFC) annual Doing Business report, along with growing evidence that the tools work. In El Salvador five times as many businesses register annually since its reforms. Many countries, including China, have dropped minimum capital requirements. The pace of reform is accelerating, with more than 40 countries making changes in the most recent year surveyed (World Bank and IFC 2006). Accelerated formation of legitimate small businesses creates benefits for individuals (owners, workers, customers), the enterprises, and the larger economy.

Coupled with reform is growing attention to enterprise development initiatives focused on BOP markets and investment capital for small and medium-size enterprises. The Inter-American Development Bank, as

BOX 1.3:
RESPONDING TO CRITICISMS OF THE MARKET APPROACH

Market-based approaches to meeting the needs of BOP households raise concerns about their appropriateness, especially among some academics, NGOs, and development professionals. Some argue that capitalism in these circumstances is unacceptable or that "profiting from the poor" is morally wrong. Others, pointing to examples of corporate exploitation of low-income workers or ill-informed consumers, argue that the poor are uniquely vulnerable and powerless and so need safeguards. Still others seek to protect the poor from "bad" products or the perceived excesses of a consumer society.

Some of these concerns are appropriate. But others may reflect misunderstanding—of the BOP or of market processes. As both consumers and producers, largely in the informal economy, those in the BOP already suffer from inefficient and uncompetitive markets (see box 1.2).

New formal business entrants can potentially improve competition, lower prices, and increase consumer choice—often bringing products and services previously unavailable or unaffordable. Some of these services, such as mobile telephony or financial services, can directly improve productivity, earning power, and access to jobs. Others, such as access to basic health care and pharmaceuticals or to means for securing clean water—often available to the BOP only from the private sector—translate directly into greater welfare. The potential benefits to BOP households and to the countries in which they live go well beyond consumption and are an essential step toward inclusive markets.

For many in the BOP, jobs are the critical missing ingredient, because cash income is increasingly essential. With few exceptions, job creation requires additional business investment and business formation. Expanded private sector engagement in the BOP, especially by small and medium-size enterprises, is the only sustainable source of large numbers of jobs.

Moreover, there is not enough charity or aid to meet the needs of 4 billion people on an ongoing basis. Without sustainable—that is, profitable—businesses involved, efforts to address unmet needs must fall short. And profitability is essential to attract additional investment and scale solutions to reach the full extent of the need. Even in areas traditionally served by government, such as health care and education, it is clear that in many countries the public sector cannot meet all the needs in the near term—and that private sector solutions are desirable and essential.

part of its Opportunity for the Majority program, is committing US$1 billion over five years to new investments to support private sector efforts for the BOP, including small and medium-size enterprises. The Asian Development Bank is launching several new investment funds for the same purpose. The Japan Bank for International Cooperation aims to increase its funds for African private sector development including small and medium enterprises. IFC is expanding its technical assistance and investment activities for small and medium-size enterprises.

These efforts, and the growing private sector interest in investing in small and medium-size enterprises in developing countries, explicitly recognize that an expanded private sector role and a bottom-up market approach are essential development strategies.

Characterizing BOP markets

Total annual household income of $5 trillion a year establishes the BOP as a potentially important global market. Within that market are significant regional and national variations in size, population structure income distribution, and other characteristics.

Market size

The BOP market in Asia (including the Middle East) is by far the largest: 2.86 billion people in 19 countries, with an aggregate income of $3.47 trillion (box 1.4). The BOP market in these countries represents 83% of the region's population and 42% of its aggregate purchasing power—a significant share of Asia's rapidly growing consumer market (figure 1.1). In rural areas the BOP is the majority of the market—representing 76% of aggregate household income in rural China and effectively 100% in rural India and rural Indonesia.

Eastern Europe's $458 billion BOP market includes 254 million people in 28 surveyed countries, 64% of the region's population, with 36% of the region's aggregate income. In Russia, the region's largest economy, the BOP market includes 86 million people and $164 billion in income.

In Latin America the BOP market of $509 billion includes 360 million people, 70% of the population in the 21 countries surveyed. The BOP market accounts for 28% of the region's aggregate household income, a smaller share than in other developing regions. In both Brazil and Mexico the BOP constitutes 75% of the population, representing aggregate income of $172 billion and $105 billion.

BOX 1.4:

ALTERNATIVE MARKET METRICS

Unless otherwise noted, the market sizes in this and subsequent chapters are denominated in international dollars, which reflect the purchasing power of local currencies and thus are the appropriate frame of reference for local companies and for BOP producers and consumers. But for multinational companies U.S. dollars provide a more useful metric. By this metric the global BOP market is US$1.3 trillion, while the Asian BOP market is US$742 billion, the Latin American market US$229 billion, the Eastern European market US$135 billion, and the African market US$120 billion. (See appendix A for BOP market sizes in both international and U.S. dollars for selected countries.)

In Africa the BOP market, $429 billion, is slightly smaller than that of Eastern Europe or Latin America. But it is by far the region's dominant consumer market, with 71% of aggregate purchasing power. The African BOP includes 486 million people in 22 surveyed countries—95% of the population in those countries.[10] South Africa has the region's strongest and most modern economy, yet 75% of the population remains in the BOP. The South African BOP market has an aggregate income of $44 billion. Other countries in the region offer even larger BOP market opportunities, notably Ethiopia ($84 billion) and Nigeria ($74 billion).

Market composition

Population distribution across BOP income groups is far from homogeneous. In Nigeria, for example, most of the BOP is concentrated in the lowest income segments. Mexico has a more even distribution of population by income within the BOP. The contrast between rural and urban China is particularly striking, showing that economic opportunities for BOP populations are significantly better in urban than in rural areas of that country—a disparity that has implications both for business and for social stability.

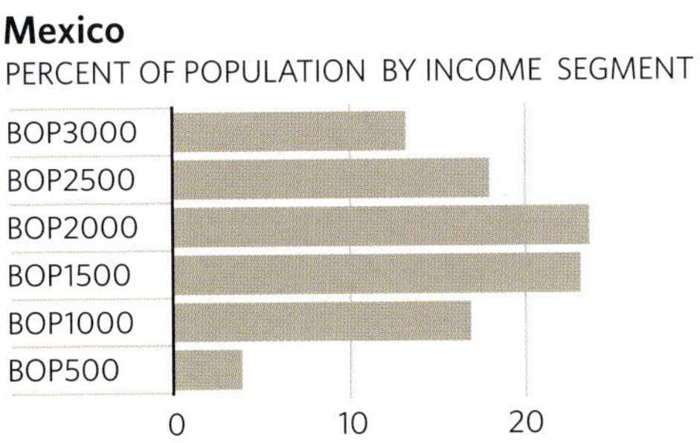

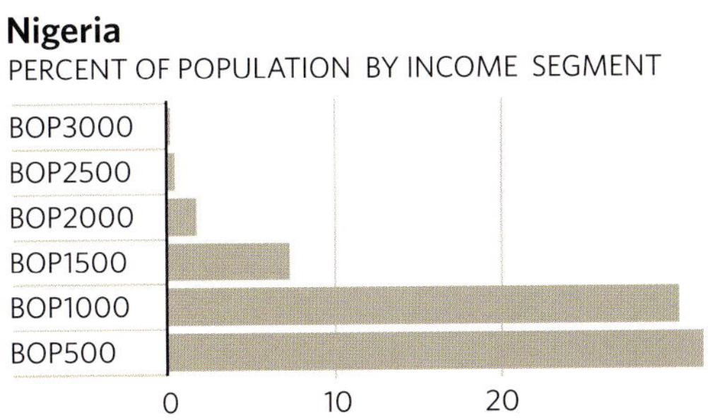

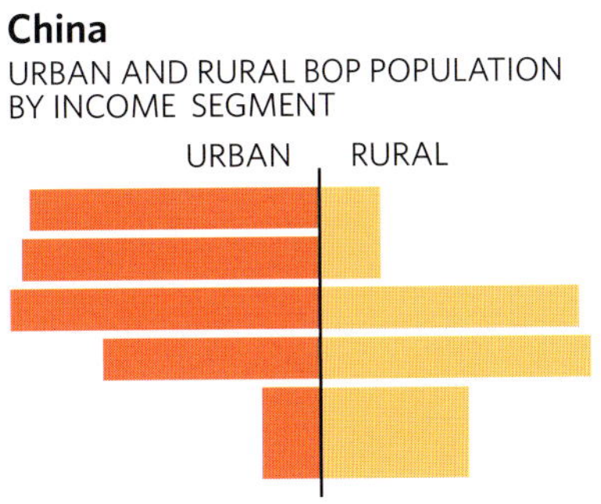

Spending patterns

Population structure by itself is not a reliable guide to market composition. Accordningly, this analysis also examines BOP spending patterns by country, sector, and income level. This analysis is based on a World Bank initiative—the International Comparison Program—to standardize the expenditures reported by national household surveys into defined categories.

The standardized data allow detailed, sector-by-sector analysis within countries, insight into how spending patterns by income level differ among countries, and more meaningful aggregation of BOP consumer markets to a regional scale, though the surveys themselves vary across countries and over time.[11] (See appendix B for a description of the standardization methodology and country tables of standardized BOP expenditure data by sector and income level.) Combining income and expenditure data allows estimation of the size of regional sector markets (box 1.5).

BOX 1.5:

ESTIMATING THE SIZE OF SECTOR MARKETS

The size of each sector market in a region is estimated by combining standardized sector expenditure data from the subset of 36 countries for which these data exist with the income-based measure of the regional market size (from 110 countries). In Africa, for example, the BOP health market measured across the 12 countries for which standardized expenditure data are available is about $8 billion, which represents about 4% of total BOP spending in those countries. Extrapolating that expenditure pattern to all surveyed countries in the region leads to an estimate of $18 billion for the total BOP health market in the region.[12]

A similar process for other regions gives $95 billion for Asia's regional BOP health market, $21 billion for Eastern Europe's, and $24 billion for Latin America's—for a total BOP health market of $158 billion.

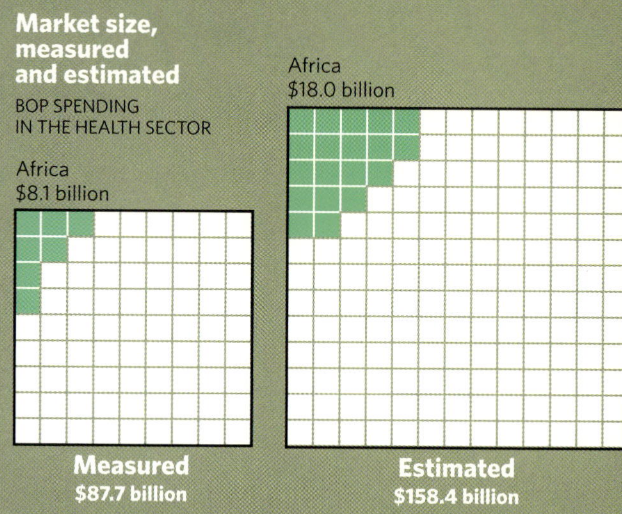

Characterizing BOP sector markets

The following chapters analyze BOP sector markets in detail, drawing on the country data tables in appendix B. Highlights from those chapters show how the data in this report can be used to characterize BOP markets.

- How large is the market? Sector markets for the 4 billion BOP consumers range widely in size. Some are relatively small, such as water ($20 billion) and information and communication technology, or ICT ($51 billion as measured, but probably twice that now because of rapid growth). Some are medium scale, such as health ($158 billion), transportation ($179 billion), housing ($332 billion), and energy ($433 billion). And some are truly large, such as food ($2,895 billion). BOP markets in Asia (including the Middle East) are the largest, reflecting the sheer weight of the population in that region. Many BOP sector markets in Africa, Eastern Europe, and Latin America and the Caribbean are roughly comparable in size, reflecting the smaller BOP populations but larger incomes in Eastern Europe and Latin America.
- How is the market segmented? BOP markets can be usefully characterized as bottom heavy, top heavy, or flat, depending on where spending is concentrated among the six income segments distinguished in the BOP. Bottom-heavy BOP markets predominate in

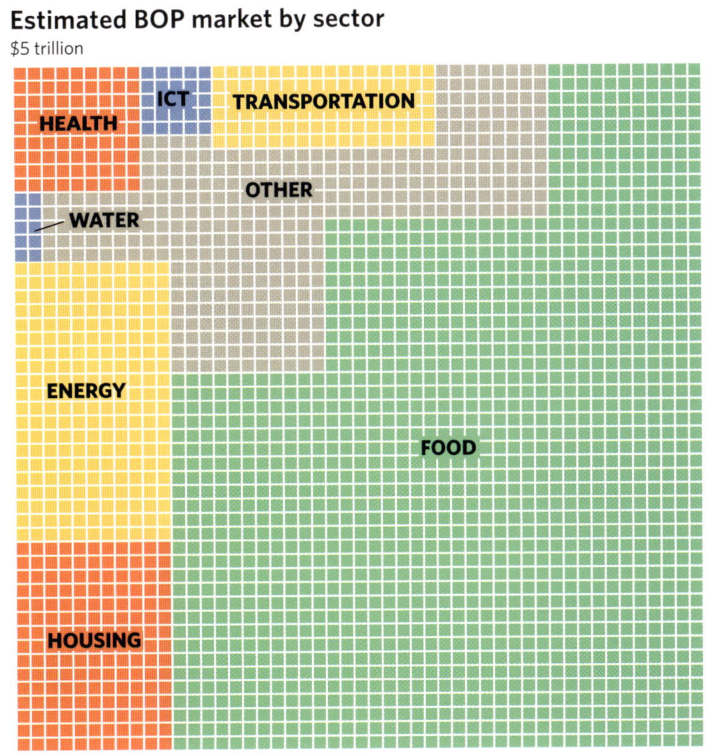

Asia and Africa, and top-heavy markets in Eastern Europe and Latin America. The ICT sector is an exception, with spending still typically concentrated in the upper income segments of the BOP in all regions.

- What do households spend? For most sectors average BOP household spending is significantly higher in Latin America than in other regions. For ICT, for example, average BOP household spending for the median country is $34 in Africa, $54 in Asia, $56 in Eastern Europe, and $107 in Latin America. Comparable numbers for health care are $154 in Africa, $131 in Asia, $152 in Eastern Europe, and $325 in Latin America—and for transportation, $211 in Africa and Asia, $141 in Eastern Europe, and $521 in Latin America. Spending is higher, but differences proportionately less, for food: $2,087 in Africa, $2,643 in Asia, $3,687 in Eastern Europe, $3,050 in Latin America.
- Where is the market? Urban areas dominate the BOP markets for water, ICT, and housing in all regions. BOP markets for transportation and energy are also heavily urban except in most of Asia, where rural areas dominate. For food and health care, rural BOP markets are larger in most countries of Africa and Asia, and urban BOP markets larger in most countries of Eastern Europe and Latin America.

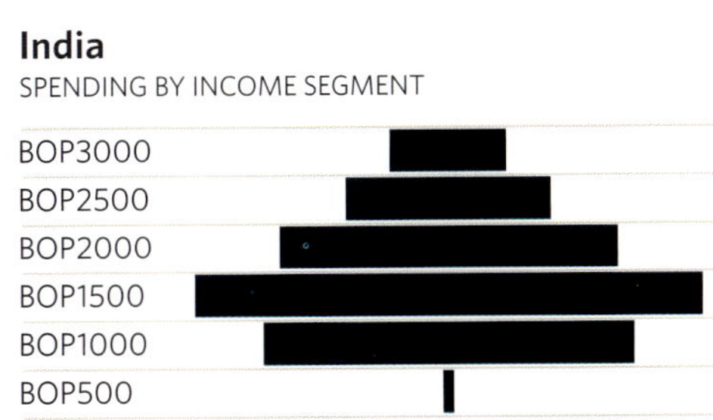

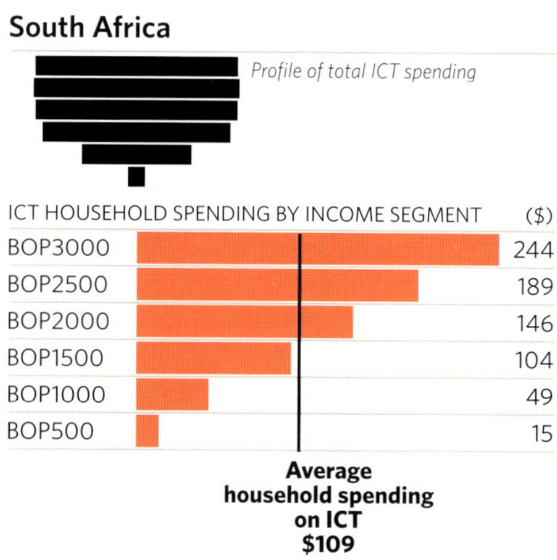

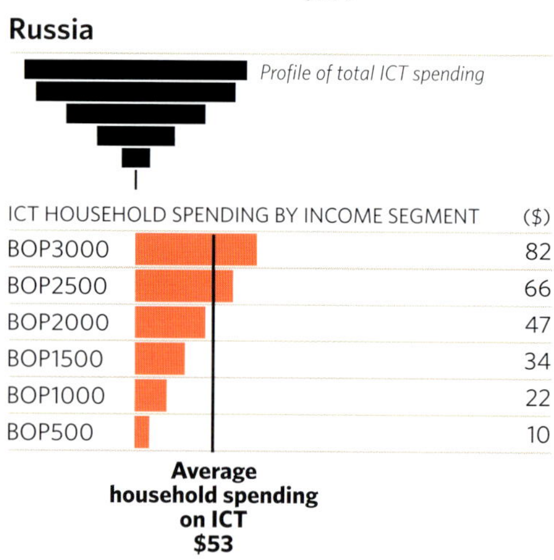

- What does the BOP buy? The survey data record interesting patterns in what BOP households buy. For health care, for example, more than half of BOP spending goes to pharmaceuticals. For ICT, phone service dominates recorded expenditures. Many BOP households don't pay cash for water: in Africa surface water is the primary source for 17% of BOP households, and unprotected wells the primary source for relatively large shares in some countries in the region. Access to electricity is virtually universal in Eastern Europe and high among BOP households in Asia and Latin America, but quite low in Africa. For all regions except Eastern Europe firewood is the dominant cooking fuel among lower BOP income segments, while propane or other modern fuels are dominant among higher BOP income segments and in urban areas.
- Is there evidence of a BOP penalty? Data for several sectors suggest a penalty—higher costs or lower quality for services, or no access at all—for BOP households. Wealthier mid-market households are seven times as likely as BOP households to have access to piped water. Some 24% of BOP households lack access to electricity, compared with only 1% of mid-market households. ICT spending and phone ownership are significantly lower among rural BOP households than either rural mid-market or even urban BOP households—consistent with the broad lack of access in rural areas confirmed by coverage data from other sources.

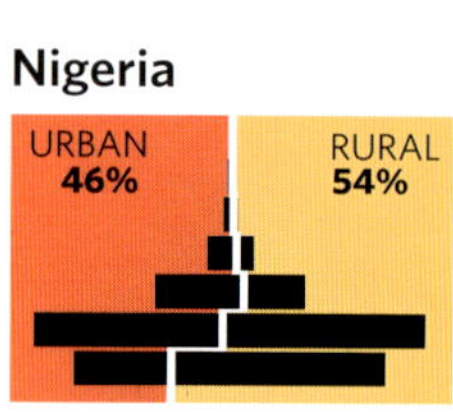

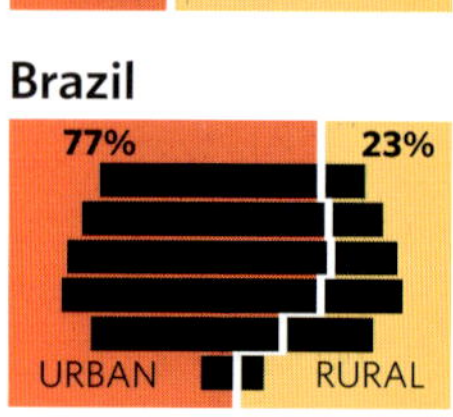

Total BOP food spending by income segment, urban and rural

BOP business strategies

The following chapters also give case studies of business enterprises that are successfully serving BOP markets. Here, four broad strategies are distinguished that are used by enterprises operating in BOP markets and that appear to be critical to their success:

- Focusing on the BOP with unique products, unique services, or unique technologies that are appropriate to BOP needs and that require reimagining the business, often through significant investment of money and management talent.
- Localizing value creation through franchising, through agent strategies that involve building local ecosystems of vendors or suppliers, or by treating the community as the customer, all of which usually involve substantial investment in capacity building and training.

Urban and rural spending—Cameroon

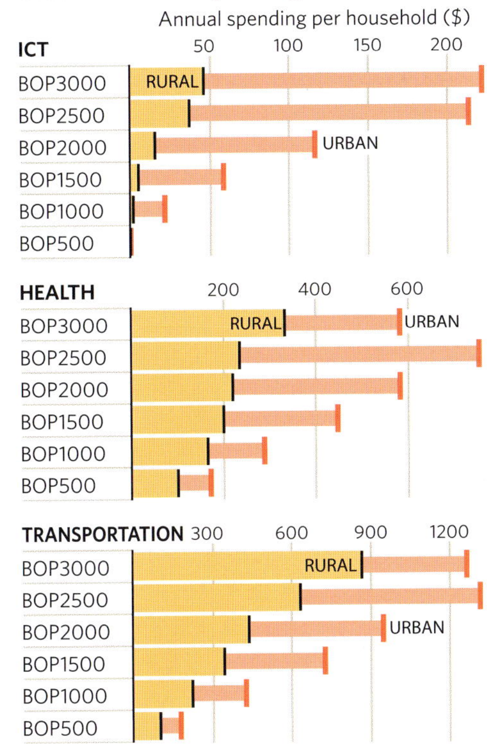

- Enabling access to goods or services—financially (through single-use or other packaging strategies that lower purchase barriers, prepaid or other novel business models that achieve the same result, or financing approaches) or physically (through novel distribution strategies or deployment of low-cost technologies).
- Unconventional partnering with governments, NGOs, or groups of multiple stakeholders to bring the necessary capabilities to the table.

Enterprises may—and often do—use more than one of these strategies.

Focusing on the BOP

In the water sector, filters and other point-of-use treatment approaches that enable BOP households to purify dirty water exemplify a strategy of focusing on the BOP, responding to BOP circumstances with unique products and technology. This strategy is also found in the food sector, in the development of healthier products that address BOP needs; in the housing sector, in the packaging of design, financing, and as-needed delivery of materials services; and in the energy sector, in the marketing of solar-powered LED lighting and high-tech home cookstoves. In financial services, microfinance and low-cost remittance systems reflect a BOP focus.

Localizing value creation

Franchising and direct marketing by agents of pharmaceuticals, health services, and preventive health materials are gaining traction in the BOP health sector, as are distribution systems (such as Shakti in India) in the food and consumer goods sectors. These approaches create jobs and help ensure local value creation as well as provide efficient, low-cost distribution. In the ICT sector mobile phone companies have built extensive ecosystems of small shops, village phone entrepreneurs, and other vendors to sell or deliver their services to BOP markets; in the Philippines even McDonald's franchises serve as points of delivery for remittances sent by phone from overseas.

Community water treatment systems and mini-hydropower systems enable the community to be the provider as well as the customer.

Data for several sectors suggest a penalty—higher costs or lower quality for services, or no access at all—for BOP households. Wealthier mid-market households are seven times as likely as BOP households to have access to piped water.

Extractive industries use a similar strategy when they source goods and services locally.

Enabling access

Sachet marketing—packaging products in single-use or other small units that make them more affordable to the BOP—is associated with fast-moving consumer goods. But the strategy is also widely used in the food sector and in ICT (pricing voice or text-messaging units at US$.50 or less and selling Internet access by the quarter hour). These packaging strategies are critical to enabling access in BOP communities, where cash is scarce.

Cross-subsidy strategies—where wealthier customers help subsidize services for BOP clients—play a big part in enabling access in the health sector. Financing strategies—microloans, consumer finance, or mortgage financing for the BOP or even community-based health insurance—play a similar part in a range of sectors, enabling access to housing, to health care, to solar power systems, and to fertilizers or advanced seeds in agricultural supply chains for the food sector.

Franchising and other local value creation strategies also are often critical to enabling access to services for the BOP, especially in rural areas.

Unconventional partnering

Public-private partnerships are common in the energy and water sectors. Less common but gaining momentum are partnerships between businesses and NGOs—to build distribution and service networks for cookstoves in the energy sector, to build and manage distribution networks for food and consumer goods, to create and manage franchise networks in health care. As banks move into providing financial services to the BOP, some are partnering with microfinance entities and community self-help groups. And partnerships between multiple stakeholders are being used to transform urban transportation systems.

Endnotes

1. In this report current U.S. dollars means 2005 dollars. Unless otherwise noted, however, market information is given in 2005 international dollars adjusted for purchasing power parity; for convenience, BOP and mid-market income cutoffs are given in international dollars for 2002 (the base year to which household surveys used in this analysis have been normalized). See appendix A for the methodology.
2. The high-income population segment is approximately 0.3 billion worldwide. But neither its size nor its very large aggregate income can be reliably measured by household surveys, because the sample of such households in national surveys, especially in developing countries, is too small.
3. In 2004 recorded remittances were the second largest source of external financing in developing countries, after foreign direct investment, and amounted to more than twice the size of official aid. Including unrecorded flows, remittances are the largest source of external financing in many developing countries. (World Bank 2006a).
4. While household surveys are regarded by economists as a source of reliable economic data, here they are applied as market research tools in ways for which they were not designed. As a result, some limitations apply: household surveys rarely capture unit prices for commodities purchased, for example, and are not standardized across countries or over time. For rapidly developing sectors, such as mobile communications, even relatively recent surveys can markedly understate use rates and expenditure.
5. Conferences include "Eradicating Poverty through Profit" (World Resources Institute, San Francisco, December 12–14, 2004; http://www.nextbillion.net/sfconference); "Business Opportunity and Innovation at the Base of the Pyramid" (World Resources Institute, Multilateral Investment Fund, and Ashoka, São Paulo, August 30, 2005); "Business Opportunity and Innovation at the Base of the Pyramid" (World Resources Institute, Multilateral Investment Fund, and Ashoka, Mexico City, September 1, 2005); and "Global Poverty: Business Solutions and Approaches" (Harvard Business School, Cambridge, MA, December 1–3, 2005; http://www.nextbillion.net/harvard05conference).
6. World Resources Institute, "News: NextBillion.net," http://www.nextbillion.net/newsroom (accessed January 12, 2007).
7. According to the International Telecommunication Union, there were 2,137 million mobile subscribers in 2005. India, China, and Brazil together accounted for 555.6 million of those, the European Union for 470.6 million, and the United States for 201.6 million.
8. East African, "Safaricom Makes $12.77 Million Profit, a Record for Region," October 30, 2006, http://allafrica.com/stories/200610301138.html.
9. Mo Ibrahim, presentation to World Bank, April, 2006.
10. Many African countries lack current household surveys. If the missing countries were included, the African BOP population and market size might be as much as twice that of the "surveyed" BOP figures given here. In other regions the missing countries would not affect reported totals significantly.
11. While the data are standardized, the household surveys are not and so do not capture the same information in each country. Direct comparisons between countries should thus be avoided or used with great caution.
12. The estimation procedure is based on the following formula applied to BOP markets: measured sector expenditure/total expenditure = estimated regional sector expenditure/total regional income, which is then solved for estimated regional sector expenditure. This amounts to assuming that the average ratio of sector expenditure to total expenditure as sampled in a measured group of countries is a good estimator for the same ratio in another group of countries in the region for which income but not standardized expenditure data are available. It also assumes that total household income equals total household expenditure, an equivalence already assumed in the methodology for assembling the income survey data.

CHAPTER TWO

The Health Market

Rural East Africa illustrates both the challenges BOP households face in obtaining health care and the potential health market they represent. Access to public health care is often very limited. Even finding medicines to buy—especially ones that work—can be difficult. Spending on health care is low—only $183 a year for a typical rural household in Uganda. Of that, half is spent on medicine, often without a doctor's prescription; self-medication is common for BOP households.

Despite the huge need for more effective distribution of medicines and other health-related consumer products—such as condoms, water filters, and antimalaria bed nets—such spending levels might not seem to suggest a promising market in which to launch a new franchise pharmacy business. Yet CFWshops Kenya is doing just that. Its 64 locally owned franchises charge prices averaging about US$0.50 a treatment for the more than 150 pharmaceuticals they stock and last year served more than 400,000 customers—and they are profitable. CFWshops Kenya and other ventures, both new and well established, are demonstrating innovative approaches to the large and largely underserved BOP health market.

BOP spending on health
$158.4 billion

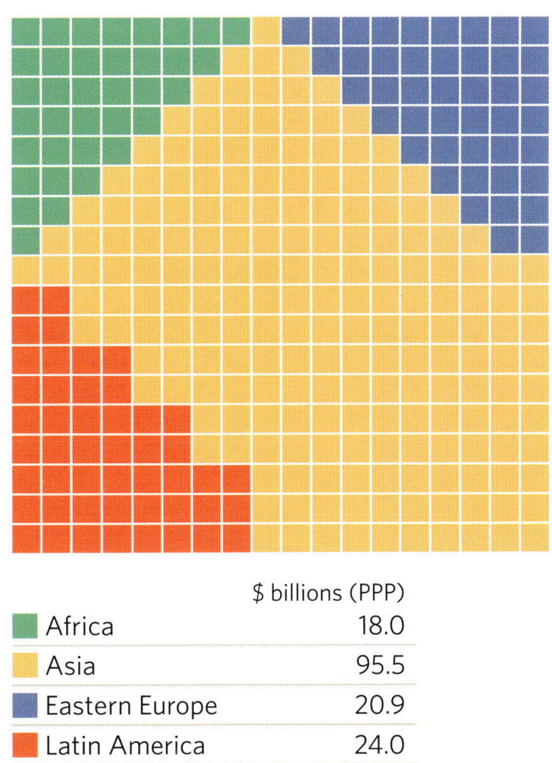

Each square represents approximately $500 million

How large is the market?

The measured BOP health market in Africa (12 countries), Asia (9), Eastern Europe (5), and Latin America and the Caribbean (9) is $87.7 billion. This represents annual household health spending in the 35 countries for which standardized data exist and covers 2.1 billion of the world's BOP population. The total BOP health market in these four regions, including all surveyed countries, is estimated to be $158.4 billion, accounting for the spending of 3.96 billion people (see box 1.5 in chapter 1 for the estimation method).[1] Asia has by far the largest measured regional BOP health market—$48.2 billion, reflecting a large BOP population (1.5 billion). The total BOP health market in Asia (including the Middle East) is estimated to be $95.5 billion, accounting for the spending of 2.9 billion people. Latin America follows, with measured BOP health spending of $20.1 billion by 276 million people and an estimated total BOP health market of $24 billion (360 million people).

Eastern Europe's measured BOP health market is $11.2 billion, covering the spending of 124 million people, and the estimated total BOP market is $20.9 billion

In Asia the extremes are represented by Pakistan, Bangladesh, and Tajikistan, where the BOP constitutes more than 98% of the health market.

(254 million people). Africa's measured BOP health market is $8.1 billion, comprising the annual spending of 258 million people, and its estimated total BOP market is $18.0 billion (486 million people).

The share of total household health spending that takes place in the BOP—and thus the relative importance of the BOP market—varies widely. In Asia the BOP dominates the market, with an 85% share. In other regions its share is far smaller: 54% in Africa, 45% in Eastern Europe, 38% in Latin America. In Eastern Europe and Latin America mid-market and high-income groups tend to dominate health markets, even though large majorities of the population in both regions are in the BOP. But Africa shows the greatest disparity between the BOP share of the total population (95%) and the BOP share of health spending (54%).

Malawi
TOTAL HEALTH SPENDING BY INCOME SEGMENT

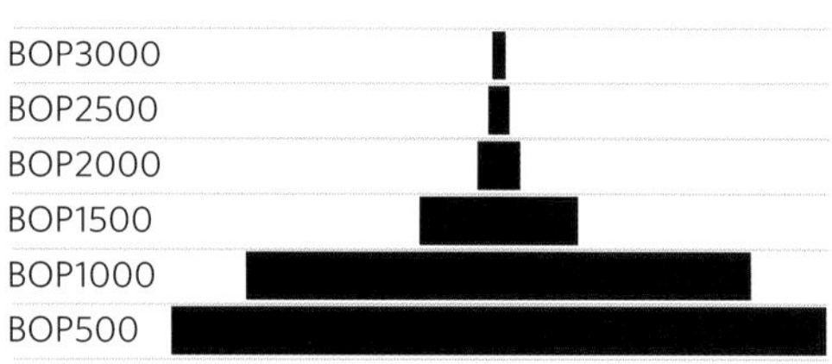

Tajikistan
TOTAL HEALTH SPENDING BY INCOME SEGMENT

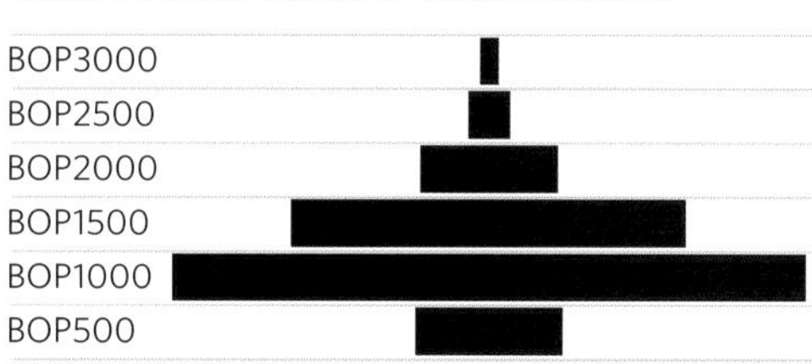

Russia
TOTAL HEALTH SPENDING BY INCOME SEGMENT

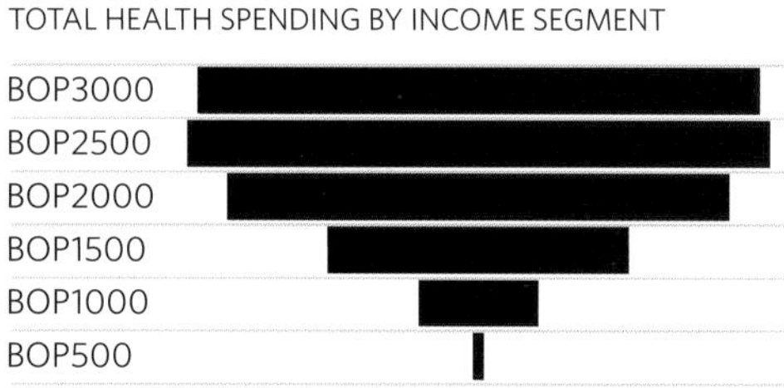

At the national level there is similarly wide disparity in the share of health spending that occurs in the BOP. In Asia the extremes are represented by Pakistan, Bangladesh, and Tajikistan, where the BOP constitutes more than 98% of the health market, and Thailand (with a substantial mid-market population), where the BOP accounts for only 44%. In Africa the extremes are Nigeria, where the BOP also accounts for 98% of the health market, and South Africa (with a market dominated by the 25% of its population that is wealthier), where BOP spending is a modest 9% of the total.

In Eastern Europe the extreme is represented by Kazakhstan with 77% of total health spending in the BOP and Macedonia, FYR (38%). In Latin America and the Caribbean the largest BOP shares of total health spending are in Jamaica (90%) and Peru (77%), and the smallest in Colombia (31%). Generally, the smaller the percentage of the population in the BOP, the greater the likelihood that wealthier population segments account for a disproportionate share of the health market.

How is the market segmented?

Bottom-heavy BOP markets—where more than half of spending occurs in the bottom three of the six BOP income segments—predominate in Africa (9 of 12 countries) and Asia (8 of 9). Malawi and Tajikistan illustrate this pattern. In two of the larger countries, India and Indonesia, while still bottom-heavy, spending is concentrated more toward the middle of the BOP income spectrum, in BOP1000–2000. India, with $35 billion in annual BOP health spending (85% of the national market), shows what this spending pattern looks like (case study 2.1). Generally in Africa and Asia the distribution of health spending across BOP income groups closely matches the distribution of the population across these groups.

In Eastern Europe and Latin America all measured countries show a top-heavy BOP spending pattern, illustrated by Russia and Peru. Another example is Mexico, with $4.1 billion in annual BOP health spending (38% of the national market; case study 2.2).

What do households spend?

The products and services that households are willing to buy depend to some degree on income. Average household spending at different income levels is thus a useful guide to product design. But spending, especially for health care, also depends on access to services. If travel to a hospital or health clinic costs more in cash or lost wages than the service itself, anecdotal evidence suggests, price-sensitive BOP households may defer treatment until a condition is relatively serious.[2] In any event, the available health dollars might be larger if health care services were relatively available and travel costs could be avoided. Current levels of household spending on health should thus be regarded as establishing a lower bound for the willingness to pay.

Average health spending by BOP households varies widely across countries. The difference depends in part on whether markets are top heavy or bottom heavy and may also reflect BOP access to public health services. But the variation can also reflect differences in the questions asked and the expenditures captured in national surveys. Both Indonesia and Pakistan have bottom-heavy health markets, for example, but their reported BOP health spending per household averages are very different: $78 and $197 (the extremes for measured countries in Asia).

A more meaningful characterization may be the regional median among average annual spending on health by BOP households. These figures are as follows: for Africa, $154 (Nigeria) and $168 (Gabon); for Asia, $131 (Sri Lanka); for Eastern Europe, $152 (Ukraine); and for Latin America, $325 (Peru). In most countries measured, household health spending increases roughly in proportion to income through the BOP. In many countries, however, health spending increases disproportionately in the highest BOP income segments, BOP2500 and BOP3000—an indication of latent demand for health care in the BOP. For the countries

CASE STUDY 2.1 **INDIA**: A SUBSTANTIAL HEALTH MARKET IN THE MIDDLE OF THE BOP

In India spending on health by BOP households is concentrated in the BOP1000, BOP1500, and BOP2000 groups. Thus the Indian BOP health market, while bottom heavy, is not dominated by the very lowest income segment, as Malawi's is, for example. These three segments account for 76% of the BOP health market in India. They also account for 65% of the total health market and 78% of all households. Indeed, with 155 million households and $26.6 billion in total annual health spending, this is a substantial market. Annual spending on health per household in these income segments averages $111, $183, and $264.

Moving up-market does not dramatically change household health spending in India. Average health spending per household in the relatively small but much wealthier mid-market population segment ($391) is only about twice that in the BOP ($192).

India

TOTAL HEALTH SPENDING BY INCOME SEGMENT

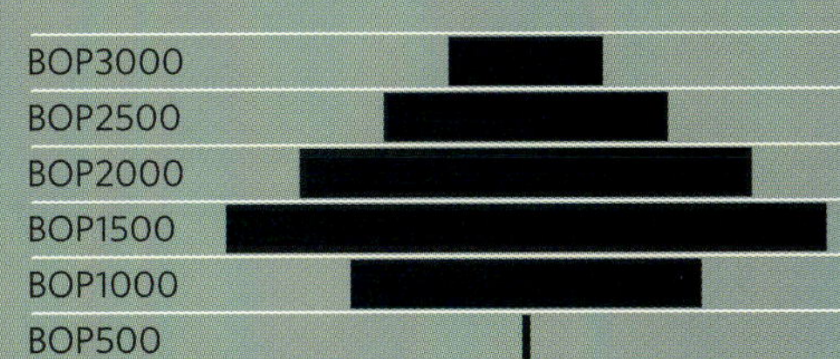

Ukraine

Sri Lanka

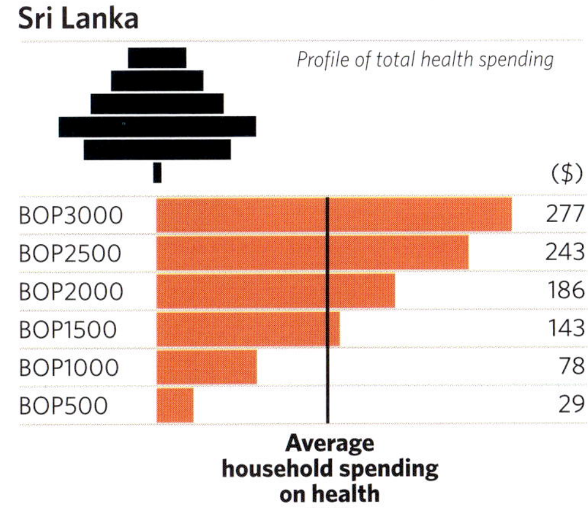

CASE STUDY 2.2 **MEXICO**: A TYPICAL TOP-HEAVY BOP HEALTH MARKET

In Mexico BOP spending on health is concentrated in the top three BOP income segments—a typical top-heavy market pattern. These three segments account for 61% of BOP households (9.5 million) and 75% of the BOP health market ($3 billion in annual spending)—but only 29% of the total health market in Mexico. Annual spending on health per household in these income segments averages $235, $359, and $394. Moving up-market more than doubles average per household spending on health, from $260 a year in the BOP to $635 in the mid-market segment. Total mid-market health spending is about 60% larger than total BOP spending.

Mexico

TOTAL HEALTH SPENDING BY INCOME SEGMENT

Peru

SHARE OF HOUSEHOLD SPENDING ON HEALTH

	(%)
BOP3000	6.0
BOP2500	5.7
BOP2000	5.5
BOP1500	5.1
BOP1000	4.5
BOP500	4.2

Sierra Leone

SHARE OF HOUSEHOLD SPENDING ON HEALTH

	(%)
BOP3000	12.1
BOP2500	8.1
BOP2000	8.4
BOP1500	7.2
BOP1000	6.8
BOP500	6.4

above, the ratio of average health spending per household in BOP3000 to that in BOP500 is 8:1 in Nigeria, 6:1 in Gabon, 9.5:1 in Sri Lanka, 3:1 in Ukraine, and 6:1 in Peru. Health care models that can tap higher income segments to cross-subsidize services to lower income segments—such as the Aravind Eye Care Hospitals in India—show much promise as a way to extend even expensive services such as surgery to the poorest parts of the BOP (case study 2.3).

As incomes rise still higher, per household health spending continues to increase—but only modestly compared with the increases in income, except in Africa. The ratio of average annual per household spending for health in the mid-market segment to that in the BOP is 1.5:1 in Russia, 2:1 in Colombia, 2:1 in India, and 3:1 in Thailand—but reaches 11:1 in Nigeria and 14:1 in South Africa.

Where is the market?

The relative sizes of urban and rural BOP health markets differ significantly across regions. In Asia the rural BOP health market is 2.4 times the size of the urban one, largely reflecting the distribution of the BOP population. Pakistan's BOP health market, for example, is 71% rural. Among measured Asian countries, only in Indonesia does BOP health spending in urban areas exceed that in rural areas. In Africa urban and rural BOP health markets are roughly comparable in size, even though rural areas generally account for a larger share of the BOP population. In Nigeria, for example, rural areas account for 52% of the BOP health market but have 22% more BOP households than urban areas. In Eastern Europe, in contrast, the urban BOP health market is 61% larger than the rural market. Russia's BOP health market is 61% urban. In Latin America the difference is far greater: the urban BOP health market is 3.5 times the size of the rural market. The urban share of the market is 85% in Brazil and 73% in Colombia.

The first response to illness in many BOP households, especially in the lower income segments that dominate bottom-heavy markets, tends to be self-medication.

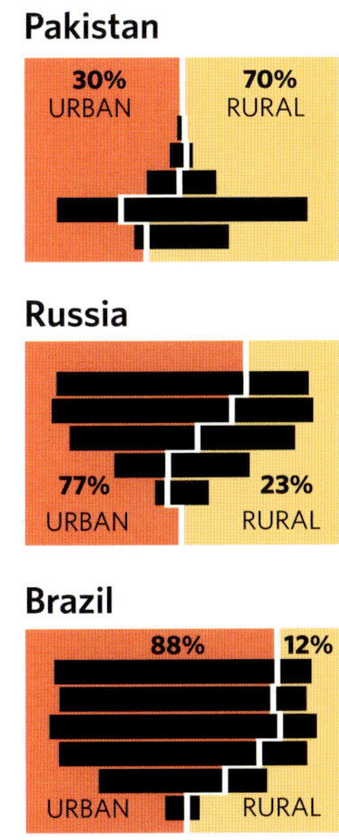

Total BOP health spending by income segment, urban and rural

Average health spending by BOP households is generally higher in urban than in rural areas—$451 a year in urban areas of Guatemala, for example, but $372 in rural areas.

The BOP share of the total urban health market is smaller in every region than the BOP share of the rural market, because of the concentration of mid-market and high-income populations in urban areas.

What does the BOP buy?

The first response to illness in many BOP households, especially in the lower income segments that dominate bottom-heavy markets, tends to be self-medication.[3] Pharmacies or other sources of medicines are thus often the front line of health care, especially in rural areas where access to clinics and hospitals may be limited. Supportive evidence for this comes from the surveys reported in this analysis: in nearly every measured country and in every BOP income segment pharmaceuticals account for more than half of all BOP health spending. As a result, the BOP often dominates national pharmaceutical markets, especially in Africa and Asia.

In Africa, except in Nigeria and South Africa, BOP households spend between 51% (Uganda) and 87% (Sierra Leone) of their health budget on pharmaceuticals. The percentage tends to be highest in the lower income segments and to decline slightly as incomes rise. In Latin America, except in Mexico, BOP households spend between 50% (Colombia) and 74% (Brazil) of their health budget on pharmaceuticals, again with higher percentages in lower income groups. The pattern is also found in most countries of Eastern Europe (69% in Russia) and in India (76%), though not in some other countries of Asia.

CASE STUDY 2.3

STREAMLINE HEALTH CARE:

BRINGING AN "ASSEMBLY LINE" APPROACH TO CATARACT SURGERY

Henry Ford standardized and streamlined automobile production to lower the cost of his cars enough so that nearly everyone could afford one. Aravind Eye Care Hospitals in India has done the same for cataract surgery. The Aravind system relies on intensive specialization in every part of the work flow to generate efficiencies. A surgeon, for example, typically performs 150 cataract surgeries every week, six times the number common among Western specialists. To further lower costs, Aravind has created a sister organization, Aurolab, to manufacture intraocular lenses locally at prices one-fiftieth of U.S. prices, as well as the sutures and drugs used in surgery.

Aravind screens millions of people each year to identify those whose eyesight is threatened by cataracts and performs nearly 200,000 surgeries a year. An important part of its business model is multitiered pricing or cross-subsidization: fees from paying patients range from $50 to $330 per operation, including the hospital stay, but it performs 65% of its operations free of charge—for those, including patients from most BOP households, who can't afford to pay.

Through its fee income, Aravind is self-supporting and also generates enough profit to fund its gradual expansion. With a 30-year record of world-class care, the Aravind model demonstrates that affordable quality health care for the BOP is possible (Prahalad 2005).

CASE STUDY 2.4 **FRANCHISING: A BUSINESS MODEL THAT DELIVERS AFFORDABLE HEALTH CARE WHERE IT'S NEEDED**

In recent years the franchise business model has proved to be a particularly suitable vehicle for delivering health services and products in both urban and rural low-income areas. A well-designed franchise structure has built-in quality control, bulk buying power, price subsidization, and expansion capabilities that can allow an enterprise to flourish in difficult BOP markets.

One example of this approach is CFWshops Kenya, with 64 financially self-sustaining franchise locations in urban, semirural, and rural areas, serving more than 400,000 patients a year. The franchises offer 150–250 government-approved health products and pharmaceuticals, priced at about US$0.50 per treatment—affordable for low-income Kenyans. Each one is located no more than an hour's walk from its intended customer base.

Forty-two locations are owned by community health workers earning an average of US$600–800 a year, and the other 22 by licensed nurses earning an average of US$1,000–1,400. In comparison, the average nurse's salary in Kenya is US$754. Clinics owned by nurses provide additional screening services and a broader range of medications, though all locations provide essential prevention and treatment products for malaria, diarrhea, amoebiasis (stomach worms) as well as mosquito nets and water treatment products.

CFWshops' headquarters, the franchisor, holds each franchise to strict standards of product quality and pricing through unannounced audits and the threat of closure. Franchise owners benefit from being part of the CFWshops system: they bear a trusted brand name, share marketing costs and best practices, and can sell drugs at prices lowered through collective bargaining and bulk buying (Fertig and Tzaras 2005).

Another successful franchise providing health products and services to the BOP is Janani, a nonprofit Indian organization using a private sector model. Janani applies a mix of techniques—subsidizing some products, generating large caseloads to obtain volume discounts, leveraging existing social and business networks, and using technology—to increase the efficiency of its operations. Its focus is on selling low-cost contraceptives through three channels—31,000 existing retail shops, a network of 40,000 rural health providers, and 520 clinics with resident doctors. In 2005 Janani sold 57.9 million condoms and 9.9 million cycles of oral contraceptives, protecting 1.6 million couples from unwanted pregnancies.[4]

Yet another is Mi Farmacita Nacional, a nationwide Mexican pharmacy chain that provides low-cost generics, purified water and powdered milk, consultations, and pre-operative services to low-income people. To supplement revenue, the independent franchises also provide such services as telephone and Internet.[5]

All these franchising operations create jobs and community-based health infrastructure and thus exemplify a strategy of **localizing value creation.**

The heavy BOP spending on pharmaceuticals points to the importance of drug distribution systems—and of quality control, since fake drugs are a problem in many developing countries.

Data from measured countries illustrate the size of markets and household spending for pharmaceuticals:

- In Africa the BOP market for pharmaceuticals is $3.9 billion—$1.3 billion in Nigeria alone. Nigerian households in the lowest three BOP income groups, which account for 87% of the national health market, spend an average of $47.99 a year on medicines.
- In Asia the BOP market for pharmaceuticals is $30.8 billion—$26.6 billion in India alone. The 155 million Indian households in the three income segments BOP1000–2000 spend an average of $134 a year on pharmaceuticals.
- In Eastern Europe the BOP market for pharmaceuticals is $9.2 billion—$8.0 billion of it in Russia. Russian BOP households spend 87.1% of their health budget on pharmaceuticals, $314 a year on average.
- In Latin America the BOP pharmaceutical market is $12.9 billion. BOP households spend 64% of their health budget, or $201 a year, on pharmaceuticals.

The heavy BOP spending on pharmaceuticals points to the importance of drug distribution systems—and of quality control, since fake drugs are a problem in many developing countries, especially in Africa. Franchise business models can add efficiency and quality control while enhancing drug distribution (case study 2.4).

Pharmaceuticals share of BOP health market
$56.7 billion

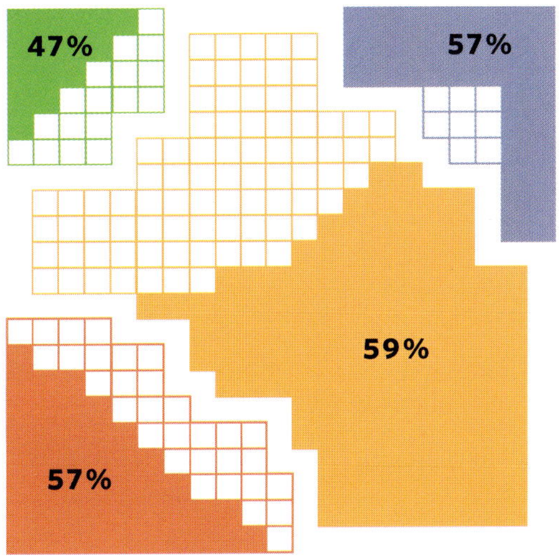

Pharmaceutical market	$ billions (PPP)
Africa	3.9
Asia	30.8
Eastern Europe	9.2
Latin America	12.9

Each square represents approximately $250 million

Endnotes

1. Reported household expenditures in a given country should be regarded as a minimum estimate of actual expenditures, because surveys may not have collected information on all types of health-related spending.
2. Participant comments at a BOP Circle meeting hosted by the World Resources Institute, Mexico City, October 19, 2006.
3. Interview with April Harding and Alex Preker, World Bank, Health Nutrition and Population. Washington, DC, May 2006 .
4. Janani, "Welcome to Janani: Overview," http://www.janani.org/overview.htm (accessed January 31, 2007).
5. Mi Farmacita, "Beneficios," http://www.tiendavirtual.ws/mifarmacita/contenido.cfm?cont=BENEFICIOS (accessed January 31, 2007). Case study 2.4

CHAPTER THREE

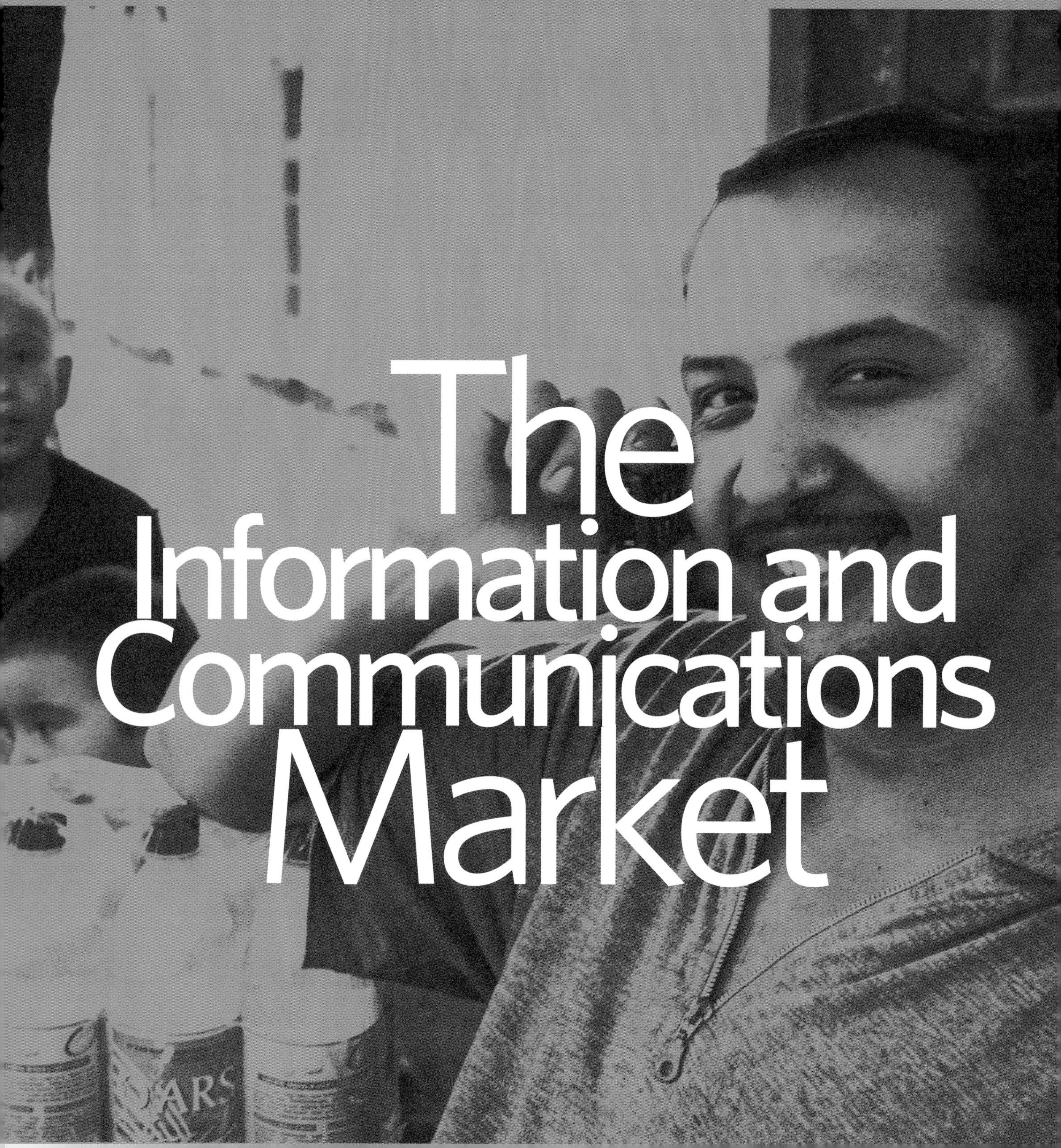

The Information and Communications Market

A small coffee grower in Costa Rica keeps in touch with international market prices, and ultimately arranges sale and pick-up of his crop, via his mobile phone. A family in the Philippines, dependent on money from a member working as a nurse in the United States, can pick it up at a local McDonald's, transferred quickly and inexpensively by a mobile phone remittance system. It may seem obvious, but those in the BOP cannot join the global economy, and benefit from it, until they are connected to it.

The household survey data reported here show significant demand for such connections and a willingness to pay—because the value proposition, for someone without connectivity, is compelling. A recent study among low-income families in Tanzania showed that access to livelihoods was a primary reason for owning a mobile phone (Vodafone 2005).

Not surprisingly, mobile phone companies in emerging markets are growing rapidly, adding hundreds of millions of customers a year (World Bank 2006b). With more than 1.5 billion mobile phone customers in developing regions—the size of the mid-market and high-income population segments—most new customers in these regions now come from the BOP.

Advanced services are starting to appear. Wizzit, a start-up in South Africa, and Globe Telecom and Smart Communications in the Philippines together are providing banking services over mobile phones to more than a million previously unbanked customers in those two countries alone (Ivatury and Pickens 2006).

A broader range of businesses is developing to provide services to the BOP. Some 1.6 million small sari-sari shops in the Philippines help customers with electronic uploads of voice or text-messaging units for their mobile phones, generating almost $1 billion in revenue. At the other end of the size spectrum, both Microsoft and Intel now have emerging-market divisions focused on developing new products for the BOP.

BOP spending on ICT
$51.4 billion

	$ billions (PPP)
Africa	4.4
Asia	28.3
Eastern Europe	5.3
Latin America	13.4

Each square represents approximately $200 million

CASE STUDY 3.1 **CELTEL: FROM START-UP TO TELECOM GIANT**

Combining a focus on underserved markets in Africa with a commitment to clean, transparent business practices, Celtel has become a leader in the highly competitive African telecom market. The company was founded in 1998 by a British entrepreneur of Sudanese descent, Dr. Mo Ibrahim. Later that year Celtel launched service in Zambia, Sierra Leone, and the Republic of Congo. The company gradually added 10 more countries to its portfolio—Malawi, Gabon, the Democratic Republic of Congo, Chad, Burkina Faso, Niger, Uganda, Tanzania, Sudan, and Kenya.

Celtel operates in some of the most difficult sociopolitical environments in the world—amid civil war and political unrest—yet the company is committed to clean, corruption-free business. Founder Ibrahim has been outspoken in his promise that Celtel will pay "not a single dollar" in bribes.

Overcoming adverse business and political environments, Celtel quickly expanded its customer base to 6 million thanks to its focus on the needs of low-income consumers. Celtel's offerings are prepaid and sold in small increments. Subsidiaries in Tanzania and Zambia offer mobile banking services over the network. Some 98% of the firm's staff are African, many of them holding company stock.

Many of those stockholding employees cashed in when Celtel was acquired by Kuwait-based MTC in mid-2005 for US$3.4 billion. Celtel, now a wholly owned subsidiary of MTC, serves 15 countries in Africa and holds licenses covering more than 30% of the continent—the largest footprint of any company in Africa. In just seven years Celtel went from start-up to telecom giant—and did so by pursuing a BOP-focused, ethically driven business strategy in some of the world's most neglected economies.[5]

Both in its use of prepaid services offered in small units and in its willingness to do business in challenging environments, Celtel exemplifies a strategy of **enabling access**.

How large is the market?

The measured BOP market for ICT—information and communication technologies and the services they provide—is $30.5 billion for Africa (11 countries), Asia (9), Eastern Europe (6), and Latin America and the Caribbean (9). This represents annual household ICT spending in the 35 low- and middle-income countries for which standardized data exist, covering 2.1 billion of the world's BOP population.

The total BOP household ICT market in these four regions, including 3.96 billion people in all surveyed countries, is estimated to be $51.4 billion (see box 1.5 in chapter 1 for the estimation method).[1] But the ICT sector has been growing explosively in developing regions in the interval since countries were surveyed, with Internet services and especially mobile phone companies adding customers at rates that may well have doubled BOP sector spending since that time.[2] Moreover, rapid market growth is expected to continue for some time: in both Africa and India less than 15% of the population have mobile phones.[3]

Asia has the largest measured regional BOP market for ICT, $14.3 billion, reflecting the region's significant BOP population of 1.49 billion. Its estimated total BOP market for ICT (including the Middle East) is $28.3 billion, including the spending of 2.9 billion people. Not far behind is Latin America's measured BOP market, $11.2 billion, accounting for the ICT spending of 276 million people. The region's estimated total BOP market is $13.4 billion (360 million people).

In Eastern Europe the measured BOP market for ICT is $3.0 billion (148 million people); the estimated total market is $5.3 billion (254

Asia has the largest measured regional BOP market for ICT, $14.3 billion, reflecting the region's significant BOP population of 1.49 billion.

Pakistan

TOTAL ICT SPENDING BY INCOME SEGMENT

Uganda

TOTAL ICT SPENDING BY INCOME SEGMENT

Belarus

TOTAL ICT SPENDING BY INCOME SEGMENT

million people). In Africa the measured BOP market is $2.0 billion (258 million people), and the estimated total BOP market $4.4 billion (486 million people). Though smallest, the African ICT market is the most rapidly growing one—and it has already generated very profitable companies and significant wealth (case study 3.1).

The BOP share of the total household ICT market in measured countries varies across regions. In Asia the BOP share is about half of the total market, 51%; in other regions it is smaller though still substantial: 36% in Eastern Europe, 28% in Africa, 26% in Latin America. Africa shows the greatest disparity between the BOP share of the population (95%) and the BOP share of ICT spending (28%).

At the national level there are wide disparities in the BOP share of ICT spending. These disparities stem in part from regulatory differences affecting the pace at which mobile phone networks expand (case study 3.2). They also reflect national differences in urban-rural demographics, since mobile networks start in urban areas and only then spread to rural areas.

In Asia the extremes are represented by Pakistan and Bangladesh, where the BOP accounts for more than 89% of the ICT market, and Thailand, where the BOP population, though substantial, accounts for only 29% of the market. In Africa the extremes are Nigeria (98%) and Burundi (12%). In Eastern Europe the extremes are represented by Belarus and Kazakhstan (74%) and FYR Macedonia (21%). In Latin America and the Caribbean, only in Jamaica does the BOP account for more than half of total ICT household spending (71%); the other extreme is Colombia, where the BOP accounts for only 12% of ICT spending.

How is the market segmented?

In Asia and Africa most BOP markets for ICT are either top heavy, like those in Sri Lanka and Uganda, or centered on the middle of the income spectrum (in the BOP1500, BOP2000, and BOP2500 segments), like those in Pakistan or Côte d'Ivoire. Indonesia, with $2.1 billion in annual BOP spending for ICT, offers another example of a market centered on the middle

CASE STUDY 3.2 **REGULATORY REFORM: OPEN MARKETS ARE BIGGER MARKETS**

A key driver of the rapid growth of ICT services in many developing countries has been the opening of markets to competition. But only about half of low- and middle-income countries have undertaken such reforms, and the difference is apparent: the Democratic Republic of Congo, with six competing mobile phone companies, has 13 times as many mobile customers per 1,000 people as does Ethiopia, with similar income per capita but only a single mobile company (World Bank 2006b). Where barriers to competition still exist, prices for ICT services are higher—twice as high on average—and market penetration is slower.

While the reform process is well advanced for mobile telephony, barriers are still the rule for newer and potentially much less expensive ICT services. In many countries Voice-over-Internet telephony remains illegal. Relatively few countries have assigned frequencies for newer, fixed wireless services, despite their potential to expand markets and make ICT services affordable and accessible to a larger share of the BOP, especially in rural areas. And only a few countries have coordinated banking and telecom regulations to pave the way for mobile phone banking, which could bring affordable financial services to hundreds of millions of people who are now unbanked. As reforms advance, so will markets and private sector investment.

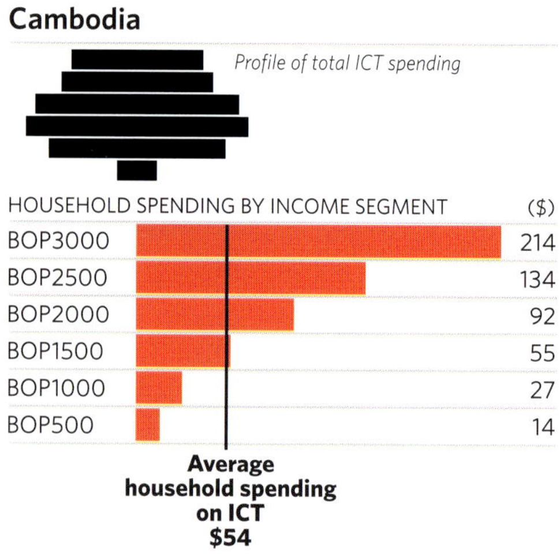

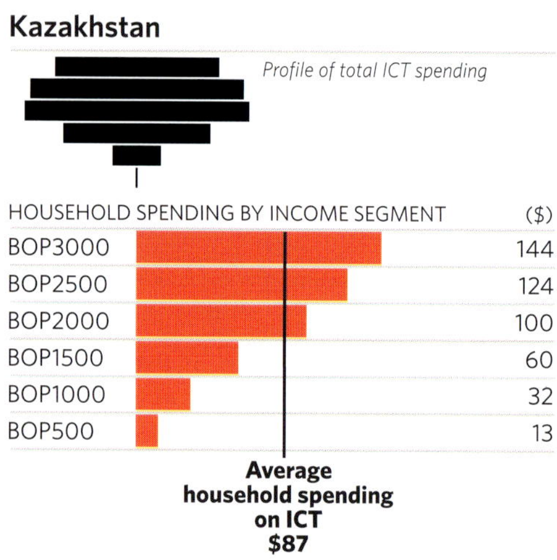

(case study 3.3). There are as yet few bottom-heavy BOP markets, reflecting the still modest penetration of ICT services into BOP populations and into rural areas.

Eastern Europe and Latin America also have top-heavy BOP markets, exemplified by Belarus and Peru. Moreover, the wealthier mid-market segment accounts for most of the total ICT market in half the measured countries of Eastern Europe and all those of Latin America. In contrast, the BOP dominates Asian and African markets; in only five countries—Thailand, South Africa, Rwanda, Malawi, and Burundi—does spending by the mid-market segment exceed that by the BOP.

What do households spend?

Business models play a big part in ICT spending. Prepaid mobile telephony in small units and Internet access by the quarter hour in cybercafes, for example, have helped to create affordability. That may account for the remarkable levels of ICT spending by BOP households documented in the surveys. Except in the very lowest BOP income segment, average ICT spending per household generally exceeds spending on water—and in the upper BOP income segments sometimes exceeds spending on health. Continuing rapid growth in the ICT sector in developing countries suggests ample untapped demand.[4] Recorded levels of household ICT spending should thus be regarded as establishing a lower bound for the willingness to pay.

Access to services also plays a big part in household spending, especially in the ICT sector—where most rural communities are still underserved—as do demographic factors. As a result, average ICT spending per BOP household varies widely across countries, but can also be similar despite quite different market characteristics. For example, Côte d'Ivoire and Sierra Leone report similar spending by BOP households—averaging $57.60 and $46.40 a year—yet Côte d'Ivoire's BOP market is decidedly bottom heavy while Sierra Leone's is more top heavy, trending toward the top two income segments (BOP2500 and BOP3000). Reported spending can also reflect differences in the

CASE STUDY 3.3 **INDONESIA: AN ICT MARKET CENTERED ON THE MIDDLE OF THE BOP**

In Indonesia ICT spending by BOP households is concentrated in the BOP1500, BOP2000, and BOP2500 income segments. These three segments account for 59% of the total ICT market and 28% of all households in Indonesia; with 15 million households and $1.6 billion in annual ICT spending, this is a substantial market. Annual ICT spending per household in these income segments averages $50, $161, and $336.

Moving up-market dramatically increases ICT spending per household—but the overall market still is decidedly concentrated in the middle BOP segments. Average annual ICT spending per household in the relatively small but much wealthier mid-market population segment ($1,238) is about eight times that in the BOP ($149).

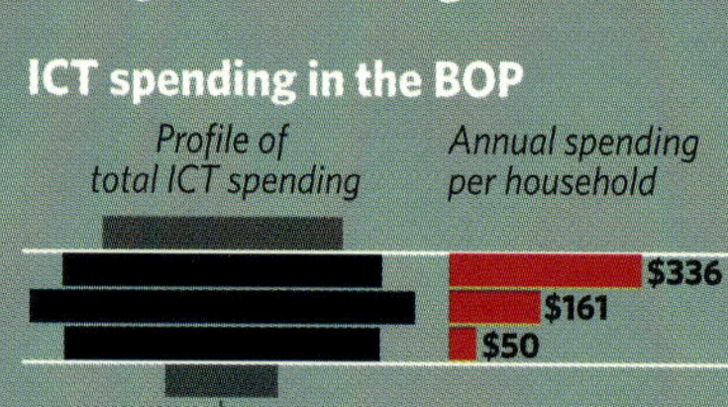

questions asked and expenditures captured in national surveys.

A more meaningful characterization may be the median of annual BOP per household spending on health for each region. These figures are as follows: for Africa, $33.89 (Cameroon); for Asia, $53.62 (Cambodia); for Eastern Europe, $55.83 (Belarus) and $87.00 (Kazakhstan); and for Latin America, $107.40 (Peru). India has the largest measured BOP market for ICT in Asia, with $7.8 billion in aggregate household spending (53% of the national ICT market); average ICT spending per BOP household is $42 a year. (No expenditure data are available for China.) In other regions the BOP market leaders are Brazil ($5.5 billion, 27% of the total market), Russia ($1.4 billion, 35% of the total market), and South Africa ($745 million, 14% of the total market). Annual BOP per household spending averages $173 in Brazil, $53 in Russia, and $109 in South Africa.

In most countries measured, ICT spending per household increases roughly in proportion to income through the BOP, especially above the lowest income segment. In many countries, however, ICT spending increases disproportionately in the highest BOP income segments (BOP2500 and BOP3000), indicating latent demand for ICT services in the BOP. Among the median countries by region discussed above, the ratio of average household ICT spending in the BOP3000 income segment to that in the BOP1000 segment is 27:1 in Cameroon, 8:1 in Cambodia, 4:1 in Belarus and Kazakhstan, and 32:1 in Peru.

As incomes rise still higher, per household ICT spending increases as well, but to an extent that varies by country—only modestly in Latin American and Eastern European countries on average, more so in most African and Asian countries. A useful measure is the ratio of average annual ICT spending by mid-market households to that by BOP households. In the above countries, mid-market households outspend BOP households by about 12:1 in Cameroon and 12:1 in Cambodia; 2:1 in Belarus and

CASE STUDY 3.4 **SMART TELECOMS: TAILORING SERVICES, TRANSFORMING MARKETS**

Most of the ICT spending recorded by household surveys is for phone service. Another spending category, generally smaller, is for ICT equipment (television sets, music players, computers, phones, cameras). A still smaller one is for repair of such equipment. Other information shows that most BOP users access the Internet from cybercafes or other shared-access points, not from home; the same is true for a large share of those using phone service.

These survey categories fail to do justice to the richness of the ICT services and business strategies propelling BOP markets. In the Philippines, for example, Smart Communications has transformed the cell phone market by allowing electronic sales of airtime through short message service (SMS) and by reducing the unit size of such sales to as little as US$0.03. This innovation has allowed access to communication services for millions of low-income Filipinos; 98% of Smart's subscribers are low-income, prepaid customers. Its SMS-based transaction system allows customers to transfer prepaid units to one another, providing an electronic "currency" that facilitates small transactions. And it allows small merchants to resell minutes, with a commission on every sale—creating a business opportunity for 800,000 microentrepreneurs.

Smart also started the world's first remittance system by text message. Expatriate Filipinos can give cash payments to international agents, who then transfer the cash to the designated recipients back in the Philippines. The recipients, alerted by an SMS message on their phone, can immediately withdraw the cash from the local McDonald's branch. Moreover, the service is cheaper than the informal, underground network often used to transport cash to the Philippines from abroad (Smith 2004b).

Smart Communications exemplifies two BOP business strategies: focusing on the BOP through its innovation of new services and localizing value creation through its extensive network of agents.

Burkina Faso

SHARE OF HOUSEHOLD SPENDING ON ICT (%)

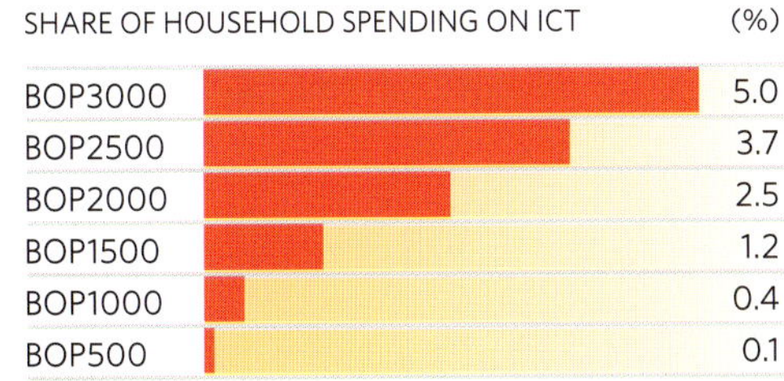

Brazil

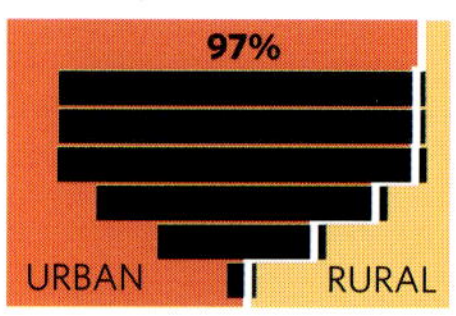

Total BOP ICT spending by income segment, urban and rural

India

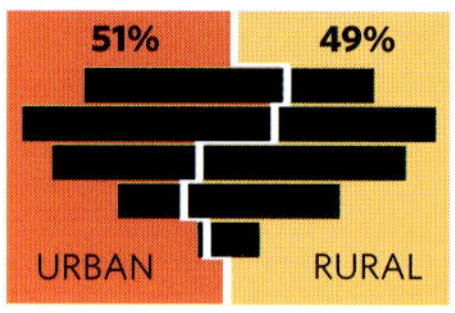

Bolivia

PERCENT OF HOUSEHOLDS WITH A TELEPHONE

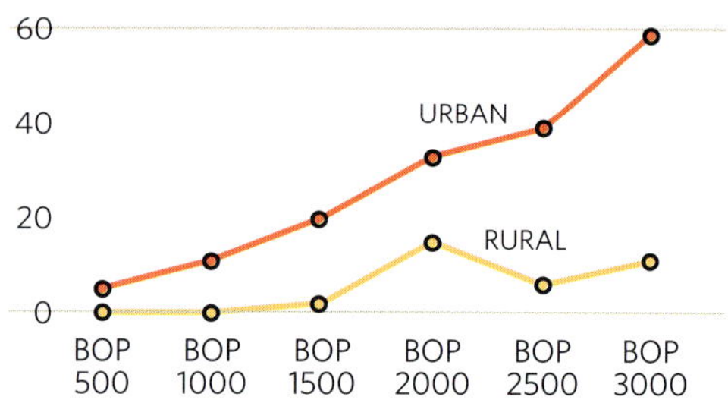

Pakistan

PERCENT OF HOUSEHOLDS WITH A TELEPHONE

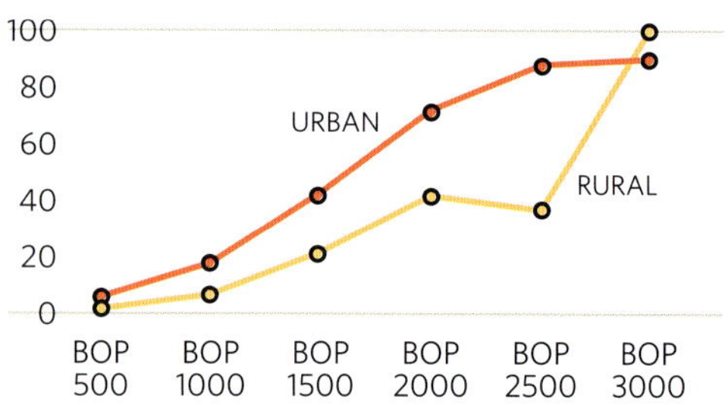

Kazakhstan; and 8:1 in Peru. These ratios are considerably higher than those in other infrastructure sectors, such as energy and water, again suggesting quite a bit of latent demand for ICT services (case study 3.4).

Where is the market?

In the still largely urban-centered ICT sector, there are vast differences in size between urban and rural markets, including their BOP segments. In all measured countries except Cambodia and Sri Lanka, urban areas dominate the overall ICT market. Urban areas also dominate the BOP market in all Eastern European and Latin American countries, in all African countries except Uganda, and in four of nine Asian countries, including India, Indonesia, and Pakistan.

In Brazil, for example, the BOP market for ICT is 97% urban, and average annual spending by urban BOP households ($203) is seven times that by rural BOP households. In Russia the urban share of the BOP market is 71%, and the ratio of urban to rural household ICT spending is 2:1. In Asia, India's BOP market for ICT is 51% urban, with urban BOP households outspending rural ones 3:1; Pakistan and Indonesia have even larger urban shares of the BOP market, 69% and 93%. In Africa, South Africa's BOP market is 68% urban, with urban households spending twice as much on average as rural households; Nigeria has a 77% urban share.

Despite generally lower levels of ICT spending in rural areas, the sheer size of the rural population in some countries means a significant rural market. Thailand's rural BOP market for ICT, for example, is $1.5 billion, with household spending averaging $160 a year. India's is $3.8 billion. Mexico's is $767 million, with average annual per household spending of $154.

Is there evidence of a BOP penalty?

Rural ICT market shares may have increased somewhat in recent years, as mobile networks have expanded out of urban centers. But the overall urban-rural pattern in BOP spending is consistent with widespread lack of access to ICT services in rural areas. The differences cannot be entirely due to higher urban incomes. In Bolivia, for example, urban BOP households spend 365% more on ICT than their rural counterparts, yet have only 94% more income (based on measured total expenditure).

Clearly, lack of access to ICT services in rural areas can be a significant BOP penalty, one that keeps rural households disconnected from markets and broader information sources and thus reinforces rural isolation and poverty.

Data on phone ownership support lack of access as a primary cause of the disparity: in Bolivia only 2% of rural BOP households report owning a fixed or cellular phone, compared with 13% of their wealthier mid-market rural neighbors and 25% of urban BOP households. This pattern is widespread. In Russia 27% of rural BOP households own a phone, compared with 48% of mid-market rural households and 53% of urban BOP households. In Pakistan 6% of BOP households in rural areas own a phone, compared with 26% of those in urban areas.

Clearly, lack of access to ICT services in rural areas can be a significant BOP penalty, one that keeps rural households disconnected from markets and broader information sources and thus reinforces rural isolation and poverty. The penalty would be more severe without the widespread—though far from universal—public or shared-access ICT services.

How shared access helps reduce the BOP penalty

While few rural BOP households in Bolivia own a phone, survey data show that such households nevertheless spend an average of $35 a year on ICT, more than $27 of it for "telephone and telefax services." Simply put, these rural households cannot afford to purchase a phone, but they will gladly pay to use one—whether a public pay phone, a neighbor's cell phone, or a shared-use phone owned by an entrepreneur.

Paraguay provides an even starker example. A survey there shows that among rural BOP households only 0.25% report owning a phone. Yet the same survey reports that annual per household ICT spending in this group averages

CASE STUDY 3.5 **COMMUNITY PHONES: ENTREPRENEURS PROVIDE SHARED ACCESS**

Vodacom Community Services, a program of South Africa's largest cellular phone company, shows how business and government can work together to achieve social and economic goals. Developed by Vodacom to meet a 1994 government mandate to provide services in BOP communities, this innovative program relies on phone shops owned and operated by entrepreneurs. The program has both provided affordable communication services to millions of South Africans and empowered thousands of previously disadvantaged entrepreneurs.

At a cost of about R 26,000 (US$3,450), prospective owners can start a Community Services franchise to operate cellular lines from inside a converted shipping container. The phone shops are independent businesses, but they offer standard products and services. At any Community Services phone shop in the country, customers can make a phone call for a set rate of R 85 (US$0.11) a minute, less than a third of the commercial rate for prepaid cellular calls.

In a good location a phone shop with five lines typically handles more than 100 hours of calling a month per line, generating total monthly revenues of R 27,000 (US$3,550); of this, R 9,000 (US$1,190) goes to the entrepreneur. The phone shops take advantage of Vodacom's extensive cellular network, which provides coverage to 93% of South Africa's 44 million citizens. Today the shops service more than 23,000 cellular lines at more than 4,400 locations throughout South Africa (Reck and Wood 2003).

The community phone shops have succeeded by harnessing local entrepreneurs, exemplifying a strategy of **localizing value creation.**

CASE STUDY 3.6 INVESTING IN THE BOP: BUSINESS STRATEGIES FOR THE NEXT BILLION

Reports from a 2006 global conference of the International Telecommunication Union suggest that telecom and information technology executives are now focusing on the BOP population in emerging markets as the source of their next billion customers. They are using a range of strategies to target the BOP.

Qualcomm, for example, is helping partners in India launch mobile phones, based on the company's technology, that cost less than US$30. While the phones may not earn much money for Qualcomm, they represent an investment in the future, according to Paul Jacobs, the company's chief executive officer. "We don't think we're going to make a lot of money on the first phone that somebody buys," he says. "But eventually [that customer] will buy more and more."

Moreover, Jacobs argues, a lot of innovation comes from focusing on developing inexpensive products for emerging markets. "It used to be that you would invest in the high-end services and they would trickle down," he says. "Now we invest equally in the low end and high end and things trickle to the middle."[6]

Motorola too believes that focusing on emerging markets results in innovation. The company sells a US$30 handset designed in India with rural users in mind. The phone can give instructions to a user by audio rather than in text form—in case the user is not literate. It also has a reflective display that people can easily see when outdoors and a battery with a standby time of two weeks (GSM Association 2005).

Such companies as Intel, Motorola, and Samsung Electronics make a case for new fixed wireless technologies, WiMax and WiFi, to connect the next billion users, arguing that wireless is far cheaper than copper, especially given the run-up in copper prices in recent years. Intel has been supporting trials in Southeast Asia. Samsung is providing equipment for trials in Latin America and plans to market the equipment in Southeast Asia and Africa.

These examples exemplify a strategy of **focusing on the BOP.**

$128 a year, with $117 of it going to telephone services.

This pattern—in which very few rural households own a phone yet most spend significant amounts on phone service—also holds in other countries. In Uganda measured annual spending for phone service averages $29 across all rural BOP households, yet just 0.10% report owning a phone. In Pakistan, where just 6% of rural BOP households own a phone, annual spending on phone services by rural BOP households averages $24. Mexico's ownership rate is higher than those in African and Asian countries, at 17%, but so is its average annual spending on phone services by rural BOP households, at $137.

In some countries public pay phones provide shared access; in others, such as India and South Africa, entrepreneur-run phone shops provide the access (case study 3.5). Cybercafes and kiosks similarly provide shared access to computers and the Internet.

New technology, new market potential

Will phones become the Internet platform for BOP households and rural communities? Several factors suggest that they will, including the business strategies adopted by some major mobile phone manufacturers and information technology companies (case study 3.6).

Mobile phones already have an enormous lead over computers in developing countries. Moreover, phones are relatively easy to master, generally require no sophisticated technical support, and, as voice-based devices, pose no literacy barrier. Phones are less expensive than computers—basic GSM models designed for developing countries are approaching US$30—and service is often offered through prepaid business models that are more affordable for BOP consumers.

The combination of powerful phones, inexpensive networks, and voice-accessible applications may open up the Internet to large numbers of new users.

Increasingly, mobile phones also offer Internet services such as e-mail and Web browsing and are becoming a platform for banking and other financial services. Driven by intense competition, mobile phone manufacturers are rapidly adding new capabilities—digital photography, voice recognition, and biometric identification, to name a few. As a result, industry observers forecast, within five years the typical mobile phone will have the processing power of today's desktop computers.

Equally important is the potential for low-cost fixed wireless networks in rural areas, bringing Internet access—and Voice-over-Internet telephony—to phones and other devices in areas too sparsely populated to support conventional cellular networks. Adding a WiFi chip to a mobile phone to allow access to such rural networks will cost only a few dollars.

The combination of powerful phones, inexpensive networks, and voice-accessible Internet applications—for obtaining market prices, health information, or government services—may open up the Internet to large numbers of new users. In any event, it is clear that ongoing innovation in technology will help increase the potential of rural—and largely BOP—ICT markets.

Endnotes

1. Reported household expenditures in a given country should be regarded as a minimum estimate of actual expenditures, because surveys may not have collected information on all types of ICT-related spending.
2. For a comprehensive overview, see the World Bank's Information and Communications for Development 2006: Global Trends and Policies (2006b). To illustrate the rapid growth in the sector, the report cites the increase in mobile phone subscribers in Nigeria from 370,000 to 16.8 million between 2001 and 2005, and the sixfold growth in the Philippines to 40 million subscribers between 2000 and 2005. Access to phones tripled in Sub-Saharan Africa and East Asia between 2000 and 2004, nearly doubled in South Asia, and doubled in Latin America and Central Asia. The numbers of Internet users grew even faster, though from a much smaller base.
3. Economist, "Out of Africa," December 9, 2006, 67–68.
4. In late 2005, for example, India was reported to be adding more than 6 million new mobile subscribers a month (Katie Allen, "Motorola's Gloomy Outlook Casts Shadow on Mobile Phone Market," Guardian Unlimited, January 6, 2006, http://business.guardian.co.uk/story/0,,1983795,00.html accessed January 18, 2006).
5. Michela Wrong, "Mo Ibrahim: Revolutionising Communications in Africa. His Tool? The Mobile Phone," New Statesman, October 17, 2006, http://www.newstatesman.com/200510170021; Mo Ibrahim, presentation to World Bank, April, 2006.
6. Bruce Einhorn, "Telecoms Hungry for Next Billion Callers," BusinessWeek, December 7, 2006, http://www.businessweek.com/globalbiz/content/dec2006/gb20061207_197764.htm.

CHAPTER FOUR

The Water Market

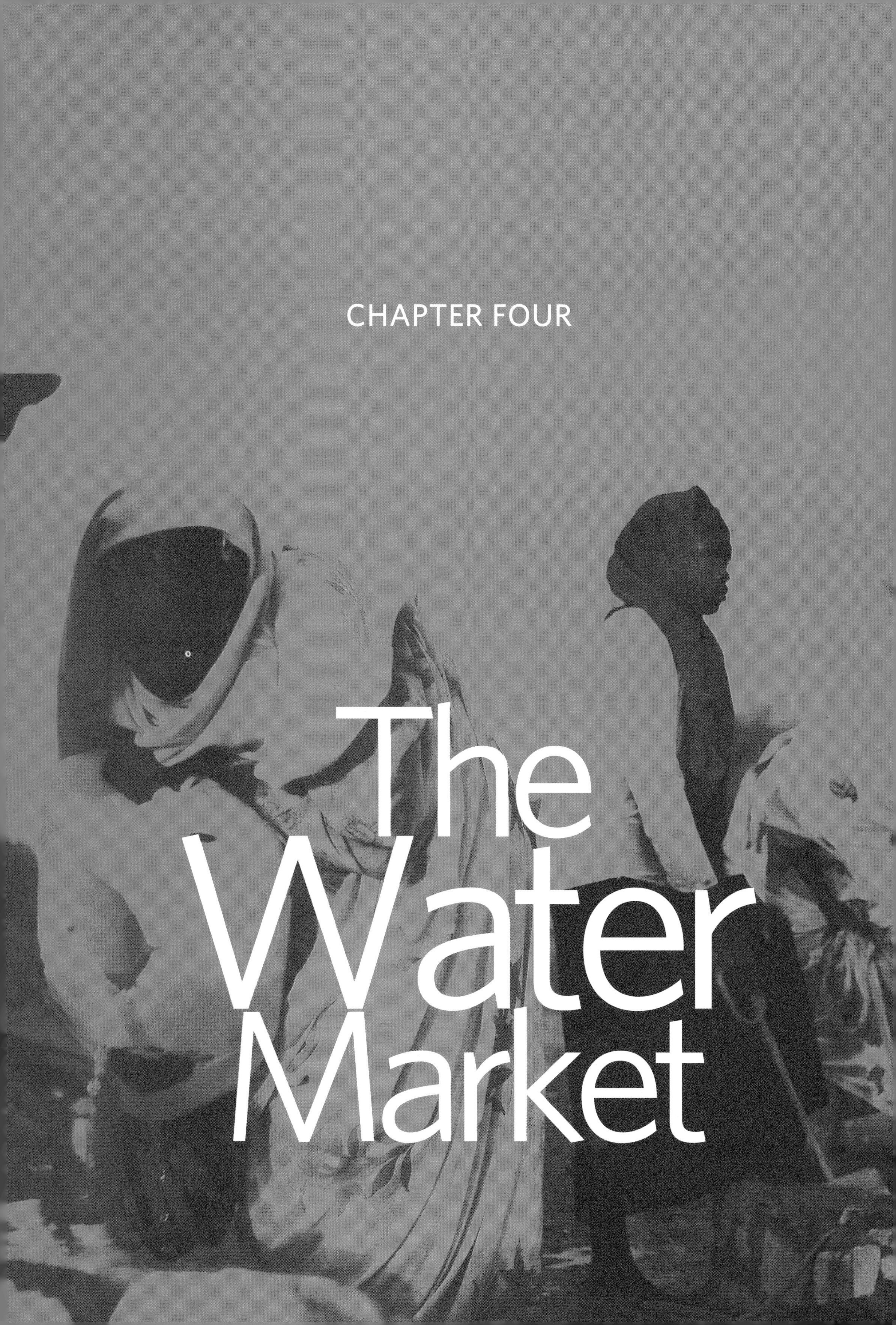

More than a billion people lack access to clean drinking water. Many more must struggle to meet their daily needs for water—or to pay the high costs for this essential commodity. The reasons for these challenges? Urban water networks are aging. Rapid urbanization is increasing demand faster than networks can expand. Many people live in water-stressed regions and water sources are being polluted by industrialization, agricultural runoff, and lack of sanitation services.

People obtain water in many ways. Some collect it at no "cost" (apart from the considerable cost of their labor) from streams or other surface sources or from wells or community standpipes. Others must pay for it. Payments to large urban water systems dominate recorded household spending on water. But households also purchase water from vendors and small-scale community water systems and pay for point-of-use services such as water purification.

The private sector is often the provider of last resort. Small-scale water vendors are often the only option in peri-urban communities. Improved point-of-use systems being devised and marketed by the private sector also show promise for giving BOP households better options for water supply, especially in rural areas. New models of community engagement and public-private partnership are emerging.

BOP spending on water
$20.1 billion

	$ billions (PPP)
Africa	5.7
Asia	6.4
Eastern Europe	3.2
Latin America	4.8

Each square represents approximately $100 million

How large is the market?

The measured BOP water market in Africa (11 countries), Asia (7), Eastern Europe (5), and Latin America and the Caribbean (7) is $11.3 billion. This represents the annual household water spending of 2.0 billion people in 30 low- and middle-income countries. The total BOP water market in these four regions, including all surveyed countries, is estimated to be $20 billion, accounting for the spending of 3.96 billion people (see box 1.5 in chapter 1 for the estimation method).

Latin America has the largest measured BOP water market, at $3.8 billion for 262.5 million people. The region's total BOP water market is estimated to be $4.8 billion, accounting for the spending of 360 million people. In

BOP water markets tend to be predominately urban, even where most BOP households are rural. Growth has been particularly rapid in peri-urban areas, which often lie beyond municipal supply networks.

Nigeria

TOTAL WATER SPENDING BY INCOME SEGMENT

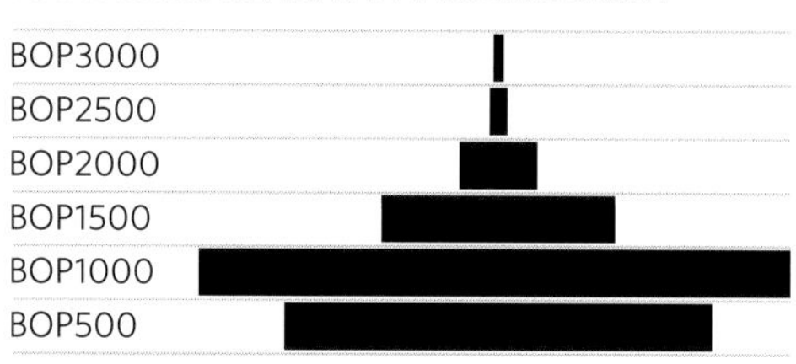

Pakistan

TOTAL WATER SPENDING BY INCOME SEGMENT

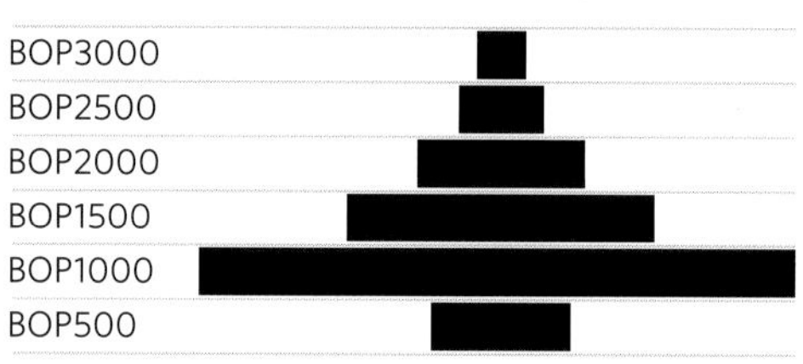

Asia the measured BOP water market is $3.2 billion (1.4 billion people), while the estimated total BOP water market in the region (including the Middle East) is $6.4 billion (2.9 billion people). In Africa the measured market is $2.5 billion (252.4 million people), and the estimated total market $5.7 billion (486 million people). Eastern Europe's measured market is $1.7 billion (138.9 million people), and its estimated total market $3.2 billion (254 million people).

The BOP share of total spending in measured markets ranges widely. Asia has the largest BOP share, at 68%. In Latin America and Eastern Europe the BOP share is 45%. In Africa the BOP share is 60%.

The regional averages mask large differences within regions. In Eastern Europe the BOP market share ranges from a low of 24% in FYR Macedonia to a high of 98% in Uzbekistan. Africa shows a similar spread: in Rwanda the BOP accounts for a mere 14% of household spending on water, while in Nigeria the BOP is effectively the entire market, accounting for more than 99%. In Latin America, among countries with larger populations, only Peru has a BOP market share of well over half, at 71%. In Asia only Thailand and Nepal have BOP market shares hovering around 50%; other countries have much larger BOP market shares.

By many measures (not just size), the BOP water market is "depressed" compared with other BOP markets. BOP households generally represent a smaller share of the national water market than of other markets, including energy and transportation. Moreover, while the BOP accounts for 71% of the population in Latin America, it accounts for only 45% of recorded water spending—and a similar pattern holds in other regions.

How is the market segmented?

Bottom-heavy BOP water markets—in which more than 50% of recorded spending occurs in the bottom three BOP income segments—are apparent in 10 of the 30 measured countries. Eight are in Asia and Africa (Indonesia, Pakistan, Tajikistan, Burkina Faso, Côte d'Ivoire, Malawi, Nigeria, and Uganda). In these countries where the bottom three BOP income segments dominate the BOP market, they often also dominate the national market—representing more of the market than both the upper BOP income segments and the mid-market segment combined.

Some cases are even more extreme, with more than 50% of all recorded national water spending occurring in the lowest two BOP income groups. Burkina Faso, Côte d'Ivoire, Nigeria, and Uganda all exhibit this pattern. In Nigeria the 22.3 million households in the BOP500 and BOP1000 segments account for 75% of the national water market—$444.6 million in annual spending.

Among Asian countries, a similar concentration occurs in Pakistan, where the BOP500 and BOP1000 groups account for 54% of the national water market, and in Tajikistan, where they account for 57%. In Indonesia, with the third largest measured water market in Asia, the lowest three BOP income groups dominate the market, accounting for 52% of total spending—$421.1 million across 125.6 million households.

Top-heavy BOP water markets, in which the top three BOP income segments account for more spending than the bottom three, predominate in Eastern Europe and Latin America—occurring in 10 of the 12 measured countries in these regions. These top-heavy BOP markets often coincide with a national market dominated by the mid-market segment. Paraguay represents an extreme case. In that country the mid-market segment represents 78% of recorded national water spending—but only 36% of the national population. In contrast, the bottom three BOP groups represent only 3% of the national water market—but 36% of the population.

Where top-heavy BOP water markets occur in Asia and Africa, they rarely coincide with mid-market dominance. Bangladesh has a top-heavy BOP water market, for example, yet the mid-market segment accounts for only 15% of national spending.

Where is the market?

BOP water markets tend to be predominantly urban, even where most BOP households are rural. Among measured markets the only exceptions to this pattern are Thailand, Uganda, and Uzbekistan. Growth in BOP water markets has been particularly rapid in peri-urban areas, which often lie beyond municipal supply networks. Here, non-networked but relatively large water purification initiatives show promise (case study 4.1).

CASE STUDY 4.1 **OUTSIDE THE NETWORK: WILLINGNESS TO PAY FOR CLEAN WATER**

WaterHealth International, a private company operating in India with both public and private funding, has developed a range of products using an ultraviolet (UV) water disinfection system—from household units to scalable community water systems and franchised water stores. A pilot in Bomminampadu, in the Indian state of Andhra Pradesh, confirmed that low-income communities are willing to pay—both for treated water and for home delivery. Indeed, 80% of households signed up—in a village where before no one had paid a thing for water.

Elsewhere in Andhra Pradesh, Heritage Livelihood Services partners with the Hyderabad Metropolitan Water Supply and Sewerage Board to bring services to peri-urban areas of the city. The company's investments, which included water tanks and working capital to provide for bulk payments for water supplies, have enabled privately-owned water trucks sub-contracted by the government to provide clean water at rates well below those charged by alternative suppliers—though still high enough to cover costs. The company also engages local community organizations to educate people about the value of improved water delivery.

WaterHealth, through its innovative efforts, illustrates a strategy of **focusing on the BOP**. Heritage Livelihood Services, in seeing the community as the customer, is employing a strategy of **localizing value creation**. Both show that private companies can implement BOP business strategies even when public entities are also involved.

Peru
TOTAL WATER SPENDING BY INCOME SEGMENT

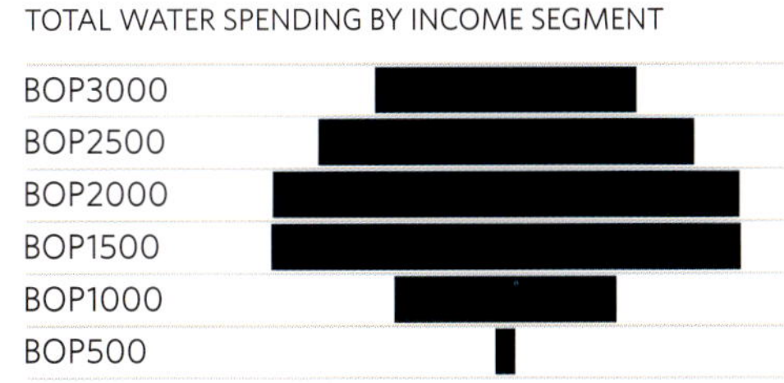

Kazakhstan
TOTAL WATER SPENDING BY INCOME SEGMENT

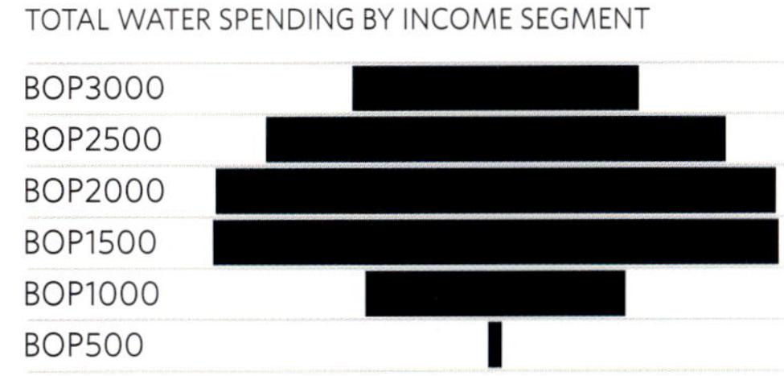

Urban BOP households spend significantly more on water than do rural BOP households.

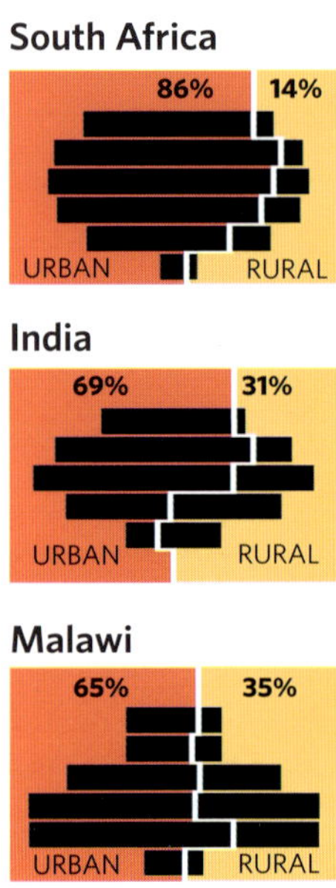

Total BOP water spending by income segment, urban and rural

In Africa the most heavily urban BOP water markets are in Djibouti, Gabon, Rwanda, and Sierra Leone, where urban spending accounts for more than 90% of the total. In Gabon the urban BOP market is 32 times the size of the rural one. At the other end of the spectrum is Uganda, whose rural market is 6 times the size of its urban market.

Urban spending also drives BOP water markets in Asia. In Pakistan, for example, urban areas account for 84% of the BOP water market, but only 29% of BOP households. Eastern Europe and Latin America, where BOP households also are mostly urban, show similar or even stronger urban dominance. In Ukraine 87% of BOP water spending is urban; in Colombia, 93%.

Urban BOP households also spend significantly more on water than do rural BOP households. In Malawi total BOP spending is twice as much in urban as in rural areas, but spending on water 16 times as much. Nepal shows a similar pattern: the urban-rural ratio for total household spending is about 2:1, while that for water spending is 22:1. Similar but much less extreme differences show up in most countries of Eastern Europe and Latin America.

What does the BOP buy?

BOP households still meet much of their need for water by gathering it from "free" sources—surface water and wells. Some of these sources are safe and protected; others are subject to serious contamination and consequently pose health hazards. The variety of contaminants—waste, heavy metals, chemical and biological agents—requires a range of solutions (case study 4.2).

BOP households in Africa are the most likely to rely on surface water. In the measured African countries 17% of BOP households report surface water as their primary source (compared with only 1% in the mid-market segment). Use of surface water is consistently highest in the BOP500 group and declines as incomes rise. In Burkina Faso, for example, 81% of households in the BOP500 segment use surface water, compared with 69% in BOP1000 and 55% in BOP1500. In Sierra Leone the rates are 47%, 38%, and 27%. In Cameroon, 49%, 40%, and 20%.

In Latin America a smaller share of BOP households rely on surface water as a primary source. Moreover, reliance on surface water drops more quickly as incomes rise. In Peru, for example, 45% of households in the BOP500 segment rely on surface water, but only 32% in BOP1000 and 15% in BOP1500.

CASE STUDY 4.2 **CLEARING UP THE WATER: NEW TECHNOLOGIES SERVING AT-RISK POPULATIONS**

A range of enterprises are developing technologies—based on desalination, disinfection, and filtering methods—to provide affordable point-of-use treatment systems for the variety of contaminants faced by BOP households and communities.

Desalination: Perhaps the simplest method of desalination is evaporation of brackish or salty water and recapture of the salt-free water through condensation. The Watercone does exactly that. Measuring 60–80 centimeters in diameter at its base, the cone can yield more than a liter of water a day under the average solar irradiation in Casablanca. Made from a UV-resistant polycarbonate plastic, the Watercone is nontoxic and recyclable and has a life expectancy of five to seven years. A new product, it is expected to sell for around US$25.

Disinfection: In Madagascar a sustainable local enterprise, Sur'Eau (safe water), is producing a dilute bleach (sodium hypochlorite) water-sanitizing solution for the mass market. Through a social marketing system and a network of more than 10,000 community-based retailers, Sur'Eau has persuaded hundreds of thousands of consumers to purchase the solution—selling more than 500,000 bottles in 2004 alone. The cost to treat enough drinking water for a family for a day, around 20 liters, is less than a penny. Recently Sur'Eau began offering a more concentrated solution in a smaller, lighter bottle, easier to transport to remote locations (PSI 2006).

The consumer products giant Procter & Gamble (P&G), working in collaboration with the U.S. Centers for Disease Control and Prevention, has also produced a dilute bleach product, marketed under the name PuR. P&G is working to make the product fully commercially viable, but it is already being sold in Bangladesh, Botswana, Chad, Haiti, Iran, Malawi, and other developing countries. The white powder comes in a small packet, sold for about US$0.10, that purifies about 2.5 gallons of water. After the tsunami in Southeast Asia in December 2004, PuR was used throughout the region to treat the contaminated water that the disaster left in its wake.

Filtering: Filtering devices have been developed for a range of water contaminants. One device, designed to rid water of bacteria, was developed in 1981 in Guatemala and has been promoted and used across the developing Another device targets arsenic contamination, widespread in much of Bangladesh—where early development initiatives led to the drilling of hundreds of thousands of bore wells, many tapping naturally arsenic-laced groundwater—and in parts of India and Nepal. Working with a Bangladeshi chemist, International Development Enterprises has developed the Shapla Arsenic Filter, based on a ferrous sulfate solution bonded to crushed brick. Incorporated into a vessel, the filter can provide 25–32 liters of arsenic-free water a day. A system sells for US$7, with replacement filters costing less than US$12 a year.

Yet another solution addresses excessive fluoride, also a problem in some parts of South Asia. Mytry, a filter technology developed at IIT-Kanpur, in India, is being sold through a local distribution network targeting a market of nearly 70 million Indians who are at risk. The business strategy calls for selling a quarter million filter units in three years (Meehan and Zaidman 2005).

Two big companies are marketing competing filter technologies in India. Hindustan Lever Limited (HLL), a division of consumer products giant Unilever, produces Pureit, which delivers six liters of purified water for a rupee. Eureka Forbes has the Acquagard line of products, representing a large share of the high-end water filter market. Both HLL and Eureka Forbes are moving steadily down-market to compete for the large BOP segment, engaging large direct sales networks. But price and consumer education remain significant barriers.

U.S. high-tech manufacturer KX Industries is developing a carbon nanofiber filter, the KX World Filter, in a gravity-flow home system, aimed at bringing the most advanced technology within reach of the BOP market. The KX system can deliver water free of dirt, chemical pollutants, and bacterial and viral contamination at US$0.008 a gallon, or US$0.03 a day for a family. The company is also developing a scaled-up village system that can deliver 2,000 gallons a day, reducing the cost to US$0.001 a gallon, with an initial capital cost of around US$150.

At the other end of the spectrum is a personal filter device, the LifeStraw, combining three technologies: a halogen-based resin that kills bacteria on contact, textile prefilters to remove particles (as small as 15 microns), and active carbon to remove parasites. Each device can purify 700 liters of water—at 2 liters a day, enough for a year. The device does not remove arsenic or excess fluoride, and constant use with saline water reduces its effective life by about half. Not yet a sustainable business endeavor, LifeStraw is promoted primarily through charitable channels.

All these initiatives, aimed at designing solutions for the unique needs of the BOP, exemplify a strategy of **focusing on the BOP.**

While BOP households are more likely to use surface water and less likely to have access to piped water, a third alternative, especially in peri-urban areas, is to buy from mobile water vendors.

Cameroon

PERCENT OF HOUSEHOLDS BY WATER SOURCE

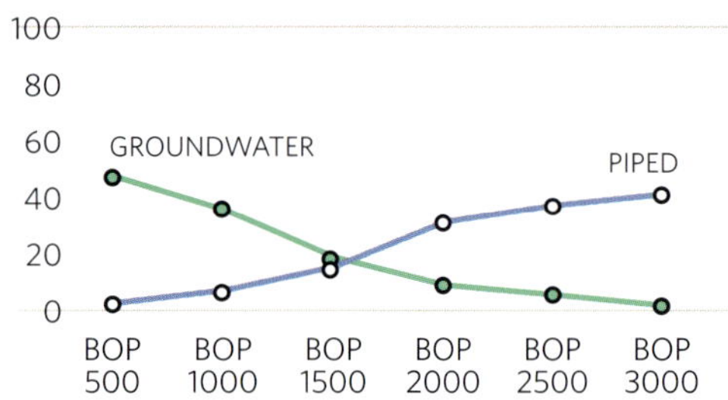

Peru

PERCENT OF HOUSEHOLDS BY WATER SOURCE

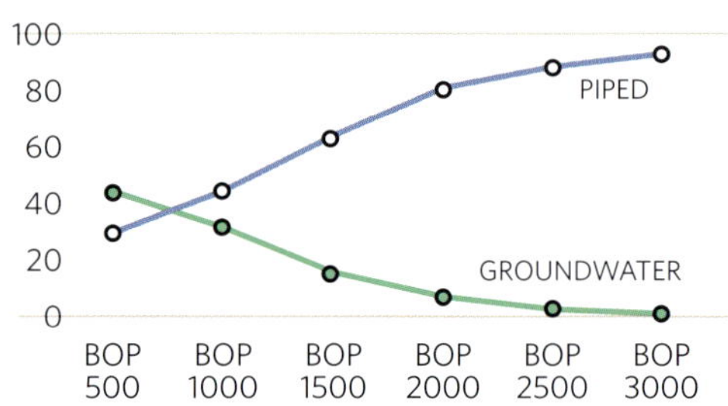

Use of unprotected wells by BOP households, where present in Asia, Eastern Europe, and Latin America, also drops off quickly as incomes rise through the lower BOP income segments. Paraguay is the lone exception, with use of unprotected wells remaining consistently high across all BOP income groups.

In Africa use of unprotected wells similarly remains high across BOP income groups in Malawi, Rwanda, Sierra Leone, and Uganda. In Malawi 26% of BOP households—and in Rwanda, 45%—report relying on unprotected wells as their primary water source.

Is there evidence of a BOP penalty?

There is a widely held view that the BOP suffers a significant penalty in access to safe drinking water—and household survey data confirm this view. Consider access to the most reliable and affordable source, piped water in the home. In 9 of the 29 countries for which sufficient data exist for a comparison, the ratio of mid-market households to BOP households with access to piped water is 6:1 or higher. Data on access to public standpipes show a similar pattern—significantly lower access in the BOP than in the mid market.

While BOP households are more likely to use surface water and less likely to have access to piped water, a third alternative, especially in peri-urban areas, is to buy from mobile water vendors. But this option typically involves a significant price penalty. One study showed that in eight major cities water vendors charge prices 8–16 times those charged by public utilities (UNDP 2006). Another study, covering 47 countries, found that mobile distributors such as tanker trucks charge unit prices up 10 times the price of piped water (Kariuki and Schwartz 2005).

Where BOP communities lack access to municipal water supply networks, point-of-use water purification and small-scale community-based water purification and waste treatment can be useful solutions. The community-based approach underlies an innovative program in Orangi, an informal settlement area in Karachi that is home to 1.2 million people. Community-managed services—latrines, neighborhood collector sewers—link to a municipal system of trunk sewers and treatment plants. Local residents provide labor and financing, and external sources provide

CASE STUDY 4.3 **THE POWER OF PARTNERSHIP: PUBLIC-PRIVATE INITIATIVES TO IMPROVE SERVICE**

Two examples—one involving a cooperative in Bolivia, the other a local government in Honduras—show that innovative approaches can make progress.

Cosmol, a cooperative providing water and sewerage service to 90,000 customers in Montero, a town in the Bolivian tropical lowlands, faced serious discontent in 2000. Members were fed up with bad service, arbitrary rules, a closed-door management, and serious financial disarray. Newly installed management renounced the old culture, promising full transparency and throwing open all records to scrutiny by members.

To secure loans to finance repair and expansion of the water and sewer network, the cooperative agreed to seek new revenues from members. Broad consultation with the community led to a conclusion that customers wanted community health insurance as well as better water supply and sanitation. A US$2 monthly surcharge—enormous in a region where the average monthly wage is only US$70—was imposed, with community approval. After each family had contributed US$150 to the water and sewer fund, the surcharge would drop to US$0.50 a month, enough to continue the health insurance program. The Cosmol experience is evidence of the value of engaging the community in the solution (Constance 2005).

In Puerto Cortés, Honduras, the hurricane of 1993 destroyed much of the already crumbling and failed infrastructure. The local government, headed by then-mayor Marlon Lara, concluded that full cost recovery would be essential for effective service provision. Lara embarked on an extensive public education campaign—and a lobbying effort to gain local control of water and sanitation. A hotly-contested election campaign turned on the question of better water and sewerage service, with higher prices and comprehensive metering of all homes, businesses, and public institutions as central issues.

It took several years, but Lara wrested control of the water and sewer authority from the national government. A new, independent public-private company was established, built on the foundations of the previously public agency, with the local government controlling the underlying assets and a private contractor managing operations under a contract setting performance goals. The company, insulated from political interference, set rates sufficient to fund proper construction and maintenance of the water and sewer system.

Marlon Lara has moved on to a national post, and the city has seen backsliding on rates and expansion of services. But the path to success—depoliticization, citizen consultation, and operational independence—has been made clear (Constance and Cortés 2004; Satterthwaite, McGranahan, and Mitlin 2005).

These examples show that the BOP business strategies of **unconventional partnering** and **localizing value creation** are available to the public as well as the private sector.

technical assistance and materials. Against all expectations and under extremely difficult conditions, the Orangi project has managed to combine cost recovery with high quality.

Similar community-based efforts are gaining traction in Bolivia. The government is finding that engaging communities early and consistently—including by educating people about fees and involving them in construction and continuing oversight—bears fruit throughout the life of a project (case study 4.3).

CHAPTER FIVE

The Transportation Market

For many in the BOP lack of transportation—or the high cost of what is available—is a constant obstacle to looking for work, getting goods to or from markets, or obtaining health care. All too often public transit systems in developing countries are run-down or nonexistent, and the costs of owning a private vehicle prohibitive.That leaves few options: walking, bicycling, animal-drawn carts, minibuses or other informal services.

Under these circumstances people cannot easily fulfill their economic potential. And sometimes, especially in rural areas, they put off seeking medical care or sending children to school because of the high cost or long hours in getting to the hospital or the school. In urban areas gridlock and pollution levy an additional toll. Deliberate transportation planning that involves multiple stakeholders is one promising route toward creating better urban transportation options (case study 5.1).

Distribution and delivery systems for merchandise operate under different constraints than public transportation systems, yet these too contribute to the economic barriers facing the BOP. The focus here is on personal transportation spending. But more efficient distribution channels for services, products, and information—from health care to consumer products to better agricultural techniques and equipment—would also help empower rural communities and reduce the need for people to

BOP spending on transportation
$179.3 billion

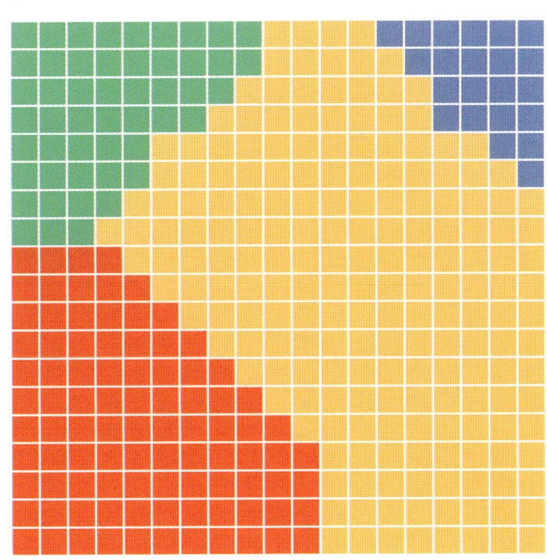

	$ billions (PPP)
Africa	24.5
Asia	98.3
Eastern Europe	10.7
Latin America	45.9

Each square represents approximately $500 million

CASE STUDY 5.1 **ALL ABOARD: TRANSIT PLANNING WITH MULTIPLE STAKEHOLDERS**

Urban migration continues to expand city populations in many developing countries: in the measured countries covered in this report around 40% of the population are urbanites. Meanwhile, such transportation issues as gridlock and pollution are generating bigger and bigger costs—fuel costs, labor hours lost in traffic, health care costs due to respiratory illnesses. Because urban transportation systems involve so many actors—from politicians to private owners, passengers, and civil and mechanical engineers—creating one that is affordable and environmentally sustainable requires involving multiple stakeholders.

Doing so can yield big benefits. Consider the Mexico City Bus Rapid Transit system, established by a public-private partnership between the city government, private bus owners, and the EMBARQ program of the World Resources Institute. In 2006, after a year in operation, the transit system carried more than 100 million passengers, had reduced commute times along its route by about 50%, and prevented around 36,000 tons of carbon dioxide emissions into Mexico City's air. Rides cost around US$0.30 each (Flores-Arias 2006).

Another project, in the Philippine city of Vigan, Luzon, is retrofitting motorbikes—the most common transportation vehicle in Asia—with less polluting and more efficient fuel injection systems. The project, which plans to retrofit thousands—potentially several tens of thousands—of motor-tricycle taxis, is being undertaken by the nonprofit organization Envirofit, working with city officials, motorbike owners, local mechanics, and manufacturers. City officials have committed to passing legislation that will require tricycle drivers to replace or retrofit their vehicles. Envirofit is training local manufacturers and mechanics in the production and installation of its fuel injection systems, building capacity for a transportation industry based on environmentally friendly technology.

Both of these examples illustrate the value of the strategy of **unconventional partnering**.

travel to obtain such essentials. Indeed, transportation impacts every sector covered in this report.

How large is the market?

The measured BOP market for transportation for Africa (12 countries), Asia (9), Eastern Europe (6), and Latin America and the Caribbean (9) is $105 billion. This represents the annual household transportation spending of 2.2 billion people in the 36 low- and middle-income countries for which standardized data exist. The total BOP transportation market in these four regions, comprising 3.9 billion people, is estimated to be $179 billion (see box 1.5 in chapter 1 for the estimation method).

The largest measured regional BOP transportation market is the $49.6 billion Asian market (1.5 billion people), followed by those in Latin America ($38.4 billion and 276 million people), Africa ($11.0 billion and 253 million people), and Eastern Europe ($6.0 billion and 148 million people). Total BOP household transportation spending is estimated to be $98.3 billion in Asia, $45.9 billion in Latin America, $24.5 billion in Africa, and $10.7 billion in Eastern Europe.

Spending by the BOP accounts for 63% of the total Asian transportation market, 41% of the Eastern European market, 39% of the African market, and 28% of the Latin American market.

In national transportation markets the BOP consistently accounts for a large share of the total in Asia. BOP spending represents more than 60% of the total market in every measured Asian country but Cambodia (42%)

The BOP share of transportation spending is consistently high in Africa. It exceeds 50% in all but three measured countries. South Africa, where the BOP market share is just 14%, is the most prominent exception.

and Thailand (30%). In Bangladesh, Indonesia, Pakistan, and Tajikistan the BOP share is more than 90%.

The BOP share of transportation spending is also consistently high in Africa. It exceeds 50% in all but three measured countries. South Africa, where the BOP market share is just 14%, is the most prominent exception. BOP market shares are largest in Côte d'Ivoire (74%), Djibouti (94%), and Nigeria (98%).

In Eastern Europe the BOP share of the market ranges from 23% in FYR Macedonia to 77% in Kazakhstan. In Russia the BOP transportation market, Eastern Europe's largest, accounts for 43% of the total.

Spending by mid-market and high-income segments dominates the transportation market in most countries of Latin America and the Caribbean. The BOP share of the national market is less than 35% in every country but Jamaica (81%) and Peru (51%). The smallest BOP shares are in Colombia (17%) and Paraguay (19%).

How is the market segmented?

In most of the measured African and Asian countries BOP transportation markets are bottom heavy. BOP transportation spending is concentrated in the BOP1000 and BOP1500 groups, as exemplified by Bangladesh and Burkina Faso. Important exceptions to this pattern include South Africa and Thailand, where BOP transportation spending is significantly top heavy,

CASE STUDY 5.2 **BRAZIL: A BIG MARKET AT THE TOP OF THE BOP**

Brazil's BOP transportation market of $19.5 billion is the largest among the nine measured countries in Latin America. Though this spending is more than 50% of the total measured BOP transportation market in the region, it is only 28% of Brazil's total transportation market of $71 billion. This kind of market distribution is common in Latin America, where the mid-market and high-income population segments account for the majority of transportation expenditures even though the population is concentrated in the BOP. In Brazil the BOP accounts for 71% of the total population.

Brazil's BOP population itself is bottom heavy, with 71% in the bottom three BOP income segments. Yet the BOP transportation spending is concentrated in the top three BOP income segments. These three constitute a $13.6 billion market, more than 70% of the BOP market and 19% of the national market. That market alone is larger than every other measured national BOP transportation market except India's.

The 13.8 million households in Brazil's top three BOP income segments spend an average of $983 a year on transportation, 12% of their household budget. Urban households account for 85% of the transportation spending by these segments.

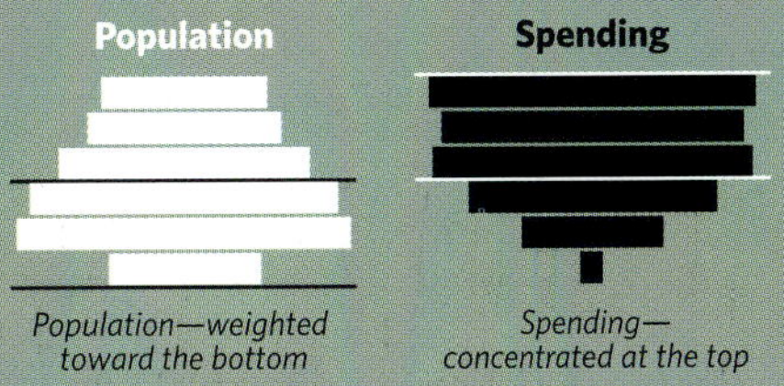

Bangladesh

TOTAL TRANSPORTATION SPENDING BY INCOME SEGMENT

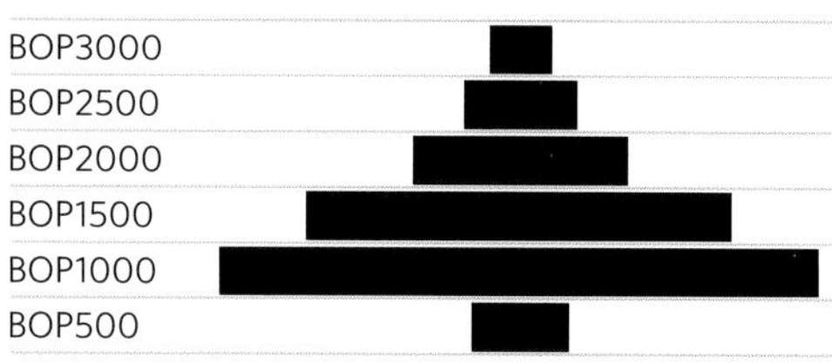

Burkina Faso

TOTAL TRANSPORTATION SPENDING BY INCOME SEGMENT

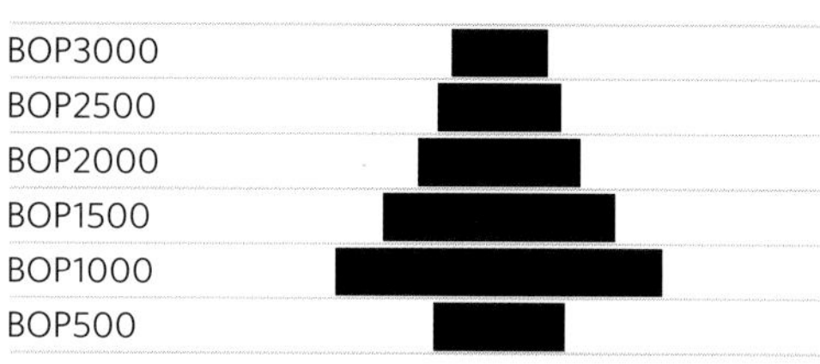

Thailand

TOTAL TRANSPORTATION SPENDING BY INCOME SEGMENT

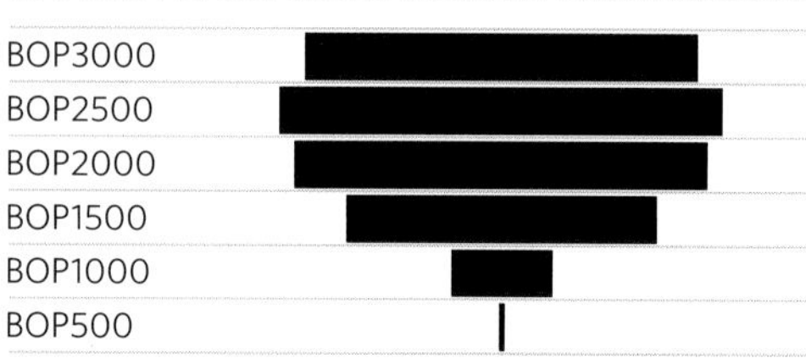

and India, where it is marginally top heavy. BOP transportation spending in Eastern Europe and Latin America is distinctly top heavy and concentrated in the BOP2500 and BOP3000 groups. This top-heavy pattern is exemplified by Brazil, which has one of the largest BOP transportation markets (case study 5.2).

What do households spend?

Average annual transportation spending per BOP household varies widely within and between regions. In Africa and Asia, however, the median for this figure among measured countries is remarkably close: in Africa, $211 (Burkina Faso) and $275 (Uganda); and in Asia, $211 (Tajikistan). In contrast, the recorded average spending in Africa ranges from $25 a year in Burundi to $157 in Nigeria, $333 in South Africa, and $517 in Gabon. In Asia the range is from $101 a year in Nepal to $136 in India and $601 in Thailand. Differences in the survey questions asked and data captured may account for some of the variation.

The median among measured countries in Eastern Europe is $141 a year (Ukraine), and in Latin America, $521 a year (Paraguay). Average transportation spending per BOP household in Eastern Europe is generally less than in Africa and Asia, probably reflecting that region's heavily urban character and its well-developed public transit systems. Russia also reflects the Eastern European median, recording an average of $141 in transportation spending per BOP household.

Within the BOP, transportation spending increases steeply— and often disproportionately—as income rises.

In contrast, in Latin America BOP transportation spending is distinctly higher than in Africa and Asia: in every measured country but Peru BOP households spend more than $270 a year on average for transportation. The range extends from $181 a year in Peru to $331 in Jamaica, $613 in Brazil, and $809 in Mexico.

Within the BOP, transportation spending increases steeply—and often disproportionately—as income rises. While the income ratio between the BOP3000 and BOP500 groups is 6:1, the transportation spending ratio is at least 10:1 in 29 of the 36 measured countries. The ratio varies across the largest BOP markets by region: in Nigeria it is 32:1; in India, 17:1; in Brazil, 13:1; and in Russia, 5:1. The pattern suggests substantial latent demand for transportation within the BOP. Clearly, those in the BOP view spending for transportation—buying that first motorbike—much as they do spending for ICT: a priority for increasing their productivity and their economic options. Data from Nigeria give additional insight into the spending of different market segments (case study 5.3).

Transportation spending in the mid-market segment is higher than in the BOP but not dramatically so. Ratios of average mid-market to average BOP per household spending for some major countries range from less than 2:1 in Russia and 3:1 in Mexico to 5:1 in India, 8:1 in Pakistan and South Africa, and 12:1 in Nigeria. Transportation, as a share of total per household spending, varies widely between BOP income segments, and between countries, as shown by the examples of India and Brazil.

Where is the market?

National transportation markets are predominantly urban in every region but Asia. In Africa more than 50% of all transportation spending is urban in every country but Uganda and Burkina Faso; in eight coun-

Uganda

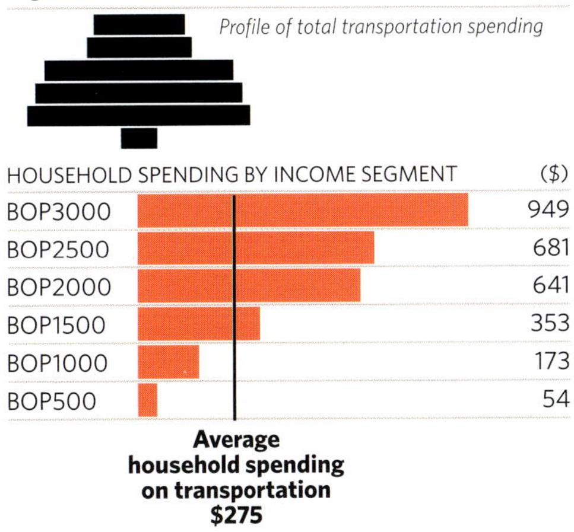

Paraguay

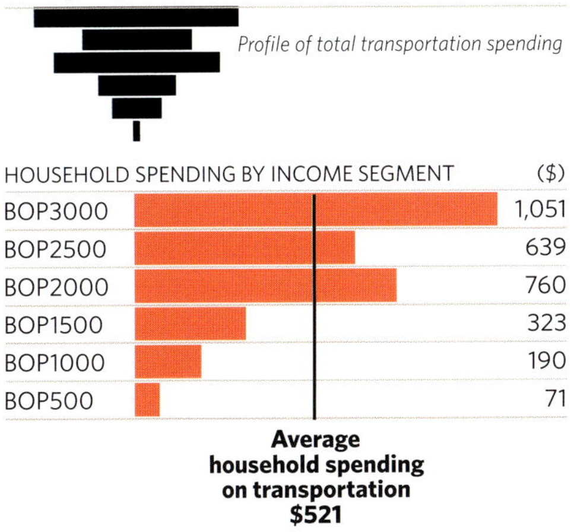

India

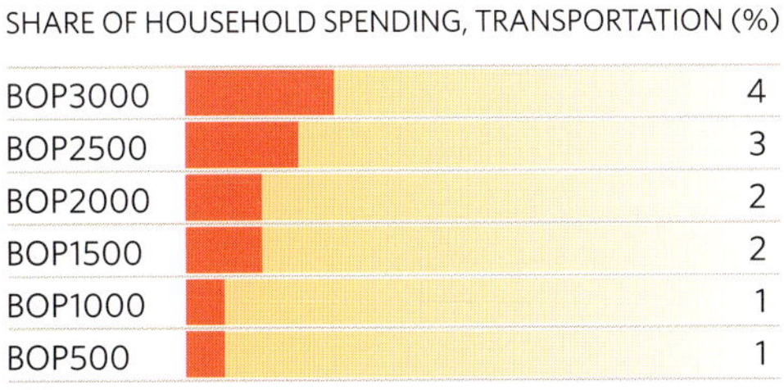

Brazil

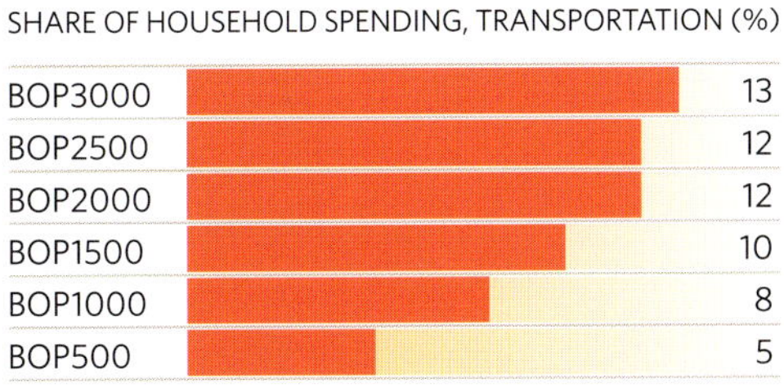

CASE STUDY5.3 **NIGERIA: THE BIGGEST BOP TRANSPORTATION MARKET IN AFRICA**

Nigeria has the largest BOP share in the total transportation market, at 98%, and the largest BOP transportation market in Africa, at $4.2 billion. Indeed, its BOP transportation market is nearly twice as large as South Africa's, the next largest recorded one in the region.

Nigeria's BOP transportation market centers on the spending of the BOP1000 and BOP1500 income segments. Together, these segments account for 39% of Nigeria's population but 62% of its BOP spending, and 61% of its total spending, on transportation. In contrast, the lowest BOP income segment, BOP500, has 59% of Nigeria's population yet accounts for only 17% of the national transportation market, spending only $55 per household a year on average.

In Nigeria, as in most countries, household spending on transportation rises significantly with income. Spending reaches $682 in the BOP 2500 segment and jumps markedly to $1746 in the BOP 3000 segment. This may reflect purchase and operating costs of a first motorbike or other vehicle. In any event, the pattern of increased spending likely reflects pent-up demand for transportation and the importance of better solutions.

TOTAL TRANSPORTATION SPENDING BY INCOME SEGMENT

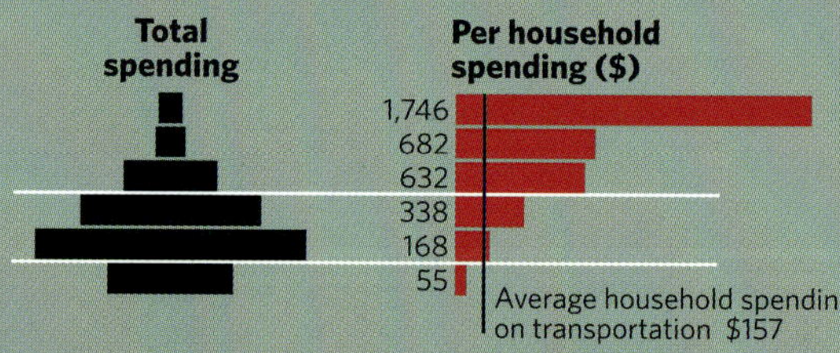

Though rural transportation markets are generally smaller than urban ones, except in Asia, the BOP share of rural markets is large: more than 60% in all but 7 countries for which standardized data exist.

tries more than 70% of transportation spending occurs in urban areas. In Eastern Europe and Latin America the urban share of the transportation market is more than 65% in all countries except Jamaica. In Asia, however, urban market shares range from 22% in Sri Lanka to 69% in Indonesia, reflecting the importance of the rural transportation market in this region.

A similar pattern appears in the BOP market, though in nearly every country the BOP transportation market is more rural than the total market. Even so, more than half of BOP transportation spending occurs in urban areas in all but four countries in Africa, two in Eastern Europe, and two in Latin America. Ukraine, with 66% of the BOP transportation spending in urban areas, and South Africa with 64% illustrate common patterns. The Asian BOP transportation market, however, is distinctly rural: 85% of BOP transportation spending in Cambodia, for example. Less than 42% of BOP transportation spending occurs in urban areas in every country but Indonesia.

Though rural transportation markets are generally smaller than urban ones, except in Asia, the BOP share of rural markets is large: more than 60% in all but 7 countries of the 36 for which standardized data exist.

Comparing urban with rural BOP markets shows urban BOP markets to be more top heavy and rural markets more bottom heavy. In 26 urban BOP markets the income segment with the largest market share is among the top three BOP segments. In 29 rural BOP markets the income segment with the largest market share is among the bottom three.

Ukraine

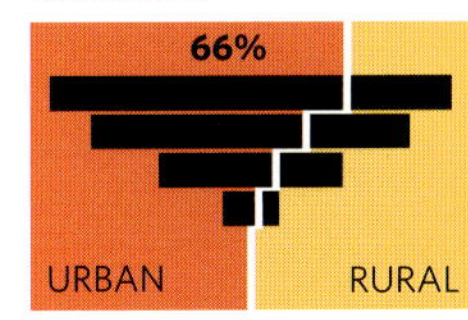

Cambodia

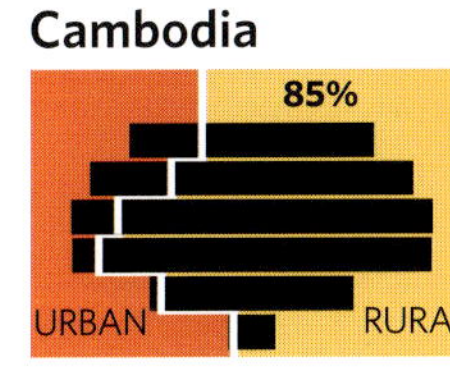

Total BOP transportation spending by income segment, urban and rural

Endnotes

1. Reported household expenditures in a given country should be regarded as a minimum estimate of actual expenditures, because surveys may not have collected information on all types of transportation-related spending.
2. EMBARQ, "Cities on the Move: Mexico City, Mexico," http://embarq.wri.org/en/ProjectCitiesDetail.aspx?id=1 (accessed January 31, 2007).
3. Envirofit, "About Vigan," http://www.envirofit.org/projects/vigan.php (accessed January 31, 2007).

CHAPTER SIX

The Housing Market

Housing is one of the larger BOP markets—larger than transportation, smaller than energy. The market encompasses major spending items—rent, mortgage payments (or imputed rents), and repairs and other services. But the BOP housing market is perhaps uniquely handicapped by informality. Both lack of legal title to housing in squatter settlements—Hernando De Soto's "dead capital"—and lack of access to mortgage financing for the BOP limit its potential size.

Despite these barriers, both private sector approaches and policy reforms—sometimes catalyzed by NGOs—are showing how to tap this market in ways that provide significant benefits for BOP households. In Asia especially, where mortgage markets are undeveloped and land prices high relative to income, the market potential—and the need—is huge (Bestani and Klein 2006).

How large is the market?

The measured BOP market for housing in Africa (12 countries), Asia (9), Eastern Europe (6), and Latin America and the Caribbean (9) is $187.5 billion. This represents recorded annual household spending on housing in the 36 low- and middle-income countries for which standardized data exist, covering 2.1 billion of the world's BOP population. The total BOP housing market in these four regions, including 3.96 billion people in all surveyed countries, is estimated to be $331.8 billion (see box 1.5 in chapter 1 for the estimation method). Because imputed rent is a major part of household spending on housing and cannot be determined precisely, these numbers should be regarded as setting a lower bound for such spending.

Asia has the largest measured regional BOP market for housing, $86.6 billion, reflecting a significant BOP popula-

BOP spending on housing
$331.8 billion

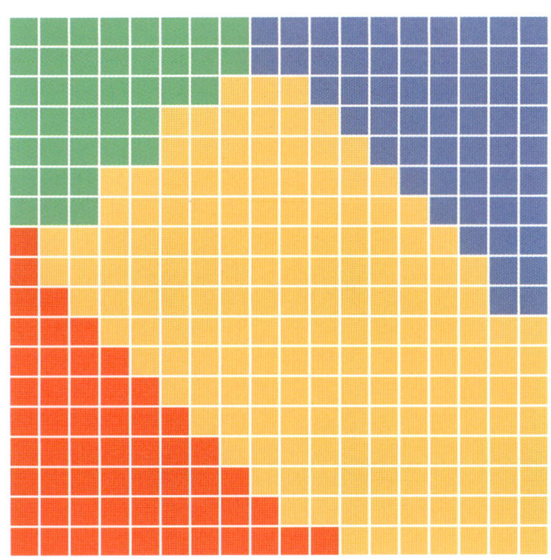

Each square represents approximately $1 billion

Rwanda
TOTAL HOUSING SPENDING BY INCOME SEGMENT

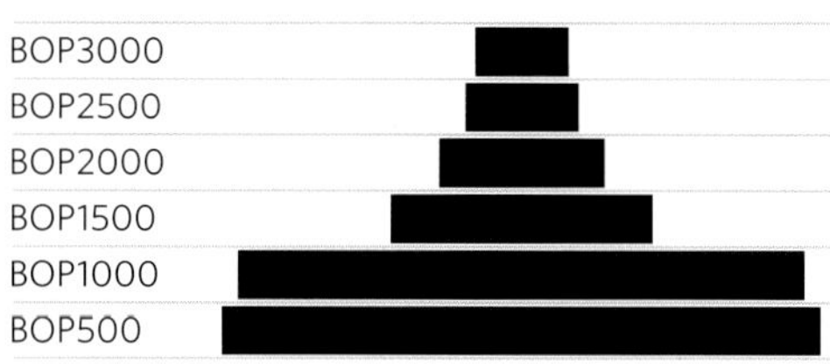

Thailand
TOTAL HOUSING SPENDING BY INCOME SEGMENT

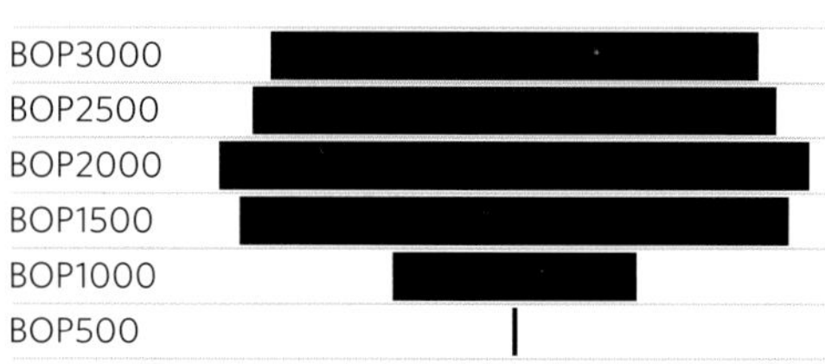

tion of 1.49 billion. The total BOP housing market in Asia (including the Middle East) is estimated to be $171.4 billion, representing the spending of 2.9 billion people. Latin America has the next largest measured market, $47.4 billion (276 million people), and an estimated total market of $56.7 billion (360 million people).

In Eastern Europe the measured BOP housing market is $34.2 billion (148 million people), and the estimated total market $60.8 billion (254 million people). In Africa the measured BOP market is $19.3 billion (258 million people), and the estimated total BOP market is $42.9 billion (486 million people).

The average BOP share of measured national housing markets varies across regions. In Asia and Africa that share is 63%. In other regions it is much smaller: 39% in Latin America, 35% in Eastern Europe. Latin America has the greatest disparity between the BOP share of the population (71%) and the average BOP share of housing spending (39%).

The BOP share of housing spending also varies across countries. These differences in part reflect the prevalence of a landed middle class in some developing countries, such as South Africa and throughout Latin America. Between mid-market landowners and disenfranchised BOP communities, the BOP share of a country's housing market is on average half that of its weight in population. Nonetheless, in countries such as Pakistan and Sierra Leone, the BOP accounts for more than 95% of the measured housing market.

In Asia one extreme is represented by Sri Lanka, Pakistan, and Bangladesh, where the BOP accounts for more than 90% of the spending on housing—the other by Thailand and India, where despite the substantial BOP population, the recorded BOP share is only 47% and 48%, respectively. In Africa the extremes are Nigeria (99% BOP) and South Africa (31%). In Eastern Europe the extremes are represented by Uzbekistan (92%) and FYR Macedonia (13%).

How is the market segmented?

Many African BOP markets for housing are relatively bottom heavy, with spending concentrated in the bottom three of the six BOP income segments. The remainder are flat, with spending distributed relatively evenly across all BOP income segments. In Asia too, most BOP housing markets are either bottom heavy or flat.

BOP spending on housing reflects consistently strong demand: people are willing to spend a fairly consistent share of their income on their home.

In Eastern Europe, in contrast, almost all countries have a top-heavy BOP market, with the top three segments accounting for more than half of BOP housing spending. The lone exception is Uzbekistan, where the bottom three BOP income segments account for 77% of spending. In Latin America spending tends to flatten out at the BOP1500 segment. In Brazil, for example, the top four segments each account for 19–23% of BOP housing spending.

In Latin America and the Caribbean some large national housing markets are dominated by the wealthier mid-market segment; in Colombia the BOP accounts for only 27% of the total. In Peru, however, the BOP segment accounts for nearly three-quarters of the total market (73%). Jamaica represents the extreme, with 88% of the national housing market in the BOP.

In contrast, the BOP dominates Asian markets, with only Thailand and India having slightly more than half of total housing spending in the mid market. Africa too is predominantly a BOP market: in only one country, South Africa, does spending in the mid-market segment exceed that in the BOP.

What do households spend?

BOP spending on housing reflects consistently strong demand: people are willing to spend a fairly constant share of their income on their home.

India has the largest measured BOP housing market in Asia, $62.1 billion; BOP spending accounts for 48% of the national housing market and averages $164 per household a year. In other regions the BOP market leaders are Mexico ($45.6 billion, 44% of the total market), with average annual spending of $1,280 per BOP household; Russia ($94.7 billion, 34% of the total market), with average spending of $1,268; and South Africa ($14.4 billion, 31% of the total market), with average spending of $652.

These expenditures by BOP households may not be large. But in Mexico they are large enough to fuel two significant and growing corporate efforts to tap BOP housing markets (case study 6.1).

Ukraine

TOTAL HOUSING SPENDING BY INCOME SEGMENT

Brazil

TOTAL HOUSING SPENDING BY INCOME SEGMENT

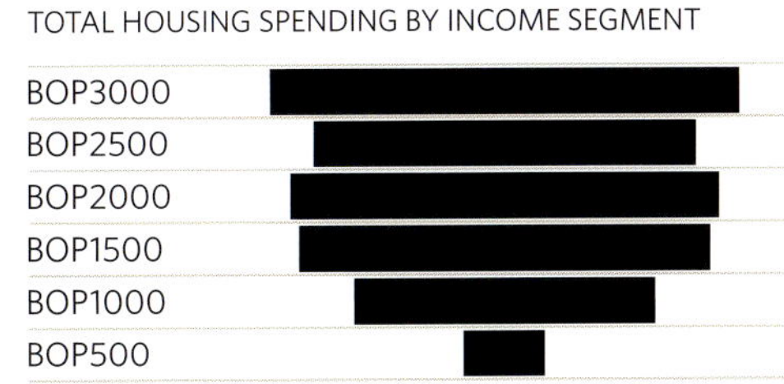

Burkina Faso

SHARE OF HOUSEHOLD SPENDING ON HOUSING (%)

India

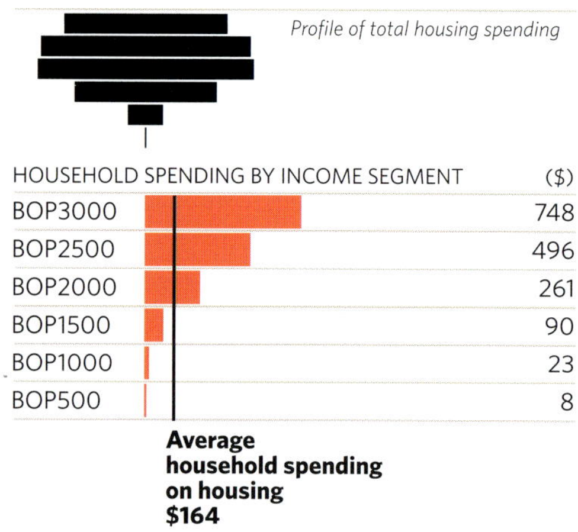

Mexico

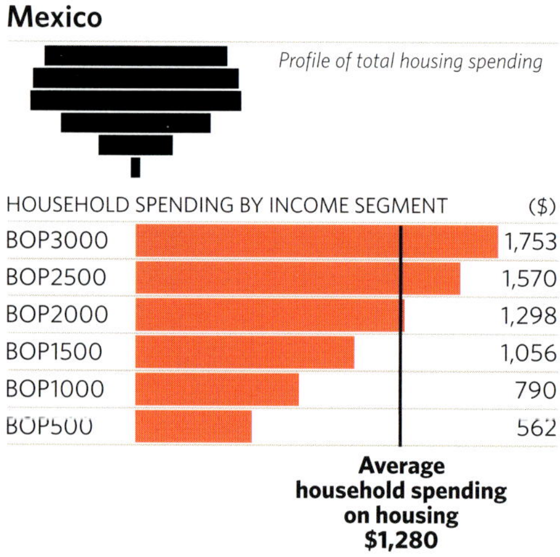

Uganda

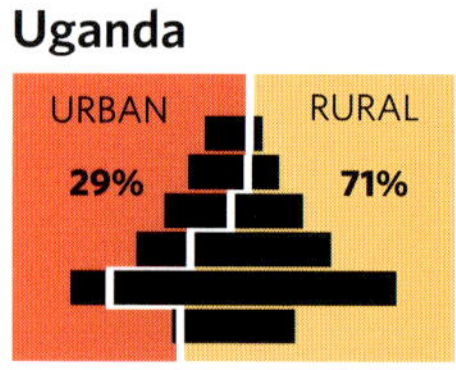

Total BOP housing spending by income segment, urban and rural

Russia

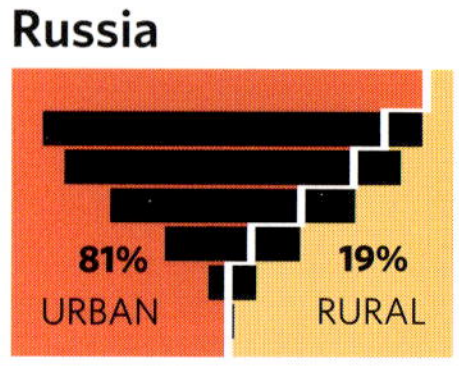

Where is the market?

In 24 of the 36 measured countries, BOP housing markets are predominately urban. However, it is often difficult for national surveys to accurately measure housing expenditure in poor rural areas—often rents must be imputed.

In Asian and African countries, housing markets are often predominantly rural. The Ugandan BOP housing market, for example, is 71% rural. Most Asian BOP housing markets also are predominantly rural. In Sri Lanka, for example, 77% of the BOP housing market is rural. Rural housing markets can be substantial—$9 billion in Thailand, for example. An exception to the pattern of rural dominance is Pakistan, where urban squatter settlements account for much of the imputed BOP rent and the BOP housing market is only 36% rural.

In Eastern Europe, where countries were so heavily urbanized under Soviet rule, much of the housing is in cities. In Russia just 19% of the BOP market is rural. Only two countries have BOP markets in which at least a quarter of the spending takes place in rural areas—FYR Macedonia (31%) and Belarus (25%).

In many Latin American countries reported spending on housing also occurs mostly in urban areas. In Colombia, for example, urban spending is 92% of the total for BOP housing. In Guatemala, however, the BOP housing market is 52% rural and 48% urban.

Large urban BOP communities represent huge untapped market opportunities. Mexico's urban BOP housing market is nearly $16 billion annually (see case study 6.1). Brazil and Colombia each report urban BOP housing spending of more than $8 billion a year.

India has the largest measured BOP housing market in Asia, $62.1 billion; BOP spending accounts for 48% of the national housing market and averages $164 per household a year.

Is there evidence of a BOP penalty?

Household surveys seek to capture all sources of income, but they do not measure the "dead capital" trapped in the informal economy. For many BOP households, their dwelling and the land it sits on is their primary capital. When they lack formal title to that asset, or when they must contend with ineffective land markets or barriers to transferring title, housing becomes dead capital. Under these circumstances BOP households face a significant BOP penalty—one that artificially curbs their potential purchasing power and often their access to services.

The problem extends to the multitude of enterprises in the informal economy. These businesses, operating outside the formal legal system, cannot easily leverage their assets into working capital. The dead capital trapped in houses and businesses together is enormous: a recent study showed that informal properties and businesses in just 12 Latin American countries are worth as much as US$1.2 trillion (ILD 2006; IDB 2006). Worldwide, the figure is estimated to be at least US$9.3 trillion, and is probably much larger (De Soto 2004).

Informal home ownership also poses a barrier to service delivery. Many governments require proof of title before a household can receive social benefits. And municipalities often are unwilling to connect undocumented homes to water, sewer, and electricity networks, since they have no legal recourse to collect un-

CASE STUDY 6.1 **MEXICO: HOUSING INNOVATIONS AT WORK**

Two competing corporate programs serve the BOP housing market in Mexico: Patrimonio Hoy and Mi Casa. Each is the initiative of a major cement manufacturer in the country.

Cemex, the third largest cement manufacturer in the world, decided it needed to move from selling materials to selling solutions. With low fixed prices, materials on credit, precosted housing designs, and even supervised construction services for Mexicans working abroad, its Patrimonio Hoy program, launched in 1998, makes housing affordable for poor people in Mexico.

The program provides consultations with architects to help would-be home owners design their project, schedules deliveries of materials over what is typically a 70-week building period, and keeps prices stable through that period. The cost is about US$14 a week over the building period. Participants in the program "found they were building homes faster, and generally cheaper, than they could on their own" (Sandoval 2005).

By late 2006, according to Cemex, the Patrimonio Hoy program had served 150,000 clients in 45 cities throughout Mexico. Now the company is expanding the strategy to other countries.

Facing strong competition from Cemex in the bagged cement market, Holcim Apasco has focused on innovation in distribution. By setting up its own Mi Casa distribution centers, it can bypass two to three distributors and thus keep prices more affordable. Since 1996 the company has established more than 120 standard Mi Casa locations, where resellers have a full range of building materials and products available locally at reasonable prices.

A parallel scheme has trained more than 10,000 people in the skills needed to build their own homes. The Mi Casa project recognizes that the real need of the market is not cement but the knowledge to build a safe and comfortable home—along with the delivery of affordable materials (WBCSD 2004).

Both of these examples illustrate a strategy of **focusing on the BOP.**

CASE STUDY 6.2 **ENTITLED: SOLUTIONS FOR SECURE HOUSING**

Hernando De Soto's Institute for Liberty and Democracy has designed land reform programs in Egypt, El Salvador, Haiti, Tanzania, and, most notably, Peru. The Peruvian program, which ran from 1982 through 1996, resulted in 1.2 million families and nearly 400,000 informal businesses receiving title to their home or business. Independent evaluations show that the reform program generated US$10 billion in net benefits for home owners. The value of newly formalized real estate increased by US$2.2 billion, for example, and that of already formalized real estate by US$3.2 billion. The program also generated US$300 million in new annual tax revenue and 560,000 new formal sector jobs.

Saiban, a housing development NGO, has taken a different approach in Pakistan, where an estimated 30% of the population live in unplanned squatter settlements. These squatters, with no legal title to the land on which they live, can be evicted at any time and also lack the collateral that could give them access to formal credit markets. Saiban's solution is to provide plots of developed land in several settlements at affordable rates, giving the former squatters secure tenure. It offers the new home owners a low-cost mortgage, with 20% (about US$175) due as a down payment and the rest (about US$525) to be repaid in monthly installments over eight years.

Saiban's success in offering mortgage products to people earning only about US$3 a day has generated interest from at least two commercial banks. Both are now experimenting with their own low-cost mortgage products aimed at this market (Azfar and Rahman 2004).

paid fees from a home that—in the eyes of the government—does not exist.

Economist Hernando De Soto (2003) has suggested that one way out of this informality trap is to make extralegal ownership more formal—for example, by offering home owners official title to their home. A different strategy, in Pakistan, has focused on providing low-cost mortgages that enable low-income families to buy new homes with secure titles (case study 6.2).

Informal home ownership poses a barrier to service delivery. Many governments require proof of title before a household can receive social benefits. And municipalities often are unwilling to connect undocumented homes to water, sewer, and electricity networks, since they have no legal recourse to collect unpaid fees from a home that—in the eyes of the government—does not exist.

Endnotes

1. Reported household expenditures in a given country should be regarded as a minimum estimate of actual expenditures, because surveys may not have collected information on all types of housing-related spending. Moreover, many surveys do not account for the expenditure value of an owner-occupied dwelling; these surveys are standardized using a rent imputation to estimate the amount of money owners would spend if they were renting the house they own.
2. Many surveys in Latin American countries suffer from measurement and imputation problems in rural areas, which may lead to underrecording of the rural housing market.
3. Institute for Liberty and Democracy, "Mapping Dead Capital.." Inter-American Development Bank, http://www.iadb.org/bop/mapping_capital.cfm (accessed January 12, 2007).
4. Cemex, "Construye tu futuro hoy," http://www.cemexmexico.com/se/se_ph_pf.html (accessed March 1, 2007), and "Patrimonio Hoy Developing and Launching a Market Transforming Innovation to Low-Income, Developing World Markets," http://www.vision.com/clients/client_stories/cemex_pat.html (accessed March 1, 2007).
5. Institute for Liberty and Democracy, "Documented Impact of ILD's Reforms," http://www.ild.org.pe/eng/facts.htm and http://www.ild.org.pe/pdf/annex/Annex_01.pdf (accessed January 30, 2007).

CHAPTER SEVEN

The Energy Market

Lack of clean, affordable energy is part of the poverty trap. Pollution from indoor use of harmful fuels for cooking and lighting leads to significant health problems. Gathering biomass fuels takes time that could be better spent—in school or at work. And the higher cost of inefficient energy-using devices and the lack of access to modern energy sources such as electricity become part of the BOP penalty—the added cost of being poor.

Together, private sector solutions and public institutional reforms are working to close the energy gap. Innovative approaches and new business investments are bringing energy services to BOP markets. While earlier efforts to extend grids beyond major urban centers often met with difficulties and even failure, rural electrification initiatives in Latin America suggest that creative solutions can be found. Where publicly regulated grids cannot reach, off-grid solutions are becoming more widespread—using hydropower, solar photovoltaics, and hybrid solutions. New technologies, such as light-emitting diodes (LEDs), and modern improvements of old ones, such as biomass-burning cookstoves, are increasingly available at affordable prices to both urban and remote rural populations.

BOP spending on energy
$433.4 billion

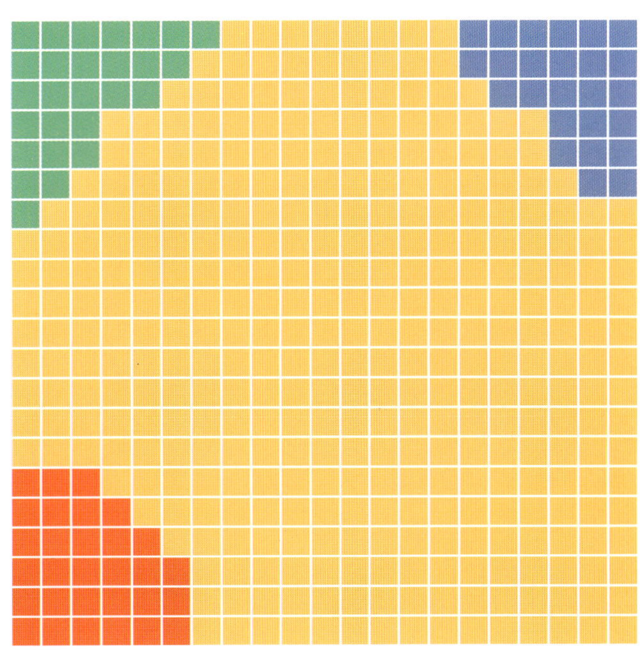

	$ billions (PPP)
Africa	26.6
Asia	350.9
Eastern Europe	25.4
Latin America	30.5

Each square represents approximately $1 Billion

How large is the market?

The measured BOP household market for energy is $228 billion, representing the annual spending of 2.1 billion people in 34 countries. The total BOP household energy market in Africa, Asia, Eastern Europe, and Latin America and the Caribbean is estimated to be $433 billion, representing the spending of 3.96 billion people (see box 1.5 in chapter 1 for the estimation method).

Asia has the largest BOP energy market, with measured annual spending of $177 billion by 1.5 billion people. The estimated total BOP energy market in the region (including the Middle East) is $351 billion (2.9 billion people). Latin America's measured BOP energy market is $25 bil-

BOP households devote an average of 7% of their expenditures to energy. In most measured countries, the share of household spending devoted to energy does not change significantly as incomes rise.

Côte d'Ivoire

TOTAL ENERGY SPENDING BY INCOME SEGMENT

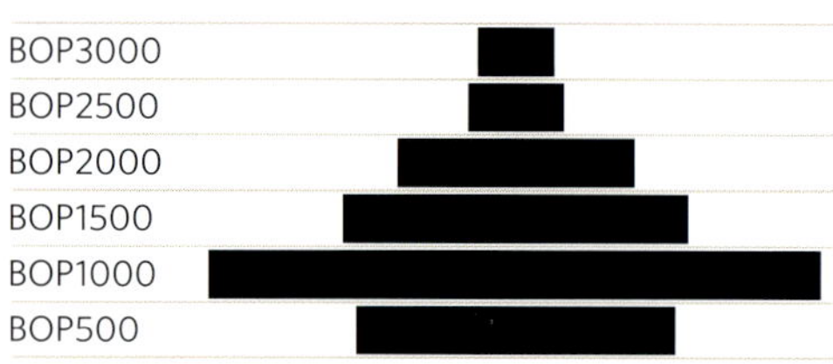

Indonesia

TOTAL ENERGY SPENDING BY INCOME SEGMENT

Ukraine

TOTAL ENERGY SPENDING BY INCOME SEGMENT

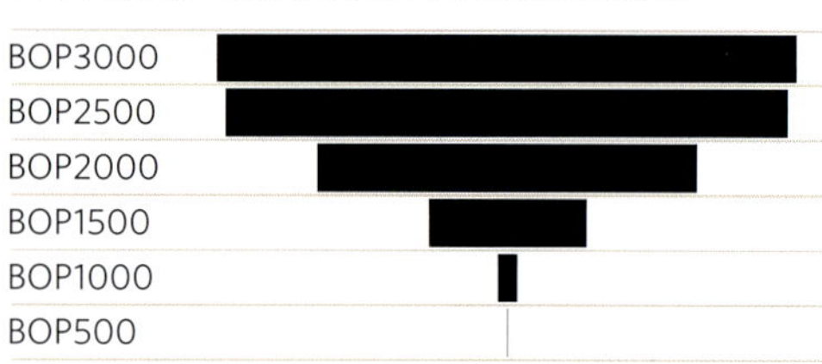

Colombia

TOTAL ENERGY SPENDING BY INCOME SEGMENT

lion (269.5 million people), and its estimated total market $31 billion (360 million people). While Africa has the smallest measured BOP energy market, at $12 billion (253.3 million people), its estimated total BOP energy market is $27 billion (486 million people). Eastern Europe, with a Soviet-era legacy of cheap and reasonably universal electricity, shows BOP energy spending of $14 billion (138.9 million people) and an estimated total BOP market of $25 billion (254 million people).

In Africa, Eastern Europe, and Latin America energy ranks third in BOP household expenditures, trailing food and housing. In Asia energy ranks second, surpassing housing, because of the high levels of energy spending reported in India.

In national energy markets the BOP represents a significant share in virtually all 34 countries for which standardized survey data exist. It accounts for more than 90% of recorded spending in such populous countries as Indonesia, Nigeria, and Pakistan—and more than 50% in Brazil, India, Sri Lanka, Uganda, Peru, and Bolivia (case studies 7.1 and 7.2). The BOP share falls short of 50% in only 7 of the 34 countries: FYR Macedonia (20%), Paraguay (30%), Colombia (35%), South Africa (41%), Russia (44%), Ukraine (47%), and Mexico (48%).

The smallest BOP market shares by region are recorded in South Africa, Thailand, FYR Macedonia, and Paraguay. The largest are in Nigeria, Tajikistan and Pakistan (a virtual tie in Asia), Uzbekistan, and Jamaica.

How is the market segmented?

Developing-country energy markets are predominantly in the BOP. Moreover, nearly a quarter of all recorded energy spending occurs in the bottom two BOP income segments—BOP500 and BOP1000, where per capita income is $1.50 and $3 a day.

Market concentration in these two income groups is most pronounced in Asia and Africa, where bottom-heavy BOP markets predominate. In Indonesia, for example, where the BOP accounts for 95% of national energy spending, 50% of the spending occurs in the BOP500 and BOP1000 segments. In Burundi, where the BOP carries similar weight, at 89% of the national energy market, the BOP500 and BOP1000 segments account for 62% of this market.

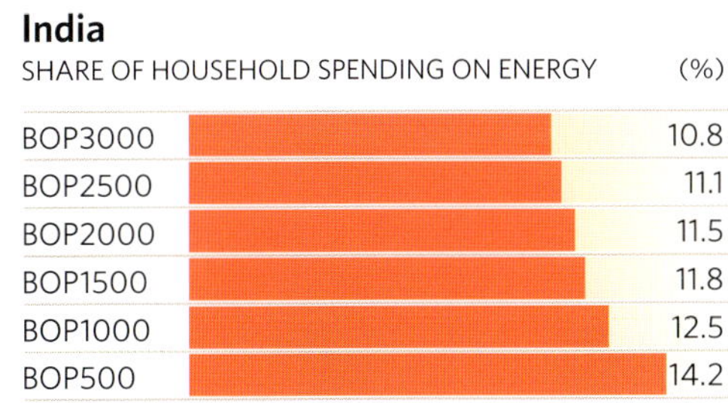

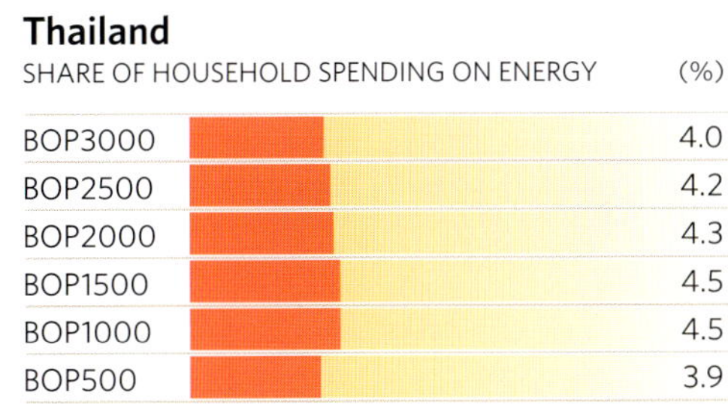

South Africa has a different market segmentation than other measured countries in Africa. While the BOP makes up 74% of the population, it accounts for only 41% of total energy spending. Distribution of the BOP energy market across income groups is more balanced, split evenly between the lower three BOP income segments and the upper three. The more dominant mid-market population segment outspends the BOP population by 32%.

Top-heavy BOP energy markets and larger mid-market spending are found in much of Eastern Europe and Latin America. In Ukraine the top three BOP income groups account for 90% of BOP spending, while the mid-market segment, 40% of the national population, slightly outweighs the BOP market. In Colombia the top three BOP income groups represent 73% of the BOP energy market, while the mid-market segment, 42% of the national population, accounts for an energy market nearly twice the size of the BOP market.

What do households spend?

Across measured countries BOP households devote an average of 9% of their expenditures to energy. Asia shows the largest share, at 10%, with all other regions clustering around the average. In most measured countries, the share of household spending devoted to energy does not change significantly as incomes rise.

Households in the BOP500 income group spend an average of $148 a year on energy, equivalent to around $0.40 a day. In the BOP1000 group the average rises to $264 a year ($0.72 a day), and in the BOP1500 segment to $379 a year ($1 a day).

These amounts may be small, but the large populations in the bottom three income segments create big markets. In the 34 countries for which standardized data on energy spending are available, energy expenditures total $9.5 billion a year in the BOP500 segment, $60.5 billion in BOP1000, and $64.0 billion in BOP1500.

Differences in access to electricity between rural and urban areas create different patterns of energy spending. In Brazil, for example, the 6.5 million rural BOP households spend $661.3 million a year on energy, or $102 per household—while the 25.3 million urban BOP households spend $10.1 billion, or $397 per household. On average, an urban BOP household in Brazil spends 289% more on energy than its rural counterpart.

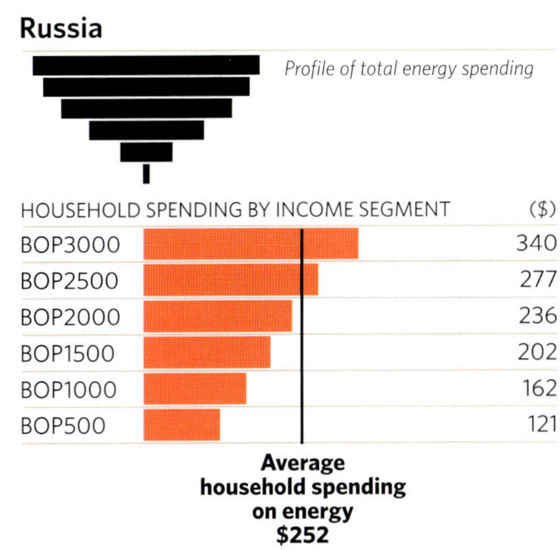

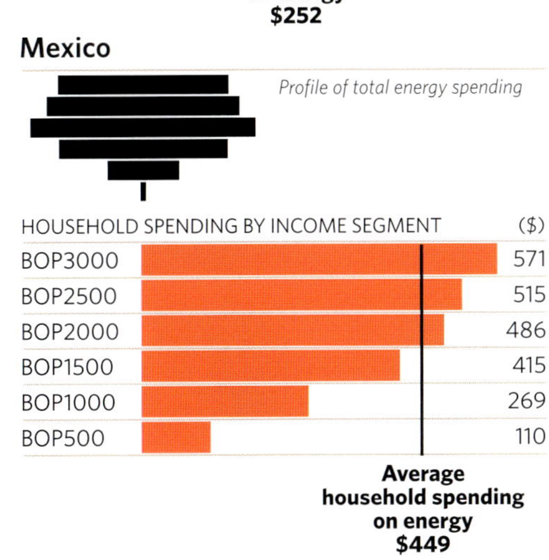

CASE STUDY 7.1 **NIGERIA:**

WHERE THE BOP IS THE MARKET

Nigeria's national household energy market has the biggest BOP share in Africa: 99.4%. At $5.1 billion, the market is also the second largest recorded in Africa (after South Africa's). The distribution of the market closely tracks the distribution of the population—both skew heavily toward the lowest BOP income groups. The BOP500 income segment accounts for 36% of national energy spending, the BOP1000 for 40%, and the BOP1500 for 16%. (Burkina Faso is the only other measured country in any region with more than a third of its national energy market in the BOP500 segment.)

Nigeria has more households in the BOP500 income group—13 million, 49% of the national total—than any other African nation has in its entire country. India, with nearly nine times the population of Nigeria, has less than a third as many households in the BOP500 segment—3.6 million.

Nigeria's BOP500 households earn between $1 and $2 a day in per capita income. Yet they spend an average of $140 a year on energy, or some $0.40 a day—for a total of $1.8 billion a year for this income segment.

This spending by BOP500 households is split roughly evenly between urban and rural markets: 52% ($940 million) in urban areas, 48% ($883 million) in rural areas. (The national energy market is somewhat more heavily urban weighted: 63% urban, 37% rural.) Rural BOP500 households report average energy spending of $130 a year, half that of their urban counterparts, at $267. But rural BOP500 households outnumber urban ones nearly two to one, equalizing the market sizes.

Only 35% of BOP500 households in Nigeria report having access to electricity, but this is still the second highest rate in this income group among surveyed African countries. The share of households with access to electricity climbs to 57% in BOP1000, 74% in BOP1500, and 82% in BOP2000. Stark differences show up between rural and urban areas: only 14% of rural BOP500 households report having access to electricity, compared with 72% of urban ones.

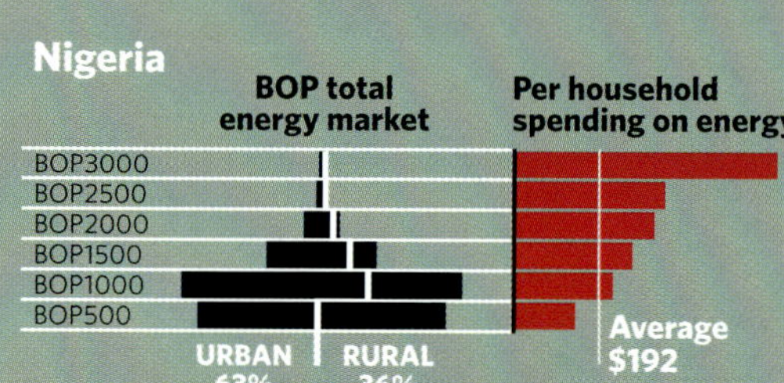

For rural BOP500 households without electricity, kerosene is the dominant fuel source for lighting: 79% report it as their primary source, compared with only 25% of urban BOP500 households. For cooking, firewood is the primary fuel source for both urban and rural BOP500 households, reported by 80% on average. Among BOP2000 households firewood use falls to 31%, replaced by kerosene for 59% of households.

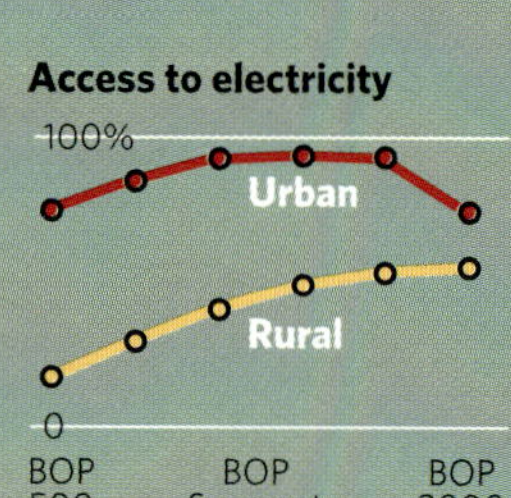

Patterns of fuel use vary across income groups as well as between rural and urban areas. In Africa, Asia, and Latin America firewood is the main fuel source used for cooking in the lower BOP income groups.

Patterns of fuel use vary across income groups as well as between rural and urban areas. In Africa, Asia, and Latin America firewood is the main fuel source used for cooking in the lower BOP income groups. In Thailand firewood is reported as the primary source by 79% of households in BOP500, 45% in BOP1000, and 27% in BOP1500.

Far more rural than urban BOP households—in all income segments—use firewood as their primary fuel source for cooking. In Gabon 48% of urban households in BOP500 report firewood as their primary fuel source, while 86% of their rural counterparts do. Across all BOP income segments, however, only 20% of urban households use primarily firewood, compared with 76% of rural households—a share nearly four times as large.

In higher income segments propane or liquefied petroleum gas (LPG) becomes the most common substitute for firewood. In Bolivia this is the primary fuel source for 87% of households in BOP2500, 87% in BOP3000, and 93% in the mid-market segment (compared with 13% in BOP500). Use in Nepal is reported by 60%, 75%, and 94% in the same groups (<1% in BOP500). In African countries fuel sources used in the mid-market segment are more varied, with the most prevalent being propane or LPG in Cameroon, Côte d'Ivoire, Malawi, and Rwanda; kerosene in Burundi, Djibouti, and Nigeria; and electricity in Malawi and Uganda.

For lighting, kerosene is the predominant fuel source in lower BOP income groups in Africa and Asia. In Malawi 89% of households in the BOP500 segment report it as their primary lighting fuel, compared with only 7% in the mid-market segment. In Bhutan the share for BOP500 households is 64%, while there is no recorded use in the mid-market segment.

Electricity replaces kerosene in the mid-market segment, where it is predominant across regions. In Burkina Faso electricity is the primary

Thailand

PERCENT OF HOUSEHOLDS BY PRIMARY COOKING FUEL

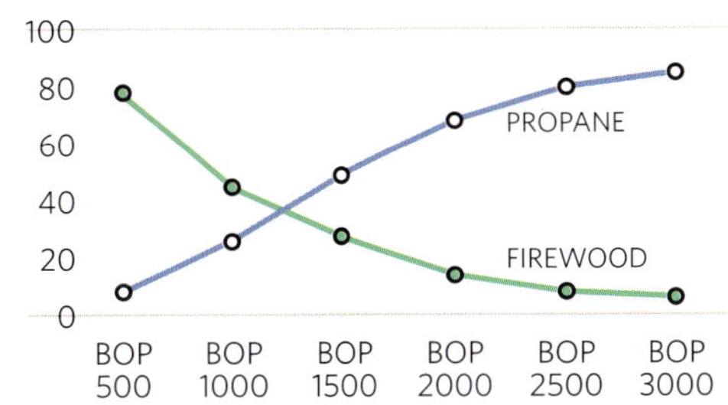

Gabon

PERCENT OF HOUSEHOLDS USING FIREWOOD AS THE PRIMARY COOKING FUEL

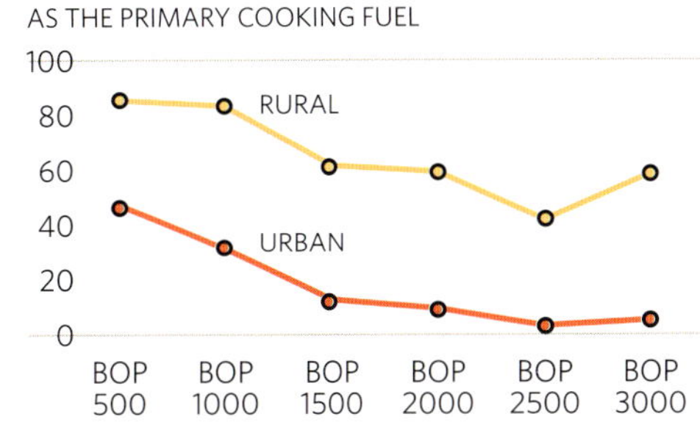

Malawi

PERCENT OF HOUSEHOLDS BY PRIMARY LIGHTING

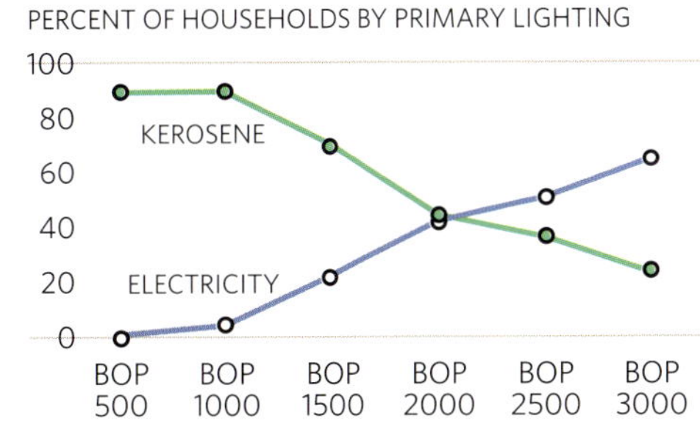

CASE STUDY 7.2 **INDIA: SMALL EXPENDITURES ADD UP TO A HUGE MARKET**

India has the largest measured energy market in Asia, with $163 billion in annual household spending. Some 52% of that market is in the bottom three BOP income groups (70% of the population), and 81% in the bottom five (92% of the population). Annual per household spending averages $342 in BOP500, $606 in BOP1000, and $751 in BOP1500.

Rural areas account for 63% of the national energy market, or $102 billion in annual spending—and 70% of the BOP market, or $99.7 billion. The urban BOP energy market represents $42.3 billion in spending.

For rural BOP households, energy spending averages around $705 a year, or $2 a day. For urban BOP households the average is $1,008 a year, around $2.75 a day. Per household spending in the mid-market segment averages $1,236 in rural areas and $1,368 in urban areas.

The rural BOP energy market shows a large concentration in the lowest BOP income groups: 69% is in the bottom three, compared with just 23% in the urban BOP energy market. This concentration is due in part to the small mid-market population in rural areas. While the mid-market population's energy spending in rural areas amounts to $2.3 billion, it is nearly nine times as much in urban areas, at $18.7 billion. In contrast, the bottom three BOP income segments in rural areas spend $70 billion on energy—nearly 45% of all national per household energy spending. Yet in each of these three BOP income segments household energy spending averages less than $2 a day.

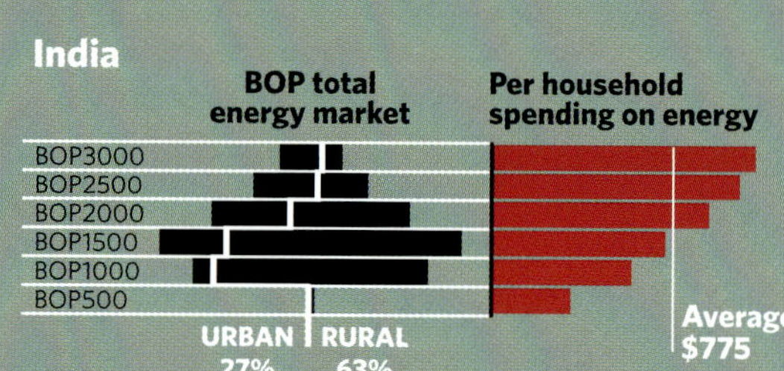

Kerosene is the most common lighting fuel for the lowest two BOP income groups—reported as the primary source by 65% of BOP500 households and 50% of BOP1000 ones. Kerosene use rates fall off dramatically in higher income segments, dropping to 7% in BOP2500 and BOP3000 and only 1% in the mid market. Electricity becomes the main lighting source in BOP2500 and higher income levels.

Firewood is the primary fuel source for cooking in the lower BOP income groups in India, reported by 75% of surveyed households in BOP500, 78% in BOP1000, and 60% in BOP1500. Use falls to only 23% of households in BOP2500 and 15% in BOP3000. Propane or LPG becomes the main fuel source for cooking in higher income groups, reported by 65% of households in BOP2500, 79% in BOP3000, and 87% in the mid market.

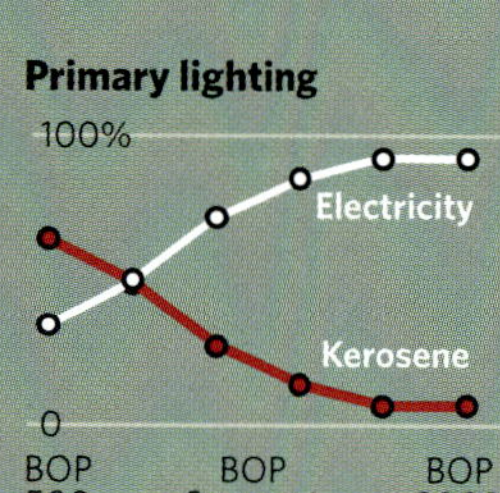

Africa's BOP energy markets maintain a roughly even split between urban and rural areas. Asia's markets, in contrast, are decidedly skewed toward rural areas.

Cambodia

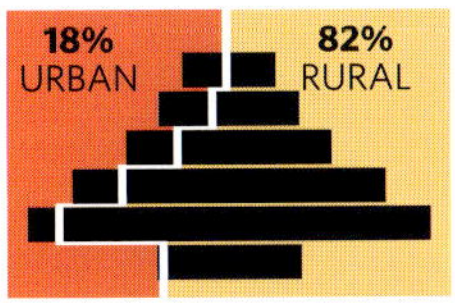

Malawi

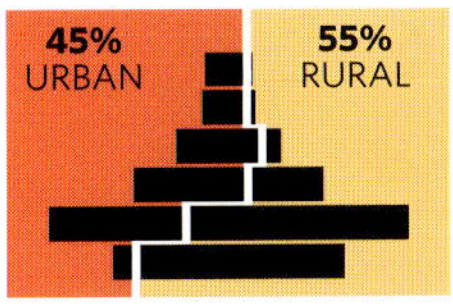

Total BOP energy spending by income segment, urban and rural

lighting source for 8% of households in the BOP; in the mid-market segment this share rises to 78%.

Where is the market?

Measured BOP spending on energy splits approximately 40% urban, 60% rural. But rural BOP households spend on average 44% less on energy than do urban BOP households. The larger populations in rural areas balance out the markets—and represent significant market opportunities for energy to power lighting, cooking, and productive enterprises (case studies 7.3–7.6).

Africa's BOP energy markets, at 55% urban, maintain a roughly even split between urban and rural areas. Yet rural BOP households spend only a third as much on energy as their urban counterparts on average, the largest such discrepancy among regions. In Malawi, for example, while the BOP energy market is 55% rural, rural BOP households spend only 15% as much on energy as their urban counterparts.

Asia's BOP energy markets, in contrast, are decidedly skewed toward rural areas (Indonesia is the lone exception). In Cambodia the BOP energy market is 82% rural.

Eastern Europe's BOP energy markets are predominantly urban. This region, where access to electricity is nearly universal, has the smallest gap between rural and urban energy spending. In Ukraine, where the BOP energy market is 67% urban, urban BOP households spend only 17% more on energy than their rural counterparts.

Latin America's BOP energy markets also tilt decidedly toward uban areas (with Guatemala

CASE STUDY 7.3 **POWERING UP: HARNESSING SUBSIDIES FOR RURAL ELECTRIFICATION IN CHILE**

In the mid-1990s Chile, an early reformer in the electricity sector, set out to achieve rural electrification through a program involving the private sector. The goal: provide electricity to 50% of the rural population—one million people. The program offered a one-time direct subsidy to private electricity distribution companies to cover part of the capital investment; operating costs would have to be covered through tariffs. Four principles guided the program: decentralized decision making, joint financing, competition, and appropriate technologies.

The program has been a success in several ways. It exceeded its target, reaching 75% of the unserved population by 1999. Projects were financially sustainable enough to allow the government to reduce its investment stake, as planned. Regional governments performed well, as did community groups and the private energy companies. While most power has come through grid extension, isolated areas have experimented successfully with wind, biomass, hydropower, and photovoltaic systems. Finally, while the average state subsidy per dwelling increased by 50% from 1995 to 1999 (from $1,080 to $1,510), the cost to government has been acceptable—especially in light of the social goal achieved—and within expected budgetary limits.

Early and continual consultation helped ensure satisfaction and support among customers. And rural communities have proved to be good customers: bill payment rates are high, and electricity use is steadily rising as economic activity grows (Jadresic 2000).

This case shows the value of the strategy of **unconventional partnering.**

CASE STUDY 7.4 **THINKNG SMALL TO SOLVE BIG:**

HARNESSING SUBSIDIES FOR RURAL ELECTRIFICATION IN CHILE

Through technological innovation, many large companies are working to solve big problems with small devices. The energy giant Shell aims to create sustainable market systems to sell 20 million affordable stoves in India by 2010. And with the support of its private sector-focused Shell Foundation, two Indian NGOs, the Appropriate Rural Technology Institute and Development Alternatives, are developing and marketing low-polluting biomass fuels and cooking devices.

Another oil giant, BP, is rolling out a stove that can use either biomass or liquefied natural gas. With NGO partners, BP is also developing innovative distribution models, micro-financing for the stoves, and small-scale entrepreneurship. Dutch multinational Philips has developed an efficient wood-burning stove that cuts emissions of pollutants by 90% over traditional wood fires (Philips Research 2006). German industrial leaders Bosch and Siemens have teamed up to develop Protos, a plant oil stove, now on the market in the Philippines.

All these efforts marry high-tech academic research and civil society engagement with a market-driven business model. They illustrate a strategy of focusing on the BOP, combined in some cases with **unconventional partnering.**

the lone exception). In Mexico urban areas account for 76% of BOP spending on energy, with urban BOP households spending roughly 50% more on energy than their rural counterparts.

Is there evidence of a BOP penalty?

Income is clearly related to access to energy and to the type of energy source used for different purposes. The BOP consistently has less access to electricity than the mid-market segment. And access increases as BOP incomes rise, a consistent pattern across countries and regions.

Rural areas show a larger and more persistent BOP penalty in access to electricity across income groups: in any income group access is invariably lower in rural than in urban areas. In Bangladesh 37% of urban households in BOP500 have access, compared with only 4% of their rural counterparts. Among households in all BOP income segments in Bangladesh, the share is 81% in urban areas, 20% in rural.

Overall, 36% of BOP households lack access to electricity—while only 6% of mid-market households lack access. Reported access rates are 51% in the BOP500 income segment, 63% in BOP1000, and 74% in BOP1500.

But these averages conceal marked differences across regions. In Eastern Europe access to electricity is virtually universal. FYR Macedonia, Russia, and Ukraine all show 99% access in the BOP and at least 95% in BOP500. Latin America and Asia show access rates similar to one another across the lowest BOP income segments, albeit lower than Eastern

Russia

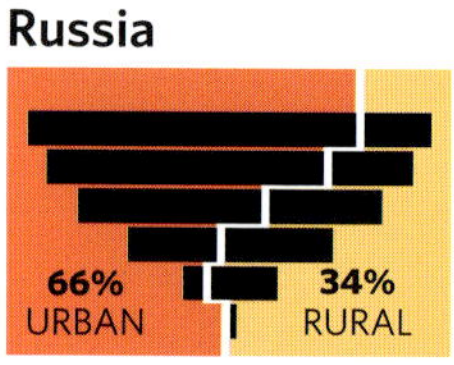

Bolivia

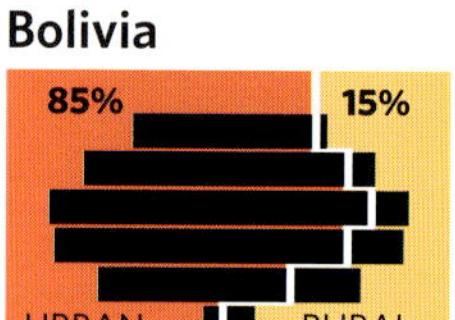

Total BOP energy spending by income segment, urban and rural

Overall, 36% of BOP households lack access to electricity— while only 6% of mid-market households lack access. Reported access rates are 51% in the BOP500 income segment, 63% in BOP1000, and 74% in BOP1500.

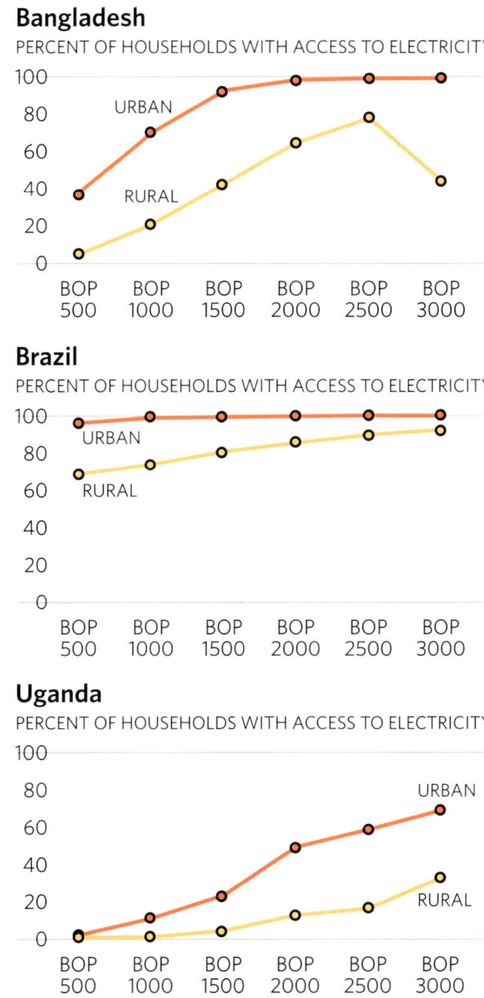

Europe and with higher variance across measured countries. High access rates occur in Brazil, where coverage in BOP500 is 85%, and in Indonesia, with 82% in the same segment.

Africa, in contrast, has severely depressed rates of access to electricity. Gabon has the largest share of BOP500 households reporting access, at 54%. But only 16% of all BOP households in Sierra Leone have access to electricity, and less than 10% in Burkina Faso, Malawi, Rwanda, and Uganda. The situation is most extreme in Africa's rural areas: the share of BOP households with access to electricity in rural areas is only a fifth that in urban areas.

Bringing electricity to low-income communities involves inherent difficulties. But new solutions are emerging for at least some of the problems related to the BOP penalty (case study 7.3).

CASE STUDY 7.5 **HERE COMES THE SUN: SOLAR BECOMING MORE EFFICIENT, MORE AFFORDABLE**

Solar photovoltaic systems are making headway for general household use in off-grid situations. Market-based enterprises are replacing earlier government-run programs. Solar panels are becoming increasingly efficient, with the cost per kilowatt-hour of electricity produced continuing to decline. And "clean tech" solutions are finding favor in the capital markets, so enterprise funding is more readily available.

The Solar Electric Light Company (Selco), a small company in India, and the Solar Electric Light Fund (SELF), an NGO, both provide household-size photovoltaic systems at an affordable cost, with financing options, in a number of countries. A well-funded new company, Orb Energy, staffed by solar power veterans, is building both commercial and residential units for the Indian market. E+Co, a pioneering energy fund, is now just one of many capital funds investing broadly in solar photovoltaic, geothermal, wind, biomass generators, and small hydropower systems.

In Brazil, IDEAAS offers a full-service solar photovoltaic system without requiring customer purchase—a business model not unlike grid utilities. This profitable social enterprise has reduced the number of rural Brazilians without electricity from 60 million in the mid-1990s to fewer than 12 million today.

All these cases, centering on context-specific innovation, illustrate a strategy of **focusing on the BOP.**

CASE STUDY 7.6 **PORTABLE POWER: LIGHT YOU CAN CARRY AND WEAR**

High-brightness, solid-state lighting produces a digital light of 80 lumens per watt, enough to read, work, or travel by. Kennedy & Violich Architecture has embedded high-brightness light-emitting diodes (LEDs) in flexible photovoltaic solar panels. The result is a light-producing textile that is lightweight, fully portable, and off the grid.

Among the devices in production is the "Portable Workshop," a foldable textile workspace weighing 14 ounces and providing 2.5 hours of light at 160 lumens. Recharging takes four hours, through a shoulder sash with photocells or a canopy that also shades the user. For nighttime use the device can be configured to provide ambient or task lighting or to light the way for travel.

The Light Up the World Foundation, in partnership with Stanford Business School, has developed LED-based products for rural use ranging from a flashlight-size device to an on- or off-grid device for ambient or task lighting. Devices can be powered in several ways—solar, hydro, wind, or human effort. One device successful in Nepal is the pedal generator—safe, rugged, economical, able to charge multiple batteries simultaneously, and easy to maintain, repair, and transport, even over difficult terrain.

The foundation now produces multiple configurations of its systems for individuals, households, and village institutions such as schools and clinics. Its systems have been installed in more than 14,000 homes, benefiting more than 100,000 people, and plans for large-scale rollout are under way.

Though a nonprofit, the foundation puts enterprise development at the core of its mission. Through "social pricing" arrangements with component suppliers, it helps new businesses get established in local markets and provides mentoring and training to support their sustainable development.

Both these cases illustrate a strategy of **focusing on the BOP.**

In Africa, rural BOP households spend only a third as much on energy as their urban counterparts on average, the largest such discrepancy among regions.

Endnotes

1. Reported household expenditures in a given country should be regarded as a minimum estimate of actual expenditures, because surveys may not have collected information on all types of energy-related spending.
2. For more on these entities, see http://www.shellfoundation.org, http://www.arti-india.org, and http://www.devalt.org.
3. BSH (Bosch und Siemens Hausgeräte GmbH), "BSH Presents Ecological Plant Oil Stove for Developing Countries," http://www.plantoilcooker.org (accessed January 13, 2007).
4. Selco, "What We Provide," http://www.selco-india.com/what-we-provide.html; Solar Electric Light Fund, "Solar Technology," http://www.self.org/shs_tech.asp (accessed January 13, 2007).
5. E+Co, "E+Co Enterprises," http://www.eandco.net/enterprise_home.php (accessed January 13, 2007).
6. IDEAAS (Instituto para o Desenvolvimento de Energias Alternativas e da Auto Sustentabilidade), "Projects," http://www.ideaas.org.br/id_proj_luz_agora_eng.htm (accessed January 13, 2007).
7. Portable Light Project, "Portable Light," http://www.tcaup.umich.edu/portablelight/portable.swf (accessed January 13, 2007).
8. Economist, "Lighting Up the World," September 21, 2006, http://www.economist.com/science/tq/displayStory.cfm?story_id=7904248.

CHAPTER EIGHT

The Food Market

Putting enough food on the table is a constant struggle for many BOP households. Purchasing food takes more than half of BOP household budgets in many countries, especially in Africa and Asia. In Nigeria, food accounts for 52% of BOP household spending—in rural Pakistan, 55%. As incomes rise, the share of household spending on food declines. Food nevertheless represents the largest share of BOP household spending and the largest BOP market.

Improving distribution to expand access to food and providing better food products, including more nutritional ones, are clearly significant business opportunities—as well as investments that could benefit the BOP. Opportunities also exist in agriculture, an essential part of the food value chain and a major source of employment and income for the BOP.

How large is the market?

The measured BOP food market in Africa (12 countries), Asia (9), Eastern Europe (6), and Latin American and the Caribbean (9) is $1.53 trillion. This represents annual household spending on food by 2.16 billion people in the 36 low- and middle-income countries for which standardized data are available. The total BOP household food market in these four regions, including all surveyed countries, is estimated to be $2.89 trillion, accounting for the spending of 3.96 billion people (see box 1.5 in chapter 1 for the estimation method).[1]

Asia has the largest measured regional BOP food market, $1.1 trillion, reflecting a large BOP population (1.49 billion). The total BOP food market in Asia (including the Middle East) is es-

BOP spending on food
$2,894 billion

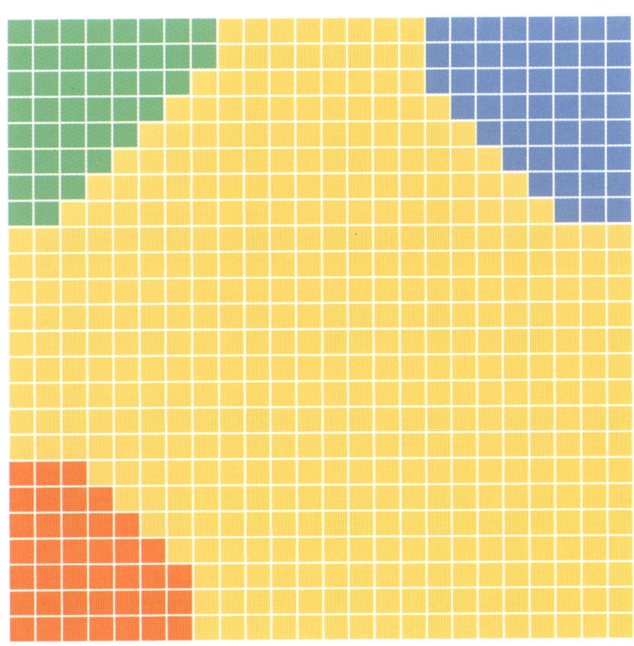

	$ billions (PPP)
Africa	215
Asia	2,236
Eastern Europe	244
Latin America	199

Each square represents approximately $5 billion

In 17 countries in Africa and Asia, the bottom three BOP income segments account for more than 50% of measured national food spending.

Nigeria

TOTAL FOOD SPENDING BY INCOME SEGMENT

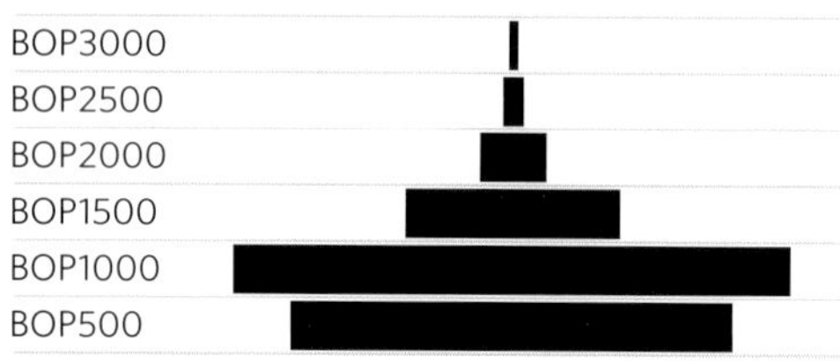

Indonesia

TOTAL FOOD SPENDING BY INCOME SEGMENT

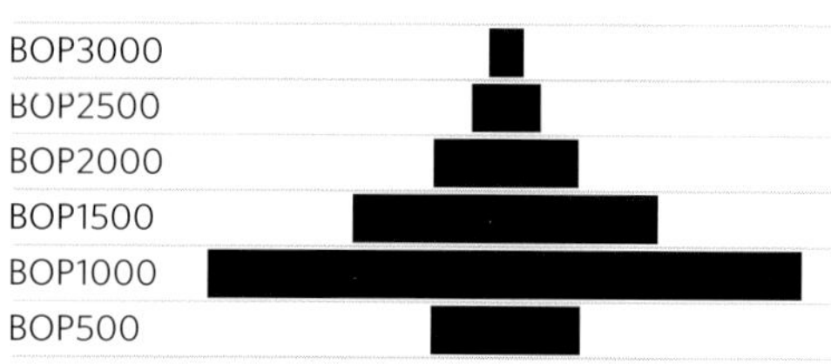

Colombia

TOTAL FOOD SPENDING BY INCOME SEGMENT

FYR Macedonia

TOTAL FOOD SPENDING BY INCOME SEGMENT

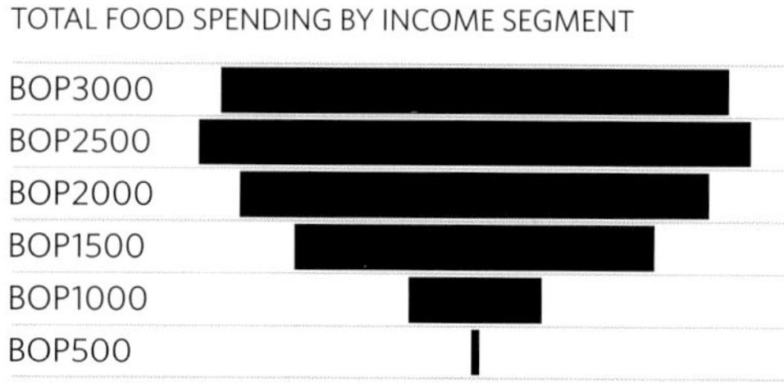

timated to be $2.24 trillion, accounting for the spending of 2.9 billion people. Latin America follows, with a measured BOP food market of $167 billion (275.8 million people) and an estimated total BOP food market of $199.4 billion (360 million people). Eastern Europe has recorded BOP food spending of $137 billion (147.8 million people) and estimated total BOP spending of $244.0 billion (254 million people). Africa's measured BOP food market is $97.0 billion (253.3 million people), and its estimated total market $215.1 billion (486 million people).

Asia also has the largest BOP share of the measured food market, at 89%. Africa follows with 80%. Latin America has a markedly smaller BOP share, at 51%—as does Eastern Europe, at 50%.

In national food markets the BOP share is consistently high across measured countries in Asia. Bangladesh, Indonesia, Pakistan, and Tajikistan all have BOP shares exceeding 95%. Thailand, with 67%, is the only country with a BOP share less than 80%. In Africa the extremes at the high end are Nigeria (99%), Sierra Leone (97%), and Burkina Faso (96%)—and at the low end, South Africa (46%). In Eastern Europe, Uzbekistan (99%) marks the high extreme—and Russia (41%), FYR Macedonia (42%), and Ukraine (44%) the low. In Latin America the extremes are Peru (78%) and Colombia (33%).

How is the market segmented?

Bottom-heavy BOP food markets—in which the bottom three BOP income segments outspend the top three—occur in 24 of the 30 countries measured in Africa, Asia, and Latin America. These countries with bottom-heavy BOP markets often also have a national market dominated by the BOP.

Indeed, in 17 of the 18 countries in Africa and Asia with bottom-heavy BOP food markets, the bottom three BOP income segments account for more than 50% of measured national food spending. The bottom two BOP groups alone account for more than 50% of national food spending in 8 of these countries in Africa (Burkina Faso, Burundi, Cameroon, Côte d'Ivoire, Malawi, Nigeria, Rwanda, and Sierra Leone) and 5 in Asia (Bangladesh, Indonesia, Nepal, Pakistan, and Tajikistan). Only one country in Eastern Europe (Uzbekistan) shows this concentration, and none in Latin America.

In Latin America five of the nine measured BOP food markets are bottom heavy, and in each case the BOP accounts for more than 50% of measured national food spending. In four countries (Guatemala, Honduras, Jamaica, and Peru) three middle BOP income segments (BOP1000–2000) account for more than 50% of national food spending.

Top-heavy BOP food markets—in which the top three BOP income segments outspend the bottom three—occur in four of the measured countries in Latin America (Brazil, Colombia, Mexico, and Paraguay) and five of the six measured in Eastern Europe (Belarus, Kazakhstan, FYR Macedonia, Russia, and Ukraine). In six of the countries with top-heavy BOP markets, the mid-market segment dominates the national market, accounting for more than 50% of total spending on food.

What do households spend?

Average annual food spending per household in the BOP varies across measured countries. The median value among these averages by region may be the most useful indicator: in Africa, $2,087 (Cameroon) and $2,548 (South Africa); in Asia, $2,643 (Pakistan); in Eastern Europe, $3,687 (Kazakhstan) and $3,744 (Uzbekistan); and in Latin America, $3,050 (Peru).

Household spending on food increases less rapidly than income. Or put another way, the share of the household budget devoted to food declines as household income rises. This can be seen by comparing measured annual food spending by BOP3000 and BOP500 households in the countries above. While BOP3000 households have 6 times as much income on average, they outspend BOP500 households in the food market by a ratio of only 2:1 in Cameroon, 2.3:1 in South Africa and Pakistan, 2.4:1 in Kazakhstan, 1.9:1 in Uzbekistan, and 3:1 in Peru.

This pattern probably reflects the simple fact that even in the lowest segments of the BOP, households must spend a minimum amount to ensure survival. Business strategies that can deliver more value for these minimum food expenditures accordingly can create significant market value—for BOP consumers and for the company (case study 8.1).

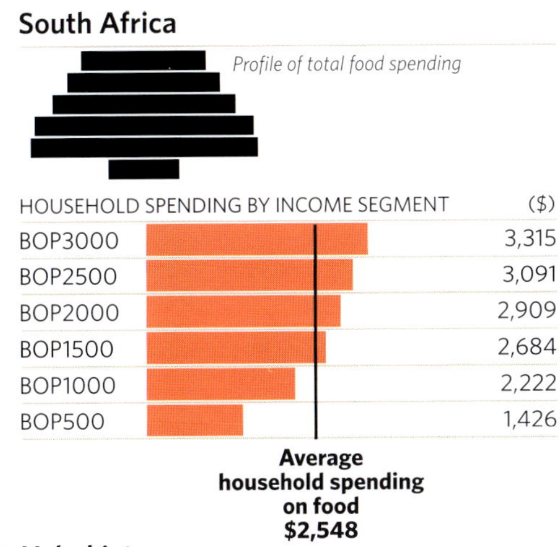

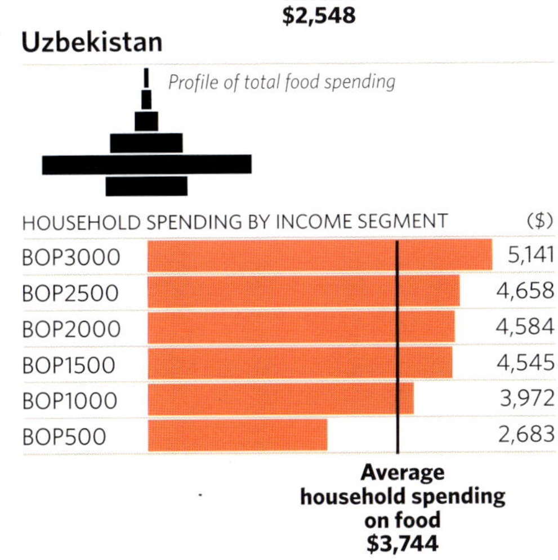

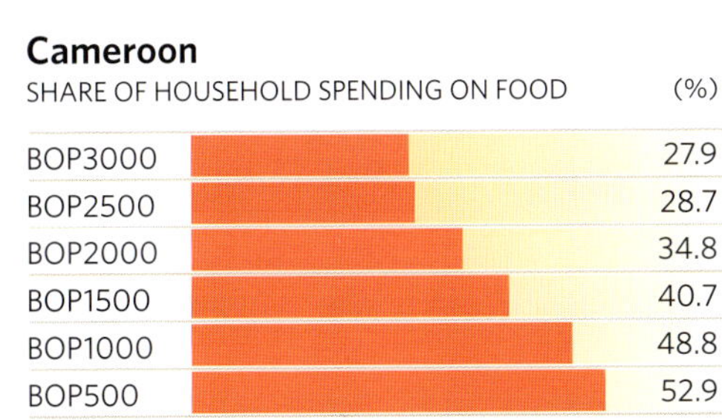

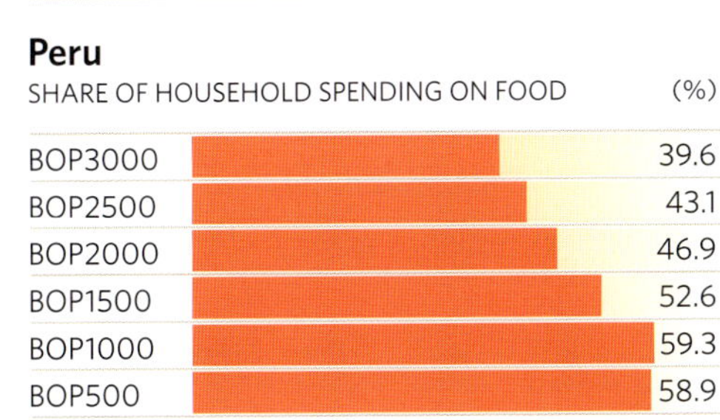

CASE STUDY 8.1 **HEALTHIER FOOD: MAKING MORE OF LESS FOR BOP MARKETS**

Making "more of less" is critical to health in the BOP. Recognizing this, private enterprises are working to find ways to help meet the nutritional needs of low-income populations. One effort has focused on insufficient dietary iodine, a leading cause of mental retardation in India. More than 70 million people in India, and 200 million globally, suffer from iodine deficiency disorder. In the developed world most salt is fortified with iodine and everyone can afford it. But in India only 20% is iodized, and this salt is priced higher than noniodized salt, putting it out of reach for many in the BOP. Moreover, climate conditions, storage practices, and traditional cooking methods in India tend to eliminate the iodine from the salt.

Hindustan Lever Limited (HLL), an Indian division of consumer giant Unilever, tackled this problem. Putting modern science and technology to work, it developed a method for producing iodized salt that would remain stable under any conditions in India—yet still be affordable to the BOP (Rajendra and Shah 2005). Its new Annapurna brand salt is profitable—and the success in India has led to initiatives in other Unilever markets. Among these are Côte d'Ivoire, Ghana, Kenya, and Nigeria, where the product has been adapted to incorporate other essential nutrients.[2]

The Bangladesh microfinance institution Grameen Bank and the French multinational Groupe Danone have partnered, in a 50:50 joint venture, to produce low-cost, high-nutrient yogurt products targeted to the BOP consumer market. What makes the model interesting is that it also focuses on BOP producers and distributors. Grameen Danone Foods will source the milk from hundreds of microfarmers, who typically own one or two cows purchased with a microloan. And it will sell the yogurt through a network of stands and food kiosks operated by microentrepreneurs. Each serving of yogurt contains three times as many nutrients as the competition, costs less than US$0.07, and comes in a 100 percent biodegradeable cup.

Still another initiative has developed a cheap source of protein. The idea got its genesis when Hector Gonzales, the founder of Cuadritos, a successful milk, cheese, and yogurt company in Mexico, established a food bank in that country. In less than two years, by harnessing efficient logistics with corporate donations, the food bank grew to feed 100,000 people a day. As Gonzales saw that thousands of tons of food were discarded daily, simply because they had not sold by their "best used by" date, he developed a technology to reprocess the protein from milk, yogurt, and vegetables. Turned into a powder, the reprocessed protein can be added to a variety of foodstuffs, such as dairy and soy milks and cookies and other baked goods (New Ventures 2006). Nutrient recycling may be the 21st-century version of the pulp and aluminum recycling of the late 20th century—profitable and beneficial.

Both of these enterprises, in innovating to address the unique conditions of the markets they encountered, illustrate a strategy of **focusing on the BOP.**

Where is the market?

The distribution of BOP food spending between urban and rural areas closely tracks the distribution of the BOP population. In Africa, where measured BOP spending on food is $97.0 billion, the BOP food market is predominantly rural in 9 of 12 countries (Djibouti, Gabon, and South Africa are the urban-tilting exceptions). Across these 12 countries the rural market is 1.6 times as large as the urban one. Significant malnutrition in the region underscores the need to improve farmers' productivity and strengthen food supply chains (case study 8.2).

Asia has similarly rural-skewed BOP food spending. At $811 billion, the region's measured rural BOP food market is 2.5 times the size of the urban market; only Indonesia has an urban market larger than the rural one. The dominance of rural markets stems from the dominance of the rural BOP population: in Asia rural BOP households outnumber urban ones by a ratio of almost 3:1. The large size of rural food markets underscores the importance of distribution strategies that can efficiently reach rural BOP households—like those being developed in India by Hindustan Lever Limited. For this company, rural BOP markets have also become a source of bottom-up learning (case study 8.3).

In Eastern Europe and Latin America BOP food markets are predominantly urban in 11 of 15 countries. In Latin America the measured urban BOP food market is $106 billion, 2.4

India

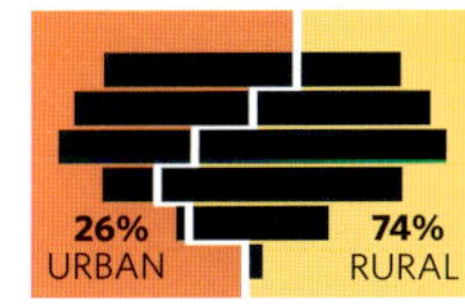

Mexico

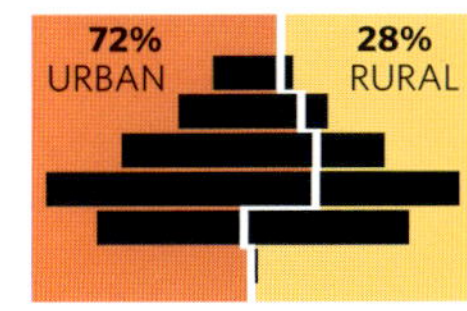

Total BOP food spending by income segment, urban and rural

times the size of the rural market. Only three countries in the region—Guatemala, Jamaica, and Paraguay—record a rural-tilted BOP food market.

Despite the mostly larger rural food markets, on average urban BOP households spend more on food than rural ones in 30 of the 36 measured countries (the exceptions are Brazil, Jamaica, Kazakhstan, Tajikistan, Ukraine, and Uzbekistan). The difference is smaller in total household spending. In Côte d'Ivoire, Nigeria, Pakistan, and Thailand, for example, the difference between urban and rural areas in BOP household spending on food is less than 10%, while the difference in spending in all markets is at least 33%.

What does the BOP buy?

In the developing world, particularly for the BOP, food is more a local than a global business. Favored foodstuffs reflect the local climate, geography, and traditions. So it is not surprising to find in household survey data—as for Brazil—that BOP spending patterns on food do not differ appreciably from those of the mid-market segment, either in the types of foods purchased

CASE STUDY 8.2
PUMPING UP PRODUCTIVITY: NEW WATER PUMPS FOR BOP FARMERS

BOP farmers can play an important part in local or even international food value chains, and innovations that improve their productivity also increase their incomes. With this in mind, the NGO International Development Enterprises has developed a family of step-action foot pumps for agricultural use, all of which can be locally manufactured from locally available metal and wood materials.[3] Since these basic pumps were introduced in 1985, more than 2 million have been installed worldwide. Different designs allow the use of different water sources—from rivers and other surface water to boreholes and other groundwater sources.

Another NGO, KickStart, has focused on developing appropriate technologies for African entrepreneurs that can be fully market driven, creating enterprises at every level of the value chain from manufacture to distribution, retailing, and end use by farmers.[4] KickStart's "MoneyMaker" line of pumps—ranging from simple treadle to more complex suction-pressure pumps—are in wide use, mostly in East Africa (John Deere 2005).[5]

These enterprises, producing meaningful innovations in response to BOP needs, exemplify a strategy of **focusing on the BOP.**

The large size of rural food markets underscores the importance of distribution strategies that can efficiently reach rural BOP households or in the allocation of spending among these types.

Still, survey data for Brazil do reveal differences. Two categories of food purchases that appear in the top 10 for the BOP do not show up in the top 10 for the mid-market segment: "other cereals, flours" and "sugar." Similarly, two categories in the top 10 for the mid-market segment—"mineral waters and soft drinks" and "fresh or chilled fruits"—rank only 14 and 15 for the BOP. It can be surmised that the calorie-rich carbohydrates of cereals and sugars are simply more important in the basic diets of people with lower incomes—and that fresh fruit and bottled beverages are more affordable alternatives for those with higher incomes.

Spending per household differs significantly, of course. Brazilian households in the bottom three BOP segments (BOP500–1500) spend an average of $1,332 a year on food, while those in the mid-market segment spend an average of $3,487. Even so, the difference is smaller than might be expected. The income ratio between mid-market households (median income $12,000) and BOP1000 households is 12:1, yet the ratio of average household food spending for these two groups is only 3:1. This is consistent with the finding from household survey data that the share of food in household spending steadily declines as incomes rise—and does so in all income groups.

FOOD CASE STUDY 8.3 **REACHING THE BOP INNOVATIONS IN DISTRIBUTION**

Some of the BOP penalty can be ascribed to the difficulties and added cost of distribution in low-income communities, whether urban neighborhoods or rural villages. Many companies are finding innovative new ways to reach BOP customers, as examples in the health and financial services markets show. What is true in these markets is also true in those for fast-moving consumer goods, consumer durables, and food: future growth will come largely from the BOP.

Convinced of this, Hindustan Lever Limited tries every angle to reach the BOP.[6] It requires new managers to spend six to eight weeks in a rural village, learning from BOP customers, as part of their training. To make products accessible—key in reaching the BOP market—HLL uses "sachet" packaging. Low-priced, single-serving sachets account for 55% of its shampoo sales (Balu 2001). HLL also uses unconventional marketing to reach the BOP. Fairs, festivals, and traveling cinema vans have all become important parts of its consumer outreach, combining entertainment with health and hygiene education.

Through innovations in distribution, HLL has reached deeper and deeper into rural markets. It has set up distribution networks that carry its products to the most remote villages by whatever means required—motorbike, bicycle, oxcart—and has also employed direct sales agents.

The approach builds brand loyalty at the same time that it creates employment—and exemplifies the business strategy of **enabling access.**

Brazil

SHARE OF HOUSEHOLD SPENDING ON FOOD (%)

The ratio of household food spending between the mid-market segment and the BOP1000 segment is consistent with the finding that the share of food in household spending steadily declines as incomes rise—and does so in all income segments.

Endnotes

1. Reported household expenditures in a given country should be regarded as a minimum estimate of actual expenditures, because surveys may not have collected information on all types of food-related spending.
2. Janet Roberts, "Project Shakti: Growing the Market While Changing Lives," Case Weatherhead School of Management, http://worldbenefit.cwru.edu/inquiry/featureShakti.cfm (accessed January 9, 2007).
3. International Development Enterprises, "Homepage," http://www.ideorg.org/ (accessed January 9, 2007).
4. KickStart, "KickStart: The Tools to End Poverty," http://www.kickstart.org/ (accessed January 9, 2007).
5. KickStart, "25 Entrepreneurs Who Are Changing the World: KickStart," FastCompany.com, http://www.fastcompany.com/social/2006/statements/kickstart.html (accessed January 9, 2007).
6. Hindustan Lever Limited, "Creating Markets: Delighting Customers Everywhere," http://www.hll.com/brands/creating_markets.asp (accessed January 9, 2007).

CHAPTER NINE

The Financial Services Market

Microcredit pioneer Muhammad Yunus received the Nobel Peace Prize in 2006, a milestone in public attention to the financial needs of the BOP. Until recently the main focus has been microcredit, historically the domain of nonprofits. Now the focus is changing—as new players and new products enter the market and new technologies transform services. A dynamic financial services sector is emerging—moving toward financial access for all.

Many microfinance institutions now offer savings as well as microcredit. Commercial banks are becoming active in the BOP market and bringing a still broader range of services, including insurance. Mobile phone banking, still at an early stage, promises to dramatically broaden access and lower transaction costs. Remittances to BOP households from family members overseas have emerged as a significant cross-border financial flow, bringing new attention and new ways to promote economic growth.

As these changes expand access to financial services for the BOP, the effects can be measured in many ways, not just in the volume or dollar value of transactions:

- New jobs and income. New types of financial services, provided through mobile phone systems, are generating new jobs and income for millions of small entrepreneurs who sell over-the-air credit.
- Formal identity. Establishing a banking relationship gives people a formal identity they often lacked before, contributing to the process of political and social inclusion critical to development.
- Greater personal safety. Cash is a burden for the poor, making them vulnerable to crime. By doing away with the need to carry a lot of cash, such services as debit cards and mobile phone–based access to cash and bill-paying facilities enhance personal safety and the quality of life.

In Indonesia women who are clients of Bank Rakyat Indonesia are more likely than other women to participate in family financial decisions.

- More education for children. In Bangladeshi families that are clients of Grameen Bank, nearly all girls are in school, compared with only 60% in nonclient families.
- More timely health care. In Uganda the Foundation for Credit and Community Assistance (FOCCAS) links its microloans to participation in child health education programs and has doubled the share of its clients using practices to prevent the transmission of HIV. In Bolivia microcredit clients of Crédito con Educación Rural (Crecer) had higher rates of child immunization in their families than did nonclients.
- Economic empowerment of women. In Indonesia women who are clients of Bank Rakyat Indonesia (BRI) are more likely than other women to participate in family financial decisions. In India borrowers from SEWA Bank have organized unions to lobby for higher wages and more rights as members of the associated Self-Employed Women's Association (Littlefield, Morduch, and Hashemi 2003).

Through these effects and many more, financial services play a critical part in reducing poverty and improving the access of the BOP to goods and services.

How large is the market?

National household surveys capture extensive data on financial matters, but little on actual spending for financial services. Moreover, the costs of these services are often not fully transparent to BOP customers, who may not know or understand the actual costs of transferring remittances from sender to recipient, for example, or the true interest rate paid to an informal village lender. As a result, robust data on spending for financial services are not available in sufficient detail for meaningful analysis.

What is known, however, clearly indicates that the financial services sector is changing—and doing so in ways that are moving it toward broad access for the BOP. Three factors are powering this transformation:

- The microfinance sector is growing up, attracting new participants and creating new services.
- Rapid changes in technology are reducing the transaction costs in financial services, expanding markets, and interesting large financial institutions in markets previously ignored.

- Remittances are approaching an estimated US$350 billion a year, and recipients, businesses, and national governments are learning how to leverage these "BOP to BOP" financial flows.

The following analysis briefly explores the financial services sector through these three lenses.[1]

The changing banking landscape

Several strategies are at work to bring financial services further into the BOP. One is to expand the microfinance institutions. A growing number of traditional microcredit banks—such as the Cooperative Bank of Kenya, Financiera Compartamos in Mexico, and BRI in Indonesia—have become profitable on a fully commercial basis, with sustainable microlending now just a part of their core business. And one relative newcomer, SKS Microfinance in India, has relied on operational efficiency to power rapid growth in lending (case study 9.1).

By the industry's own estimate, however, microcredit had reached only 82 million households by the end of 2006. Even the industry's new target for 2015, 175 million households, would represent only 31.5% of today's 556 million BOP households.[2]

Clearly, other strategies are needed to reach scale. Some are already in play. Major financial institutions are discovering that they can go "down-market" profitably, leveraging their capital, their expertise, and their back-office systems. In one of many examples, Citi in late 2006 announced plans to expand into low-income neighborhoods of India with automated teller machines (ATMs) using thumbprints to identify customers.[3] Banks also are beginning to

CASE STUDY 9.1 BOTTOM UP BANKING: DEEPENING FINANCIAL SERVICES ONE SMALL LOAN AT A TIME

In 1998, with US$52,000 in "family and friends" funding, Vikram Akula[14] started SKS Microfinance, a microcredit institution in India. Akula had a very specific goal in mind: use modern, efficient back-office systems to lower transaction costs so radically that microloans could be handled profitably and at scale.[15] Going well beyond the Grameen "lending circle" approach, SKS targeted a massive market—the 800 million people of the BOP in India.

SKS created simple loan management software with help from friends at consulting firms. And it developed simple rules for borrowers that cut transaction time and complexity—for example, requiring standard regular repayments in multiples of five rupees (the smallest paper bill in India, worth around US$0.11).

SKS has carefully tracked its risk profile, balancing its loan portfolio when in danger of becoming overexposed in one sector or another. When loans for buffaloes rose rapidly, for example, it quickly responded by finding borrowers in such areas as retail, construction, and auto and truck repair.

Big banks are now lining up to lend SKS funds to relend to its own clients.[16] ICICI Bank, India's largest private sector bank, has given SKS an open line of credit. ICICI assesses the risk to be low—SKS has a 98% on-time repayment rate. Moreover, SKS earns a higher return on capital than ICICI's large corporate borrowers.

SKS has loaned more than US$57 million to more than 200,000 women. Besides its income-generating loans, SKS offers interest-free loans for emergencies and life insurance for its clients. An SKS affiliate, SKS Education, provides education services to poor children.

SKS now has 85 microfinance branches in five Indian states and plans to open in five more as it pursues its goal of serving 700,000 clients by early 2007. By its own account it is already among the world's fastest-growing microfinance organizations.[17]

All these efforts add up to a significant deepening of the financial services sector for the BOP—and illustrate a strategy of **enabling access**.

Nontraditional players are entering the BOP market. Retail giant Wal-Mart has received regulatory approval in Mexico to create its own bank collocated with its stores. Grameen Foundation USA and India's largest private bank, ICICI Bank, have formed Grameen Capital India to assist microfinance institutions in raising funds.

view those receiving remittances as potential customers for a range of financial services.

Nontraditional players are entering the BOP market. Retail giant Wal-Mart has received regulatory approval in Mexico to create its own bank, Banco Wal-Mart, colocated with its stores.[4] If the venture is successful, other Wal-Mart banks will follow elsewhere.

Some microfinance institutions and big commercial banks are meeting in the middle. Grameen Foundation USA and India's largest private sector bank, ICICI Bank, have formed Grameen Capital India to assist microfinance institutions in raising funds. The joint venture will help microfinance institutions access primary and secondary debt markets and sell portfolios of microloans to other banks—and will also supply guarantees and credit enhancements for these portfolios where appropriate.[5]

ICICI has many similar ventures in the pipeline aimed at reaching the BOP. One is a partnership with microfinance institutions and technology provider n-Logue to harness thousands of entrepreneur-run Internet kiosks as the first touch point for savings accounts, mutual fund purchases, insurance, and even equity loans—and to provide branches, franchise operators, and ATMs throughout rural India.[6] Partnerships like these are spreading across the financial sector as a way to broaden access to services for the BOP.[7]

Steady growth of savings accounts in the BOP provides compelling evidence of its appetite for more than microcredit. Savings accounts for low-income customers in developing and transition economies are estimated to number more than a billion (Peachey and Roe 2006).[8] Indeed, for BRI and Financiera Compartamos, savings accounts represent a much larger part of their BOP portfolio than do microloans. Savings vehicles are often hampered by outdated laws and regulations. But where permitted, they can play a powerful new role in deepening the financial sector for the BOP.

Finance for small and medium-size enterprises is growing. While this development does not bring financial services to the BOP, it does expand opportunity by creating jobs and services. The financing comes in the form of loans and equity investment beyond the limits of microfinance but too small for the traditional lending windows of large banks. The Asian Development Bank is developing a series of investment funds for small and medium-size enterprises in Asia, and the Japan Bank for International Cooperation has increased by several million dollars its pledge for private sector investment in Africa, including money for small and medium enterprises. Shell Foundation has helped launch several investment funds in Africa that focus on small enterprises, bringing in local financial institutions as coinvestors.[9] The most effective new models combine the provision of capital with mentoring, business education, and skills training.

Commercial banks are seeking new ways to participate in small and medium-size enterprise finance, driven by such structural factors as low rates of return on government debt in much of the developed world and stiff competition among banks at the high end of the market. The global banks usually partner with local banks, able to provide the risk assessment and community relationships critical to success. Meanwhile, the availability of capital and the support of big money-center banks are driving local banks to better serve local small and medium-size enterprises, a market many have long ignored.

Technology as a driver

Technology does two key things that help drive the development of financial services: it cuts costs, and it bridges physical distance. For BOP customers, technology in financial services can address four important concerns: convenience, accessibility, safety, and transferability (Wright and others n.d.). A mobile phone–based transaction system offers far more convenience and accessibility than a traditional financial institution, whose use may require that clients find a bank branch or attend a weekly microfinance group meeting. Electronic forms of money, less prone to theft, are safer than cash. They also are more easily transferred, especially overseas.

Technology is bringing nontraditional players into the financial services market. Most notably, mobile phone operators are introducing new products and services over their networks that look and feel like traditional financial services (case study 9.2). Start-ups are finding ways to combine mobile networks and traditional banks (case study 9.3).

The resulting hybrids—banks partnered with mobile phone operators, or companies that market both financial and mobile phone services—pose issues for banking and telecommunications regulators. But the benefits seem so great as to demand solutions, and Pakistan, for example, has instructed the two sets of regulators to work out effective solutions.[10]

The emerging technology-driven financial services include bank-centric models, electronic currency, and mobile commerce systems. The services are being provided through a range of technologies: ATMs, mobile phones, handheld computers, and credit, debit, and smart cards.

CASE STUDY 9.2 **BANKING ON PHONES: MOBILE OPERATORS AS BANKING PIONEERS IN THE PHILIPPINES**

Filipinos are avid users of text-messaging services. By recognizing and building on this appetite, Smart Communications and Globe Telecom have become pioneers in mobile financial platforms.

Starting with the simple notion of refilling prepaid airtime debit cards electronically, Smart has created a suite of services that operate seamlessly with other company systems. The company's "Smart Money" allows a subscriber to transfer cash from a bank account to a cell phone; to pay for goods and services in thousands of shops and restaurants; to order and, using system credits, pay for goods and services over the phone; to load airtime onto any Smart system phone; to transfer money from one Smart Money card to another; to pay utility bills; and even to send remittances from abroad (Smith 2004a).

Globe Telecom provides similar services. In 2004 it launched the "G-Cash" program, which allows users to send and receive cash and to make payments to a variety of services and businesses through text-messaging. The system also allows domestic and international money transfers. Unlike with Smart's system, the user does not need to have a separate bank account: Globe's system uses banks but also relies on a network of retail locations for users to "cash in" or "cash out" (Vega).

Globe and Smart are succeeding in the marketplace because they meet real needs of customers. They provide safety: the electronic currency relieves customers of the burden and danger of carrying cash. They enhance security: values are stored centrally, protecting customers against loss if a card or phone is lost or stolen. They provide accessibility: through the remote banking applications, they bring the bank to the customer rather than requiring the customer to go to a physical location. And they allow transferability: their systems enable customers to transfer money to another customer—a service often used within families and for business transactions.

Beyond all this, the two companies have created more than 1.5 million new entrepreneurs, engaged in reselling airtime and facilitating mobile financial services. Their approach exemplifies two strategies: **localizing value creation** and **focusing on the BOP.**

In Kenya, Vodafone is partnering with local mobile operator Safaricom and local microfinance institutions to roll out a financial transaction system called M-Pesa. The system is based on a new mobile phone card, developed for the purpose, that enables microfinance clients to make deposits, check balances, and fully manage their accounts. Neighborhood banking agents can turn electronic transactions into cash and take deposits and payments on behalf of clients, earning commissions along the way. Vodafone has plans to rapidly add more countries.[11]

Prodem FFP in Bolivia is a sector-leading example in the advanced use of ATMs to provide savings accounts to low-income, illiterate customers in rural areas. Technology, it understood, would be the key to providing affordable service. Unable to find the low-cost, high-quality technology it sought, Prodem partnered with a local firm to create it. The result: an ATM that uses visual and audio prompts in four languages, including three indigenous ones, and a smart card that captures and stores account information and biometric identification. ATMs aimed at the BOP are now being taken up by big banks, such as Citi in its ATM venture in India.

Visa International has partnered with FINCA International, a microfinance institution in Latin America, in a retail banking program for FINCA's BOP microfinance clients. The program automatically deposits loans into a savings account opened by the client at a retail bank and issues the client a Visa debit card and a personal identification number (PIN) to access the funds. Visa and FINCA have found that the program makes clients more inclined to save now that their money is in a secure place. The program

At the same time that banks are discovering that the BOP want and need full access to financial services, financial sector analysts are discovering that the funds flowing in and out of the BOP are much greater than previously thought.

also increases security by eliminating the need for a loan check, which could be lost or stolen. And it gives clients a feeling of prestige associated with carrying a Visa card.

Remittances as a new tool for promoting growth

At the same time that banks are discovering that the BOP want and need full access to financial services, financial sector analysts are discovering that the funds flowing in and out of the BOP are much greater than previously thought. The Multilateral Investment Fund of the Inter-American Development Bank took the lead in tracking remittances to Latin America and the Caribbean, and now others are adding to the data.

The new understanding of the size of remittances brought policy and commercial attention. Reforms were launched to bring more of the flows into official channels, and new competition emerged among transfer services (Orozco 2006). With competition have come better service and lower cost. The results have been especially noticeable in Latin America, where the reported flows from the United States have risen every year, reaching US$53.6 billion in 2005.[12] Worldwide the total is now thought to approach US$350 billion, with significant flows to every developing region. Indeed, reported remittances doubled between 1999 and 2004 (World Bank 2005).

This stable flow of funds provides a large share of income for many in the BOP as well as a direct "BOP to BOP" financing mechanism that helps pay for new houses, new businesses, and children's educations. But governments and development agencies are only beginning to understand the national and local effects of remittance flows—and to find ways to increase the benefits from them.

One benefit: at the national level remittances significantly improve country risk ratings, as recent research by World Bank economist Dilip Ratha (2005) shows. Higher ratings encourage more private sector investment, which can help create jobs and fuel growth. Another benefit: several banks in developing countries have been able to "securitize" remittance flows—that is, use these dependable flows to back a financial instrument sold in international capital markets—and thereby lower their cost of borrowing. Both these benefits mean greater national financial capacity for domestic investment, increasing the growth effect of remittances beyond their impact at the household level.

Recognizing the potential in transferring remittances, businesses are launching new services. At the 3GSM World Congress in Barcelona in

Remittance flows, U.S. to Latin America

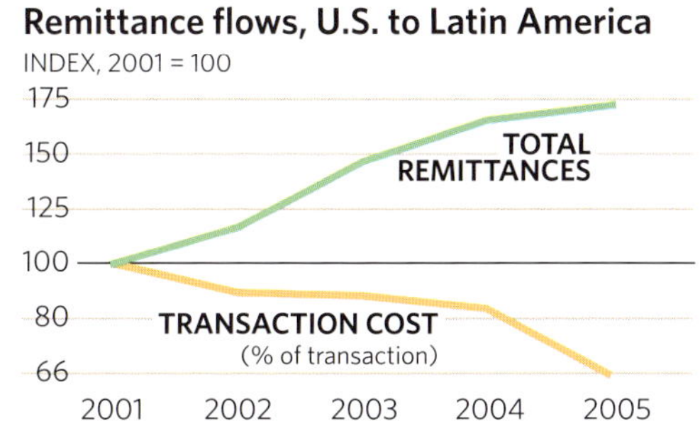

Source: Inter-American Development Bank, "Remittances to Select LAC Countries in 2005 (US$ Millions)," http://www.iadb.org/mif/remittances/index.cfm (accessed February 1, 2007).

CASE STUDY 9.3 **VIRTUAL BANKING: A BANK FOR THE BOP IN SOUTH AFRICA**

Wizzit operates a virtual banking service in South Africa—relying on mobile phones, not physical branches. Its aim is to provide access to financial services to 14 million unbanked citizens. (Kramer and Paul 2006) Wizzit operates as a division of the South African Bank of Athens. It is also an accredited issuer of a debit card and offers a secure mobile payments channel for mobile phone payments. The Wizzit system enables customers to:

- Transfer money from a Wizzit account to any other bank account holder.
- Purchase cell phone airtime.
- Pay bills with utilities and other businesses.
- Get cash at ATMs worldwide.

Conscious of the barriers that have inhibited the BOP from participating in the formal financial sector, Wizzit has adopted policies to encourage new customers:

- Multilingual customer service centers.
- Ability to open accounts at any time, any day of the week—in just two minutes.
- Full compliance with the country's "know your customer" requirements for banks—without using this as an excuse not to open accounts.
- Community-based "WIZZkid" representatives who will come to the client to open an account, rather than requiring the client to travel.
- Accounts for minors as well as adults.

Wizzit also applies its socially conscious attitude to its hiring policy. It aims to hire only unemployed people and so far has provided jobs for more than a thousand. The Wizzit business model exemplifies a strategy of **enabling access.**

February 2007, a consortium of 19 mobile operators, serving more than 600 million customers in 100 countries, announced a system that will transfer remittances entirely through their mobile phone systems, radically reducing cost. The consortium predicts global remittances of more than $1 trillion a year by 2012.[13]

These developments notwithstanding, there is still a serious shortage of infrastructure on the ground to provide financial services to the BOP. Carefully mapping where remittances are sent in Mexico and where formal banking institutions exist, the Inter-American Development Bank has identified many locations with substantial remittances but no banking services. This lack of presence represents a lost opportunity for traditional financial institutions and a barrier to full financial citizenship for the BOP. It also creates a significant opening to this unserved market for non-traditional players and branchless banking enterprises.

Endnotes

1. There are, of course, many other important aspects of financial services for the BOP not addressed here, such as supply chain finance, the deepening of credit service analysis, and the provision of all types of insurance, from crop insurance to flood, health, and business liability policies.
2. Associated Press, "Microcredit Campaign Launches New Goal of Reaching 175 Million of World's Poorest by 2015," International Herald Tribune, November 1, 2006,
3. http://www.iht.com/articles/ap/2006/11/01/america/NA_GEN_Canada_Microcredit_Summit.php (accessed November 1, 2006).
4. Joe Leahy, "Citi Plans Thumbprint ATMs for India's Poor," Financial Times, December 1, 2006, http://www.ft.com/.
5. BusinessWeek, "In Mexico, Banco Wal-Mart," November 20, 2006, http://www.businessweek.com/magazine/content/06_47/b4010076.htm?chan=search.
6. Jyoti Sunita, "ICICI Bank, Grameen of USA Set Up JV for Micro-Finance," Financial Express, November 16, 2005, http://www.financialexpress.com/fe_full_story.php?content_id=108757 (accessed January 17, 2007).
7. Anand Giridharadas, "In India, Thinking Big by Thinking Small," International Herald Tribune, September 30, 2005, http://www.iht.com/articles/2005/09/30/business/wbbank.php (accessed January 17, 2007); Sumit Sharma and Cherian Thomas, "ICICI Seeks 25 Million Rural Clients to Lift Growth (update 1)," Bloomberg, November 1, 2006, http://www.bloomberg.com/apps/news?pid=20601091&sid=aHZH6TpOSmJM.
8. AME Info, "Visa Encourages Banks to Partner with Microfinance Institutions," November 7, 2006, http://www.ameinfo.com/101075.html.
9. In fact, Peachey and Roe (2006) come up with an eye-popping estimate of 1.4 billion. Christen, Rosenberg, and Jayadeva (2004, 1) are more cautious, but their estimate too is large: "over 750 million [savings and loan] accounts in various classes of financial institutions that are generally aimed at markets below the level of commercial banks."
10. John Oyuke, "Sh900 Million Fund Targets Small Traders," The Standard (Nairobi), May 17, 2006; Shell Foundation, "ASPIRE Kenya Launches," http://www.shellfoundation.org/index.php?newsID=337 (accessed January 17, 2007).
11. DAWN: The Internet Edition, "Efforts Geared up to Introduce Mobile Banking," October 20, 2006, http://www.dawn.com/2006/10/20/ebr8.htm.
12. Based on private conversations with Vodafone managers in November 2006; and MicroSave (2006).
13. Inter-American Development Bank, "Remittances to Select LAC Countries in 2005 (US$ Millions)," http://www.iadb.org/mif/remittances/index.cfm (accessed February 1, 2007).
14. Reuters, "Mobile Carriers Facilitate Cash Transfers," CNET News.com, February 11, 2007,
15. http://news.com.com/Mobile+carriers+facilitate+cash+transfers/2100-1039_3-6158314.html?tag=nefd.top (accessed February 13, 2007).
16. Time Magazine, "The Lives and Ideas of the World's Most Influential People," special issue, May 8, 2006.
17. SKS Microfinance, "SKS," http://www.sksindia.com/ (accessed January 22, 2007).
18. Eric B. Shivnoor, "Entrepreneur Gets Big Banks to Back Very Small Loans," Wall Street Journal, May 15, 2006, http://www.wsj.com/.
19. MIX Market, "Profile of SKS," http://www.mixmarket.org/en/demand/demand.show.profile.asp?ett=25 (accessed January 10, 2007).

References

Annamalai, Kuttayan, and Sachin Rao. 2003. What Works: ITC's E-Choupal and Profitable Rural Transformation. Washington, DC: World Resources Institute. http://www.nextbillion.net/node/1433.

Azfar, Asad, and Aun Rahman. 2004. Housing the Urban Poor. New York: Acumen Fund. http://www.acumenfund.org/pdf/saiban_study.pdf.

Balu, Rekha. 2001. "Strategic Innovation: Hindustan Lever Ltd." Fast Company (May). http://www.fastcompany.com/online/47/hindustan.html.

Banerjee, Abhijit V., and Esther Duflo. 2006. "The Economic Lives of the Poor." Working Paper 06-29, Department of Economics, Massachusetts Institute of Technology, Cambridge, MA. http://ssrn.com/abstract=942062/.

Bestani, Robert, and Johanna Klein. 2006. "Housing Finance in Asia." Asian Development Bank, Manila.

Brugmann, Jeb and C. K. Prahalad. 2007. "Cocreating Business's New Social Compact." Harvard Business Review (February): 80-90.

Christen, Robert P., Richard Rosenberg, and Veena Jayadeva. 2004. Financial Institutions with a Double Bottom Line. Washington, DC: Consultative Group to Assist the Poor. http://www.cgap.org/docs/OccasionalPaper_8.pdf.

Cohen, Nevin. 2001. What Works: Grameen Telecom's Village Phones. Washington, DC: World Resources Institute. http://www.nextbillion.net/node/1429.

Commission on the Private Sector and Development. 2004. Unleashing Entrepreneurship: Making Business Work for the Poor. New York: United Nations Development Programme.

Constance, Paul. 2005. "A Water Service Based on Trust." IDBAmérica (May). http://www.iadb.org/idbamerica/index.cfm?thisid=3493.

Constance, Paul, and Puerto Cortés. 2004. "Service Worth the Price." IDBAmérica (September). http://www.iadb.org/idbamerica/index.cfm?thisid=2981.

De Soto, Hernando. 2003. The Mystery of Capital: Why Capitalism Triumphs in the West and Fails Everywhere Else. New York: Basic Books.

———. 2004. 2004–05 Frank Porter Graham Lecture, University of North Carolina, Chapel Hill, October 26. http://www.johnstoncenter.unc.edu/events/desoto.html (accessed January 16, 2007).

Dunston, Chris, David McAfee, Reinhard Kaiser, Desire Rakotoarison, Lalah Rambeloson, Anh Thu Hoang, and Robert E. Quick. 2001. "Collaboration, Cholera, and Cyclones: A Project to Improve Point-of-Use Water Quality in Madagascar." American Journal of Public Health 91 (10): 1574–76. http://www.ajph.org/cgi/content/full/91/10/1574.

Fertig, Michelle, and Herc Tzaras. 2005. What Works: HealthStore's Franchise Approach to Healthcare. Washington, DC: World Resources Institute. http://www.nextbillion.net/node/1643.

Flores-Arias, Elda S., ed. 2006. "Metrobús: Welcome Aboard." Special issue, Sustainable Mobility 1 (October). http://embarq.wri.org/documentupload/BRTingles.pdf.

Gamser, Matthew, ed. 2005. "Discovering Hidden Assets—Financing the Base of the Pyramid." Special issue, Developing Alternatives 10 (1). http://www.dai.com/pdf/developing_alternatives/developing_alternatives_winter_2005.pdf.

GSM Association. 2005. "GSM Association Forges Sub-$30 Mobile Phone Segment for Developing Countries." Press release, Emerging Market Handset Programme, September 27. http://www.gsmworld.com/emh/news/emh2_press_gsma270905.html.

Hart, Stuart L. 2005. Capitalism at the Crossroads: The Unlimited Business Opportunities in Solving the World's Most Difficult Problems. Upper Saddle River, NJ: Wharton School Publishing.

Hart, Stuart L., and C. K. Prahalad. 2002. "The Fortune at the Bottom of the Pyramid." Strategy + Business, no. 26: 2–14.

IDB (Inter-American Development Bank). 2006. Building Opportunity for the Majority. Washington, DC: IDB.

ILD (Institute for Liberty and Democracy). 2006. "Evaluación preliminar de la economía extralegal en 12 países de Latinoamérica y el Caribe." Lima, Peru. Also available at http://www.iadb.org/NEWS/articledetail.cfm?artid=3123&language=En.

ILO (International Labour Organisation). 2002. Key Indicators of the Labour Market, 2nd ed. Geneva: ILO.

ITU (International Telecommunication Union). 2006. "Cellular Subscribers." http://www.itu.int/ITU-D/ict/statistics/at_glance/cellular05.pdf (accessed January 12, 2007).

Ivatury, Gautam, and Mark Pickens. 2006. Mobile Phone Banking and Low-Income Customers: Evidence from South Africa. Washington, DC: Consultative Group to Assist the Poor, United Nations Foundation, and Vodafone Group Foundation.

Jadresic, Alejandro. 2000. "A Case Study on Subsidizing Rural Electrification in Chile." In Energy Services for the Poor, ed. Penelope J. Brook and Suzanne Smith, 76–82. Washington, DC: World Bank.

JBIC (Japan Bank for International Cooperation). 2006. "JBIC ODA Loans under Enhanced Private Sector Assistance (EPSA) for Africa." Document distributed at African Development Bank Group Annual Meeting, Ouagadougou, Burkina Faso, May 17–18.

John Deere. 2005. "John Deere Grants $3 Million to Provide Basic Tools to African Farmers." Press release, June 8. http://www.deere.com/en_US/newsroom/2005/releases/corporate/2005_0608kickstart.html (accessed January 17, 2007).

Kahane, Michele, Jessica Landis, Steve Rochlin, and John Weisner. 2005. Untapped: Creating Value in Underserved Markets. San Francisco: Berrett-Koehler.

Kariuki, Mukami, and Jordan Schwartz. 2005. "Small-Scale Private Service Providers of Water Supply and Electricity." Policy Research Working Paper 3727, World Bank, Washington, DC.

Kramer, William J., and John Paul. 2006. "Mobile-Enabled Transactions for the Base of the Economic Pyramid: A Brief Review of the 2006 'State-of-Play'." In Economic Empowerment through Mobile, ed. Charlotte Grezo. Vodafone CR Dialogues. Newbury, Berkshire, England: Vodafone.

Littlefield, Elizabeth, Jonathan Morduch, and Syed Hashemi. 2003. Is Microfinance an Effective Strategy to Reach the Millennium Development Goals? Washington, DC: Consultative Group to Assist the Poor. http://www.cgap.org/.

Lodge, George, and Craig Wilson. 2006. A Corporate Solution to Global Poverty. Princeton, NJ: Princeton University Press.

Meehan, Bill, and Yasmin Zaidman. 2005. Acumen Fund and Mytry De-Fluoridation Filter Technologies. Cambridge, MA: Harvard Business School Publishing.

MicroSave. 2006. "M-Pesa Pilot Implementation Report." Vodafone and MicroSave, Nairobi.

Milanovic, Branko. 2005. Worlds Apart: Measuring International and Global Inequality. Princeton, NJ: Princeton University Press.

New Ventures. 2006. "Cuadritos." Rising Ventures (August–October). http://www.new-ventures.org/?fuseaction=content&IDdocumento=251#cuadritos.

Orozco, Manuel. 2006. International Flows of Remittances: Cost, Competition and Financial Access in Latin America and the Caribbean—Toward an Industry Scorecard. Washington, DC: Inter-American Dialogue.

Peachey, Stephen, and Alan Roe. 2006. Access to Finance: What Does It Mean and How Do Savings Banks Foster Access. Brussels: World Savings Banks Institute. http://www.savings-banks.com/content/default.asp?PageID=181.

Philips Research. 2006. "Philips Develops a Woodstove That Saves Lives and Preserves Energy Resources." Press release, February 27. http://www.research.philips.com/newscenter/archive/2006/060227-woodstove.html (accessed January 16, 2007).

Prahalad, C. K. 2005. The Fortune at the Bottom of the Pyramid: Eradicating Poverty through Profits. Upper Saddle River, NJ: Wharton School Publishing.

Prahalad, C. K., and Allen Hammond. 2002. "Serving the World's Poor, Profitably." Harvard Business Review (September): 4–11.

PSI (Population Services International). 2006. Disinfecting Water, Saving Lives. Washington, DC: PSI. http://www.psi.org/resources/pubs/Water-sep05.pdf.

Ratha, Dilip. 2005. "Leveraging Remittances for International Capital Market Access." Working paper, World Bank, Washington, DC, November 18. http://siteresources.worldbank.org/INTACCESSFINANCE/Resources/Ratha-leveragingRemittances.pdf.

Reck, Jennifer, and Brad Wood. 2003. "What Works: Vodacom's Community Services Phone Shops." World Resources Institute, Washington, DC.

Sandoval, Ricardo. 2005. "Block by Block: How One of the World's Largest Companies Builds Loyalty among Mexico's Poor." Stanford Social Innovation Review (summer). http://www.ssireview.org/articles/entry/block_by_block/.

Satterthwaite, David, Gordon McGranahan, and Diana Mitlin. 2005. Community-Driven Development for Water and Sanitation in Urban Areas. Geneva: International Institute for Environment and Development and Water Supply and Sanitation Collaborative Council.

Schneider, Friedrich. 2005. "Size and Measurement of the Informal Economy in 110 Countries around the World." Working Paper 2005-13, Center for Research in Economics, Management and the Arts, Johannes Kepler University of Linz.

Smith, Sharon. 2004a. Smart Communications: Expanding Networks, Expanding Profits. Washington, DC: World Resources Institute.

———. 2004b. "What Works: Smart Communications' BOP-Driven Business Model." World Resources Institute, Washington, DC.

Sullivan, Nicholas P. 2007. You Can Hear Me Now. San Francisco: Jossey Bass.

UNDP (United Nations Development Programme). 2006. Human Development Report 2006: Beyond Scarcity—Power, Poverty and the Global Water Crisis. New York: Palgrave Macmillan.

Vega, Jose. 2006. "Improving Access to Financial Services: Mobile Money Transfer and Beyond—Reaching Rural Households through Technology." Paper presented at State Bank of Pakistan seminar, Karachi, October 12.

Vodafone. 2005. Africa: The Impact of Mobile Phones. London: Vodafone. http://www.vodafone.com/africa.

WBCSD (World Business Council for Sustainable Development). 2004. Holcim Apasco: Concrete Innovation with Mi Casa. Geneva: WBCSD. http://www.wbcsd.ch/web/publications/case/holcim_apasco_mi_casa_full_case_web.pdf.

Wilson, Craig, and Peter Wilson. 2006. Make Poverty Business. Sheffield, England: Greenleaf.

Wireless Intelligence. 2005. "Worldwide Cellular Connections Exceeds 2 Billion." Press release, GSM World News, September 15. http://www.gsmworld.com/news/press_2005/press05_21.shtml (accessed January 12, 2007).

World Bank. 2005. "Global Economic Prospects 2006: Economic Implications of Remittances and Migration." PowerPoint presentation at press launch for Global Economic Prospects 2006, World Bank, Washington, DC, November 16. http://siteresources.worldbank.org/INTGEP2006/Resources/GEP06PressConference-Short.ppt.

———. 2006a. Global Economic Prospects 2006: Economic Implications of Remittances and Migration. Washington, DC: World Bank.

———. 2006b. Information and Communications for Development 2006: Global Trends and Policies. Washington, DC: World Bank.

World Bank and IFC (International Finance Corporation). 2006. Doing Business 2007: How to Reform. Washington, DC: World Bank and IFC.

World Resources Institute, World Bank, United Nations Development Programme, and United Nations Environment Programme. 2005. World Resources Report: The Wealth of the Poor. Washington, DC: World Resources Institute.

Wright, Graham A. N., Nick Hughes, Brian Richardson, and David Cracknell. n.d. "Mobile Phone–Based E-Banking: The Customer Value Proposition." Briefing note 047, MicroSave, Nairobi. http://www.microsave.org/Briefing_notes.

APPENDIX A

INCOME DATA

METHODOLOGY

COUNTRY LIST

COUNTRY SURVEYS

POPULATION AND INCOME TABLE

Appendix A

Income data

Methodology

The analysis of the size of the BOP is based on data derived from national income and consumption surveys conducted by national statistics offices in 110 countries (see table A.1a). The analysis of the total income of the BOP is based on an income inequality methodology developed by Branko Milanovic, lead economist with the World Bank's Research Department, and described in *Worlds Apart: Measuring International and Global Inequality* (Milanovic 2005). Dr. Milanovic "lines up" all the world's people, assigning each an annual income based on the relevant national household survey, to measure global inequality among individuals.

The analysis undertaken for this report uses the same methodology in determining relative income levels. People with incomes of $3,000 and below (in 2002 international dollars, adjusted for purchasing power parity, or PPP) are defined as the BOP. Those with incomes up to $20,000 but more than $3,000 are defined as the mid-market segment. And those with incomes greater than $20,000 are defined as the high-income segment. Purchasing power parity conversions are made using data from the World Bank's World Development Indicators database.

The income cutoffs are given in 2002 international dollars for convenience and ease of reference. Unless otherwise indicated, however, actual income or expenditure figures in this report are given in 2005 international dollars, inflated from the 2002 figures using the U.S. consumer price index. (Where such data are also reported in U.S. dollars, they are given in 2005 U.S. dollars.) In 2005 international dollars the income cutoff for the BOP is $3,260, and that for the mid-market segment $21,731.

Surveys

A selected list of surveys included in the income analysis is shown in table A.1b. For a complete list of surveys used please contact Dr. Milanovic.

Size of market

Data on the size of the BOP population and on the total income of the BOP—assumed in this report to be equivalent to expenditure and thus used to define market size—are shown by selected regions and for selected countries within these regions in table A.2. The regional totals comprise selected countries listed in table A.1a. These data are provided by Dr. Milanovic and have not been previously published.

Table A.1a

Income Countries

Asia	Africa	Eastern Europe	Latin America and the Caribbean	Additional Countries
Bangladesh	Benin	Albania	Argentina (urban)	Australia
China	Burkina Faso	Armenia	Bolivia	Austria
East Timor	Cameroon	Azerbaijan	Brazil	Belgium
India	Cape Verde	Belarus	Chile	Canada
Indonesia	Comoros	Bosnia	Colombia	Finland
Iran	Egypt	Bulgaria	Costa Rica	France
Jordan	Ethiopia	Croatia	Dominican Republic	Germany
Laos	Guinea	Czech Republic	Ecuador	Greece
Malaysia	Ivory Coast	Estonia	El Salvador	Ireland
Nepal	Madagascar	Georgia	Guatemala	Israel
Pakistan	Malawi	Hungary	Haiti	Italy
Philippines	Mali	Kazakhstan	Honduras	Japan
Sri Lanka	Mauritania	Kyrgyz Rep	Jamaica	Korea, South
Syria	Mozambique	Latvia	Mexico	Luxembourg
Thailand	Nigeria	Lithuania	Nicaragua	Netherlands
Vietnam	Sao Tomé and Principe	FYR Macedonia	Panama	Norway
	Senegal	Moldova	Paraguay	Singapore
	Sierra Leone	Montenegro	Peru	Spain
	South Africa	Poland	Suriname	Sweden
	Tanzania	Romania	Uruguay (urban)	Switzerland
	Uganda	Russia	Venezuela	Taiwan
	Zambia	Serbia		United Kingdom
		Slovakia		USA
		Slovenia		
		Tajikistan		
		Turkey		
		Ukraine		
		Uzbekistan		

Table A.1b

Selected surveys used in the income analysis

Year	Country	Survey
2002	Albania	Living Standards Measurement Study Survey
2004	Armenia	Armenian Household Survey (Integrated Living Conditions Survey)
2002/3	Australia	Survey of Income and Housing
2000	Austria	European Community Household Panel (LIS Database)
2000	Belgium	Panel Study of Belgian Households (LIS Database)
2001	Bosnia and Herzegovina	Living Standards Measurement Study Survey
2003	Bulgaria	Household Income Survey
2000	Canada	Survey of Labour and Income Dynamics (LIS Database)
2001/2	Cape Verde	Inquerito as Despensas e Receitas Familiars
2004	Croatia	Household Budget Survey
2002	Czech Republic	Mikrocensus
2003	Ecuador	Encuesta de Condiciones de Vida
2004	Egypt	Income and Expenditure Survey
2000	Estonia	Household Income and Expenditure Survey (LIS Database)
2000	Finland	Income Distribution Survey (LIS Database)
2002	France	Revenus Fiscaux des Ménages
2000	Germany	German Social Economic Panel Study (LIS Database)
2000	Greece	Household Income and Living Conditions Survey (LIS Database)
2001	Haiti	Encuesta sur les Conditions de Vie en Haiti
2002	Hong Kong, China	General Household Survey
1999/2000	India (rural)	National Sample Survey
1999/2000	India (urban)	National Sample Survey
2002	Indonesia (rural)	National Socioeconomic Survey (SUSENAS)
2002	Indonesia (urban)	National Socioeconomic Survey (SUSENAS)
2000	Ireland	European Community Household Panel (LIS Database)
2001	Israel	Family Expenditure Survey (LIS Database)
2000	Italy	Bank of Italy Survey (LIS Database)
2003	Jamaica	Jamaica Survey of Living Conditions
2002	Japan	Family Income and Expenditure Survey
2003	Jordan	Household Expenditure Survey
2003	Korea	Household Income and Expenditure Survey
2002	Lao PDR	Lao Expenditure and Consumption Survey III
2002	Latvia	Household Survey
2004	Malawi	Second Integrated Household Survey
2000	Malaysia	Malaysian Household Income Survey
2002	Moldova	Household Budget Survey
2000	Montenegro	Household Income and Expenditure Survey (LSMS data)
2003/4	Nepal	Nepal Income and Expenditure Survey
2000	Norway	Income and Property Distribution Survey (LIS Database)
2000	Philippines	Family Income and Expenditure Survey
2002	Poland	Household Budget Survey
2002	Russia	Household Budget Survey
2000	São Tomé and Principe	Inquérito Condições de Vida das Familias
2003	Serbia	Living Standards Measurement Study Survey
2003	Sierra Leone	Sierra Leone Living Standards Survey
2003	Singapore	Household Expenditure Survey
2003	Slovakia	Mikrocensus
1999	Slovenia	Household Budget Survey (LIS Database)
2000	South Africa	Income and Expenditure Survey
2000	Spain	European Community Household Panel (LIS Database)
2002	Sri Lanka	Household Income and Expenditure Survey
2000	Sweden	Income Distribution Survey (LIS Database)
2002	Switzerland	Income and Expenditure Survey (LIS Database)
2003/4	Syria	Family Income and Expenditure Survey
2003	Tajikistan	Living Standards Measurement Study Survey
2003	Turkey	Household Budget Survey
1999	United Kingdom	Family Resources Survey (LIS Database)
2000	United States	March Current Population Survey (LIS Database)
2002/3	Uzbekistan	Uzbekistan Household Survey
2002/3	Zambia	Zambia Living Conditions Monitoring Survey

Note: LIS is Luxembourg Income Study. LSMS is Living Standards Measurement Study. For complete survey list see Branko Milanovic.

Table A.2

BOP population and income

	BOP population (millions)	BOP share of total population (%)	BOP income (millions)		BOP share of total income (%)
			PPP	US$	
Africa	**486**	**95.1**	**429,000**	**120,000**	**70.5**
Cameroon	14.7	95.0	15,354.1	4,710.1	75.6
Côte d'Ivoire	15.6	95.0	14,242.9	6,536.1	75.9
Ethiopia	65.6	95.0	83,544.1	10,151.1	85.8
Mali	12.6	100.0	9,202.7	2,769.2	100.0
Mozambique	17.6	95.0	12,917.6	2,408.3	71.1
Nigeria	121.0	100.0	74,419.2	27,572.1	100.0
Senegal	9.3	95.0	9,303.8	2,942.6	72.6
South Africa	33.6	75.0	43,511.1	10,072.7	30.9
Tanzania	36.2	100.0	11,318.0	5,408.2	100.0
Uganda	23.8	95.0	22,303.5	3,696.5	76.8
Zambia	18.5	100.0	9,315.3	4,008.3	100.0
Asia	**2858**	**83.4**	**3,470,000**	**742,000**	**41.7**
Bangladesh	144.0	100.0	142,293.9	29,187.9	100.0
China	1,046.2	80.8	161,127.6	32,986.1	55.2
India	1,033.9	98.6	93,710.1	16,962.1	92.7
Indonesia	213	97.8	24,035.8	6,177.1	92.2
Malaysia	19.2	80.0	38,072.3	16,274.6	43.0
Nepal	23.4	95.0	22,981.7	3,736.0	74.2
Philippines	23.6	30.0	56,023.7	13,096.4	10.8
Sri Lanka	17.1	90.0	21,788.9	5,325.2	67.3
Thailand	46.6	75.0	79,632.7	23,383.6	46.7
Vietnam	76.2	95.0	84,582.8	16,003.3	82.9
Eastern Europe	**254**	**63.8**	**458,000**	**135,000**	**36.0**
Georgia	4.9	95.0	5,546.6	1,613.4	82.6
Kazakhstan	13.1	85.0	23,933.6	6,720.7	69.1
Poland	17.4	45.0	37,423.4	17,489.1	22.6
Romania	20.2	90.0	34,471.8	10,741.8	78.3
Russia	86.4	60.0	16,423.0	4,741.6	33.4
Ukraine	29.4	60.0	65,818.4	11,673.0	41.5
Uzbekistan	23.9	95.0	22,936.9	5,273.9	82.9
Latin America & Caribbean	**360**	**69.9**	**509,000**	**229,000**	**28.2**
Argentina (urban)	17.1	45.0	28,990.7	7,318.4	13.4
Bolivia	7.7	90.0	7,473.0	2,700.9	56.0
Brazil	114.5	65.0	171,585.3	58,272.0	22.6
Chile	8.6	55.0	15,927.1	7,019.0	20.1
Colombia	30.5	70.0	41,979.7	12,061.2	28.2
Costa Rica	2.4	60.0	4,086.7	2,394.3	27.1
Dominican Republic	5.6	65.0	9,746.0	3,666.2	28.6
Ecuador	11.5	90.0	12,558.6	6,740.4	61.0
El Salvador	4.5	70.0	5,928.2	2,679.0	25.8
Guatemala	10.2	85.0	13,472.0	6,395.4	54.9
Haiti	7.8	95.0	4,260.6	958.2	62.9
Honduras	5.8	85.0	7,435.4	2,768.8	50.3
Jamaica	2.2	85.0	2,304.6	1,879.0	46.9
Mexico	76.5	75.0	105,075.0	75,052.0	39.8
Nicaragua	4.3	80.0	5,647.9	1,319.6	36.7
Panama	2.2	70.0	2,988.2	1,972.5	28.3
Paraguay	3.8	65.0	5,552.6	1,223.8	25.4
Peru	21.4	80.0	33,797.2	14,243.7	54.1
Suriname	0.3	85.0	360.6	108.2	50.4
Uruguay (urban)	1.4	45.0	2,705.6	1,271.9	16.4
Venezuela	21.4	85.0	26,741.4	18,784.6	57.9

Note: Regional totals include selected countries detailed in table A.1a.

APPENDIX B

EXPENDITURE DATA

METHODOLOGY

COUNTRY SURVEYS

COUNTRY TABLES

Standardization methodology

Expenditure data are derived from household consumption surveys conducted by national statistics offices. All surveys have been standardized as part of the 2003–06 round of the International Comparison Program. Standardization of the surveys used in this report was overseen by Olivier Dupriez, senior statistician and economist with the World Bank's Development Data Group.

The International Comparison Program is a global statistical initiative established to produce internationally comparable price levels, expenditure values, and purchasing power parity (PPP) estimates. Purchasing power parities are a form of exchange rate that takes into account the cost and affordability of common items in different countries.

The project has classified products and services consumed by households into 110 groups called "basic headings." The objective of the project is to derive, for as many participating countries as possible, the share of each basic heading in total household consumption for different population categories (sorted by level of wealth, between urban and rural areas, or using other criteria). The aim is to generate poverty-specific purchasing power parities that take into account the spending patterns of the poor.

To obtain the share of each basic heading, the project produces a standardized data set for each country. It generates these data sets by mining existing survey data—drawing on the most recent available nationally representative household budget survey (or on another survey with a detailed questionnaire on household expenditure).

Because the source data sets are not standard (different questionnaires and methods are used in different countries), the standardization process has some limits. The formatting of the resulting subsets is standardized, but total comparability of the data cannot be achieved. To the extent possible, uniform methods are used to process the data, particularly for aggregating household expenditure. But significant differences in the design of questionnaires make it impossible to fully harmonize the aggregation procedures (for example, some questionnaires do not collect enough information for estimating the annual consumption value for durables).

Surveys

Table B.1 shows the 36 surveys that have been standardized in the way described and that serve as the basis for the sector analyses in this report and for the country data tables that follow.

Country data tables

The country data tables show standardized expenditure data for each of 36 countries—the measured BOP expenditure data for the analysis presented in this report.

Table B.1
Surveys used as sources of expenditure data

Year	Country	Survey
2000	Bangladesh	Household Budget Survey
2002	Belarus	Income and Expenditure Survey
2002	Bolivia	Encuesta de Hogares (MECOVI Program)a
2002	Brazil	Pesquisa de Orçamentos Familiares
2003	Burkina Faso	Enquête Burkinabé sur les Conditions de Vie des Ménages
1998	Burundi	Enquête Prioritaire
2003/4	Cambodia	Socioeconomic Survey
2001	Cameroon	Enquête Camerounaise auprès des Ménages II
2003	Colombia	Encuesta de Calidad de Vida
2002	Côte d'Ivoire	Enquête Niveau de Vie des Ménages
2004	Djibouti	Enquête Djiboutienne auprès des Ménages Indicateurs sociaux
2005	Gabon	Enquête Gabonaise pour l'Evaluation et le Suivi de la Pauvreté
2000	Guatemala	Encuesta Nacional sobre Condiciones de Vida
2004	Honduras	Encuesta Nacional de Condiciones de Vida
2004	India	National Sample Survey 60th Round
2002	Indonesia	National Socioeconomic Survey (SUSENAS)
2002	Jamaica	Jamaica Survey of Living Conditions
2003	Kazakhstan	Household Budget Survey
2003	FYR Macedonia	Household Budget Survey
2004	Malawi	Second Integrated Household Survey
2004	Mexico	Encuesta Nacional de Ingresos y Gastos de los Hogares
2003	Nepal	Nepal Living Standards Survey II
2003	Nigeria	QUIBB+
2001	Pakistan	Pakistan Integrated Survey
2000/1	Paraguay	Encuesta Integrada de Hogares
2003	Peru	Encuesta Nacional de Hogares—Condiciones de Vida y Pobreza
2003	Russia	NOBUS
2000	Rwanda	Enquête Intégrale sur les Conditions de Vie
2003	Sierra Leone	Sierra Leone Integrated Household Survey
2000	South Africa	Income and Expenditure Survey
2002	Sri Lanka	Sri Lanka Integrated Survey
2003	Tajikistan	Living Standards Measurement Study Survey
2002	Thailand	Socioeconomic Survey
2002/3	Uganda	National Household Survey
2003	Ukraine	Household Budget Survey
2003	Uzbekistan	Living Standards Measurement Study Survey

a. MECOVI (the Spanish acronym for Mejoramiento de las Encuestas de Hogares y la Medición de Condiciones de Vida) is the Program for the Improvement of Surveys and the Measurement of Living Conditions in Latin America and the Caribbean.

BANGLADESH

Total national household market $108,611.1 million
Population 126.0 million
Households 24.2 million

BOP segment	Population: Total (millions)	Population: Share (% of national)	Population: Urban (% of segment)	Annual expenditure: Total ($ millions)	Annual expenditure: Share (% of national)	Annual expenditure: Urban (% of segment)
BOP3000	1.0	0.8	91.6	2,739.7	2.5	91.9
BOP2500	2.2	1.7	85.4	5,129.7	4.7	85.3
BOP2000	6.3	5.0	57.4	11,295.7	10.4	57.7
BOP1500	18.4	14.6	33.1	23,406.9	21.6	34.3
BOP1000	66.3	52.6	14.9	49,444.8	45.5	15.7
BOP500	31.3	24.8	6.8	13,272.9	12.2	7.0
BOP total	125.4	99.6	19.5	105,289.7	96.9	28.6

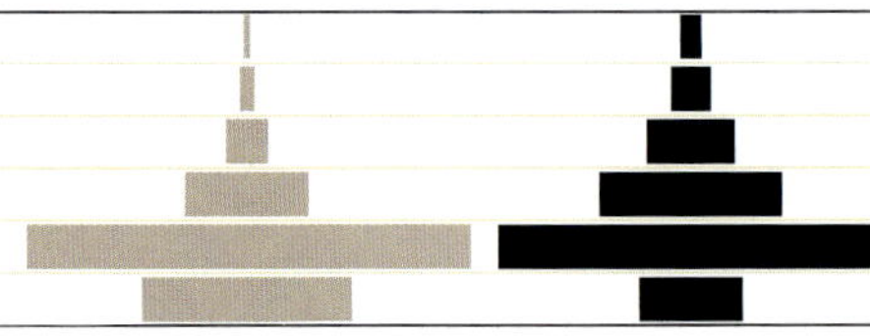

BOP expenditure by sector

$ (**Boldface** numbers are millions)	Total BOP	BOP 500	BOP 1000	BOP 1500	BOP 2000	BOP 2500	BOP 3000	Urban / rural (% of BOP)
Food	**57,581.5**	**8,574.7**	**29,078.1**	**11,964.8**	**5,045.8**	**1,999.4**	**918.7**	24/76
Per capita	459	274	439	650	803	916	947	
Per household	2379	1486	2272	3234	3890	4562	4488	
Housing	**9,512.9**	**734.7**	**3,445.6**	**2,314.6**	**1,447.7**	**939.6**	**630.7**	49/51
Per capita	76	23	52	126	230	430	650	
Per household	393	127	269	626	1116	2144	3081	
Water	**102.8**	**0.1**	**11.6**	**24.8**	**27.1**	**25.2**	**14.0**	98/2
Per capita	1	0	0	1	4	12	14	
Per household	4	0	1	7	21	57	69	
Energy	**7,537.3**	**1,168.3**	**3,839.6**	**1,466.7**	**654.2**	**273.5**	**134.9**	26/74
Per capita	60	37	58	80	104	125	139	
Per household	311	203	300	396	504	624	659	
Household goods	**10,753.8**	**1,176.2**	**4,754.5**	**2,489.0**	**1,352.2**	**652.9**	**328.9**	29/71
Per capita	86	38	72	135	215	299	339	
Per household	444	204	371	673	1042	1490	1607	
Health	**2,201.4**	**267.1**	**1,072.5**	**497.4**	**217.4**	**82.6**	**64.4**	25/75
Per capita	18	9	16	27	35	38	66	
Per household	91	46	84	134	168	188	315	
Transportation	**3,322.2**	**213.3**	**1,316.4**	**938.2**	**469.8**	**247.9**	**136.6**	32/68
Per capita	26	7	20	51	75	114	141	
Per household	137	37	103	254	362	566	667	
ICT	**426.9**	**4.0**	**88.0**	**84.4**	**122.2**	**57.5**	**70.8**	58/42
Per capita	3	0	1	5	19	26	73	
Per household	18	1	7	23	94	131	346	
Education	**2,833.0**	**98.6**	**898.5**	**808.9**	**530.2**	**325.7**	**171.0**	49/51
Per capita	23	3	14	44	84	149	176	
Per household	117	17	70	219	409	743	835	
Other	**11,017.9**	**1,036.0**	**4,940.0**	**2,818.0**	**1,429.0**	**525.3**	**269.6**	28/72
Per capita	88	33	75	153	227	241	278	
Per household	455	180	386	762	1102	1199	1317	
Total	**105,289.7**	**13,272.9**	**49,444.8**	**23,406.9**	**11,295.7**	**5,129.7**	**2,739.7**	29/71

Note: All dollar amounts in 2005 PPP

Household expenditure by sector

	National ($ millions)	BOP (%)
Food	58,544.3	98.4
Housing	10,179.4	93.5
Water	120.3	85.4
Energy	7,676.6	98.2
Household goods	11,234.3	95.7
Health	2,236.6	98.4
Transportation	3,666.4	90.6
ICT	476.0	89.7
Education	3,013.1	94.0
Other	11,464.1	96.1
Total	108,611.1	96.9

Sector shares of household expenditure
(%)

	National	BOP
Food	53.9	54.7
Housing	9.4	9.0
Water	0.1	0.1
Energy	7.1	7.2
Household goods	10.3	10.2
Health	2.1	2.1
Transportation	3.4	3.2
ICT	0.4	0.4
Education	2.8	2.7
Other	10.6	10.5
Total	100.0	100.0

BELARUS

Total national household market $15,636.0 million
Population 10.2 million
Households 3.2 million

BOP segment	Population: Total (millions)	Population: Share (% of national)	Population: Urban (% of segment)	Annual expenditure: Total ($ millions)	Annual expenditure: Share (% of national)	Annual expenditure: Urban (% of segment)
BOP3000	1.0	10.3	68.8	2,223.7	14.2	68.8
BOP2500	1.8	17.9	69.4	3,178.8	20.3	69.4
BOP2000	2.6	25.9	68.9	3,589.4	23.0	68.7
BOP1500	2.4	23.1	68.0	2,322.2	14.9	67.8
BOP1000	1.0	9.7	68.2	634.1	4.1	68.4
BOP500	0.0	0.4	84.2	12.8	0.1	87.8
BOP total	8.9	87.3	68.7	11,960.9	76.5	68.8

BOP expenditure by sector

$ (**Boldface** numbers are millions)	Total BOP	BOP 500	BOP 1000	BOP 1500	BOP 2000	BOP 2500	BOP 3000	Urban / rural (% of BOP)
Food	**8,850.9**	**10.1**	**494.3**	**1,771.0**	**2,641.4**	**2,319.6**	**1,614.5**	67/33
Per capita	994	239	498	753	999	1267	1541	
Per household	2789	1018	1924	2378	2801	3128	3379	
Housing	**526.1**	**0.8**	**31.9**	**101.1**	**162.0**	**134.4**	**95.9**	75/25
Per capita	59	19	32	43	61	73	92	
Per household	166	82	124	136	172	181	201	
Water	n.a.	n.a.	n.a.	n.a.	n.a.	n.a.	n.a.	
Per capita								
Per household								
Energy	n.a.	n.a.	n.a.	n.a.	n.a.	n.a.	n.a.	
Per capita								
Per household								
Household goods	**1,437.8**	**0.8**	**59.1**	**254.0**	**442.3**	**398.3**	**283.2**	72/28
Per capita	161	19	60	108	167	218	270	
Per household	453	82	230	341	469	537	593	
Health	**125.5**	**0.2**	**5.6**	**23.7**	**38.2**	**33.7**	**24.0**	75/25
Per capita	14	4	6	10	14	18	23	
Per household	40	18	22	32	40	45	50	
Transportation	**156.1**	**0.1**	**8.0**	**28.1**	**48.6**	**42.9**	**28.5**	75/25
Per capita	18	2	8	12	18	23	27	
Per household	49	9	31	38	52	58	60	
ICT	**177.2**	**0.1**	**6.0**	**31.3**	**52.4**	**47.5**	**39.9**	75/25
Per capita	20	1	6	13	20	26	38	
Per household	56	6	24	42	56	64	84	
Education	**75.6**	**0.1**	**4.3**	**15.6**	**25.0**	**20.0**	**10.6**	87/13
Per capita	8	3	4	7	9	11	10	
Per household	24	12	17	21	27	27	22	
Other	**611.7**	**0.7**	**24.8**	**97.3**	**179.4**	**182.5**	**126.9**	71/29
Per capita	69	16	25	41	68	100	121	
Per household	193	70	97	131	190	246	266	
Total	**11,960.9**	**12.8**	**634.1**	**2,322.2**	**3,589.4**	**3,178.8**	**2,223.7**	69/31

Note: All dollar amounts in 2005 PPP

Household expenditure by sector

	National ($ millions)	BOP (%)
Food	11,441.6	77.4
Housing	675.5	77.9
Water	n.a.	n.a.
Energy	n.a.	n.a.
Household goods	1,970.9	73.0
Health	164.0	76.5
Transportation	203.5	76.7
ICT	237.9	74.5
Education	88.2	85.7
Other	854.4	71.6
Total	15,636.0	76.5

Sector shares of household expenditure
(%)

	National	BOP
Food	73.2	74.0
Housing	4.3	4.4
Water	n.a.	n.a.
Energy	n.a.	n.a.
Household goods	12.6	12.0
Health	1.0	1.0
Transportation	1.3	1.3
ICT	1.5	1.5
Education	0.6	0.6
Other	5.5	5.1
Total	100.0	100.0

BOLIVIA

Total national household market $19,429.5 million
Population 8.5 million
Households 1.5 million

BOP segment	Population: Total (millions)	Population: Share (% of national)	Population: Urban (% of segment)	Annual expenditure: Total ($ millions)	Annual expenditure: Share (% of national)	Annual expenditure: Urban (% of segment)
BOP3000	0.4	4.2	87.7	1,068.1	5.5	87.8
BOP2500	0.7	7.7	80.6	1,590.8	8.2	80.6
BOP2000	1.0	12.2	81.4	1,968.0	10.1	81.7
BOP1500	1.5	17.9	68.5	2,042.8	10.5	69.0
BOP1000	2.1	25.1	46.8	1,704.3	8.8	48.2
BOP500	1.3	15.6	12.8	489.6	2.5	15.4
BOP total	7.1	82.7	55.4	8,863.7	45.6	69.2

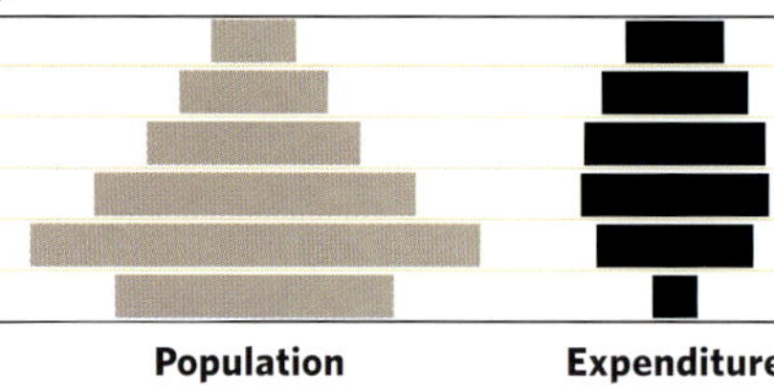

BOP expenditure by sector

$ (**Boldface** numbers are millions)	Total BOP	BOP 500	BOP 1000	BOP 1500	BOP 2000	BOP 2500	BOP 3000	Urban / rural (% of BOP)
Food	**4,174.5**	**298.4**	**965.1**	**996.2**	**880.9**	**642.3**	**391.6**	66/34
Per capita	590	223	451	650	842	979	1097	
Per household	2732	1260	2251	2929	3512	3827	3781	
Housing	**730.0**	**53.1**	**134.2**	**169.8**	**161.7**	**122.5**	**88.8**	73/27
Per capita	103	40	63	111	155	187	249	
Per household	478	224	313	499	645	730	857	
Water	**n.a**	**n.a**	**n.a**	**n.a**	**n.a**	**n.a**	**n.a**	n.a
Per capita								
Per household								
Energy	**348.1**	**11.8**	**60.6**	**80.6**	**83.2**	**66.9**	**44.8**	85/15
Per capita	49	9	28	53	80	102	126	
Per household	228	50	141	237	332	399	433	
Household goods	**1,178.2**	**51.3**	**208.9**	**265.8**	**255.2**	**236.9**	**160.1**	65/35
Per capita	167	38	98	174	244	361	448	
Per household	771	217	487	782	1018	1411	1546	
Health	**667.9**	**20.7**	**90.1**	**167.8**	**153.4**	**139.8**	**96.1**	61/39
Per capita	94	16	42	110	147	213	269	
Per household	437	88	210	494	612	833	927	
Transportation	**455.6**	**10.5**	**66.9**	**88.5**	**110.8**	**99.5**	**79.4**	75/25
Per capita	64	8	31	58	106	152	222	
Per household	298	44	156	260	442	593	766	
ICT	**159.3**	**1.8**	**14.0**	**26.1**	**41.3**	**40.1**	**36.1**	84/16
Per capita	23	1	7	17	39	61	101	
Per household	104	8	33	77	164	239	348	
Education	**63.9**	**1.7**	**8.3**	**17.0**	**16.1**	**12.0**	**8.8**	88/12
Per capita	9	1	4	11	15	18	25	
Per household	42	7	19	50	64	71	85	
Other	**1,086.2**	**40.2**	**156.2**	**231.1**	**265.4**	**230.9**	**162.5**	76/24
Per capita	154	30	73	151	254	352	455	
Per household	711	170	364	679	1058	1376	1569	
Total	**8,863.7**	**489.6**	**1,704.3**	**2,042.8**	**1,968.0**	**1,590.8**	**1,068.1**	69/31

Note: All dollar amounts in 2005 PPP

Household expenditure by sector

	National ($ millions)	BOP (%)
Food	6,079.9	68.7
Housing	1,168.3	62.5
Water	n.a	n.a
Energy	604.6	57.6
Household goods	2,651.2	44.4
Health	1,509.8	44.2
Transportation	1,566.0	29.1
ICT	531.9	29.9
Education	139.6	45.8
Other	5,178.2	21.0
Total	19,429.5	45.6

Sector shares of household expenditure
(%)

	National	BOP
Food	31.3	47.1
Housing	6.0	8.2
Water	n.a	n.a
Energy	3.1	3.9
Household goods	13.6	13.3
Health	7.8	7.5
Transportation	8.1	5.1
ICT	2.7	1.8
Education	0.7	0.7
Other	26.7	12.3
Total	100.0	100.0

BRAZIL

Total national household market $527,873.5 million
Population 176.0 million
Households 31.8 million

BOP segment	Population: Total (millions)	Population: Share (% of national)	Population: Urban (% of segment)	Annual expenditure: Total ($ millions)	Annual expenditure: Share (% of national)	Annual expenditure: Urban (% of segment)
BOP3000	12.3	7.0	87.8	36,764.9	7.0	87.6
BOP2500	15.2	8.6	86.2	37,016.1	7.0	86.3
BOP2000	20.8	11.8	85.1	39,323.9	7.4	85.1
BOP1500	26.7	15.2	79.8	36,068.5	6.8	79.8
BOP1000	32.7	18.6	73.1	26,733.6	5.1	73.7
BOP500	16.8	9.5	62.5	6,037.8	1.1	64.3
BOP total	124.5	70.7	78.2	181,944.9	34.5	82.4

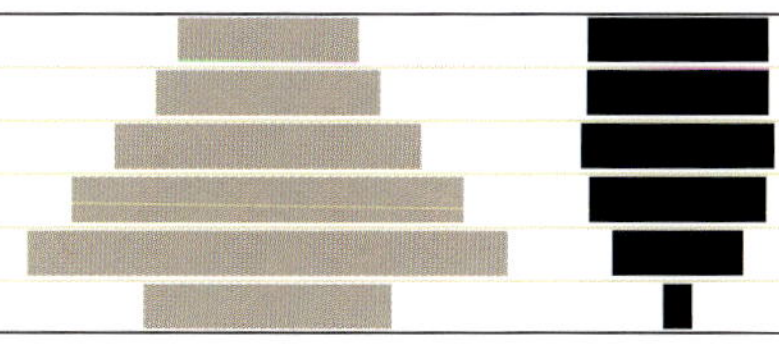

BOP expenditure by sector

$ (**Boldface** numbers are millions)	Total BOP	BOP 500	BOP 1000	BOP 1500	BOP 2000	BOP 2500	BOP 3000	Urban / rural (% of BOP)
Food	**55,278.1**	**2,212.3**	**9,867.6**	**11,898.7**	**11,515.2**	**10,511.3**	**9,272.9**	77/23
Per capita	444	132	302	446	554	692	754	
Per household	1736	638	1304	1707	2030	2396	2462	
Housing	**9,535.7**	**367.3**	**1,392.6**	**1,887.9**	**1,965.8**	**1,774.1**	**2,148.1**	86/14
Per capita	77	22	43	71	95	117	175	
Per household	300	106	184	271	346	404	570	
Water	**1,630.2**	**88.1**	**291.4**	**352.7**	**350.5**	**293.5**	**254.1**	96/4
Per capita	13	5	9	13	17	19	21	
Per household	51	25	38	51	62	67	67	
Energy	**12,153.8**	**916.8**	**2,648.6**	**2,711.4**	**2,374.9**	**1,871.8**	**1,630.3**	83/17
Per capita	98	55	81	102	114	123	133	
Per household	382	264	350	389	419	427	433	
Household goods	**25,959.3**	**740.5**	**3,574.3**	**5,181.6**	**5,701.2**	**5,482.3**	**5,279.4**	82/18
Per capita	209	44	109	194	274	361	429	
Per household	815	214	472	743	1005	1250	1401	
Health	**11,981.2**	**333.4**	**1,651.3**	**2,434.1**	**2,619.9**	**2,422.7**	**2,519.8**	83/17
Per capita	96	20	50	91	126	159	205	
Per household	376	96	218	349	462	552	669	
Transportation	**19,520.4**	**320.3**	**2,039.2**	**3,571.8**	**4,578.5**	**4,334.7**	**4,676.0**	82/18
Per capita	157	19	62	134	220	285	380	
Per household	613	92	269	512	807	988	1241	
ICT	**5,521.7**	**99.1**	**583.7**	**1,010.9**	**1,282.4**	**1,272.4**	**1,273.3**	93/7
Per capita	44	6	18	38	62	84	104	
Per household	173	29	77	145	226	290	338	
Education	**2,359.2**	**6.5**	**101.9**	**256.3**	**467.7**	**659.4**	**867.5**	96/4
Per capita	19	0	3	10	22	43	71	
Per household	74	2	13	37	82	150	230	
Other	**38,005.3**	**953.6**	**4,583.2**	**6,763.2**	**8,467.8**	**8,394.0**	**8,843.5**	86/14
Per capita	305	57	140	253	407	552	719	
Per household	1194	275	606	970	1492	1913	2348	
Total	**181,944.9**	**6,037.8**	**26,733.6**	**36,068.5**	**39,323.9**	**37,016.1**	**36,764.9**	82/18

Note: All dollar amounts in 2005 PPP

Household expenditure by sector

	National ($ millions)	BOP (%)
Food	113,684.6	48.6
Housing	26,683.5	35.7
Water	3,220.2	50.6
Energy	21,028.8	57.8
Household goods	71,972.0	36.1
Health	34,249.5	35.0
Transportation	70,786.0	27.6
ICT	20,263.3	27.2
Education	27,820.6	8.5
Other	138,165.0	27.5
Total	527,873.5	34.5

Sector shares of household expenditure
(%)

	National	BOP
Food	21.5	30.4
Housing	5.1	5.2
Water	0.6	0.9
Energy	4.0	6.7
Household goods	13.6	14.3
Health	6.5	6.6
Transportation	13.4	10.7
ICT	3.8	3.0
Education	5.3	1.3
Other	26.2	20.9
Total	100.0	100.0

BURKINA FASO

Total national household market $7094.5 million
Population 11.4 million
Households 1.7 million

BOP segment	Population: Total (millions)	Population: Share (% of national)	Population: Urban (% of segment)	Annual expenditure: Total ($ millions)	Annual expenditure: Share (% of national)	Annual expenditure: Urban (% of segment)
BOP3000	0.1	0.6	92.5	190.8	2.7	92.8
BOP2500	0.1	1.1	78.5	294.2	4.1	78.7
BOP2000	0.3	2.4	64.0	494.9	7.0	64.9
BOP1500	0.7	6.4	45.2	932.8	13.1	46.0
BOP1000	3.2	27.7	23.8	2,306.4	32.5	25.2
BOP500	6.9	60.7	8.0	2,311.5	32.6	9.1
BOP total	11.3	98.8	17.5	6,530.6	92.1	29.9

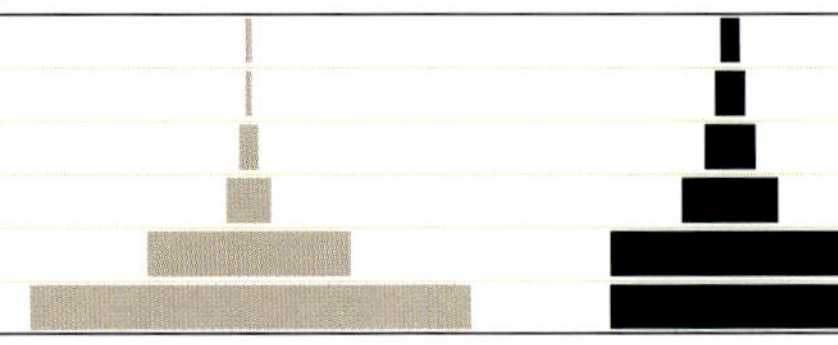

BOP expenditure by sector

$ (**Boldface** numbers are millions)	Total BOP	BOP 500	BOP 1000	BOP 1500	BOP 2000	BOP 2500	BOP 3000	Urban / rural (% of BOP)
Food	**3,520.9**	**1,437.6**	**1,259.8**	**443.5**	**207.2**	**109.0**	**63.8**	24/76
Per capita	312	208	399	609	768	881	970	
Per household	2021	1623	2201	2638	3117	3394	3677	
Housing	**594.9**	**223.8**	**201.6**	**83.0**	**43.3**	**26.5**	**16.7**	35/65
Per capita	53	32	64	114	160	214	255	
Per household	341	253	352	494	651	825	965	
Water	**86.4**	**17.2**	**30.7**	**17.0**	**10.3**	**6.9**	**4.3**	70/30
Per capita	8	2	10	23	38	56	66	
Per household	50	19	54	101	155	214	251	
Energy	**452.4**	**166.7**	**150.7**	**64.0**	**34.9**	**21.7**	**14.5**	36/64
Per capita	40	24	48	88	129	175	220	
Per household	260	188	263	381	524	676	833	
Household goods	**588.6**	**138.8**	**237.4**	**108.1**	**61.6**	**28.3**	**14.4**	20/80
Per capita	52	20	75	148	228	229	219	
Per household	338	157	415	643	927	882	830	
Health	**259.0**	**58.0**	**98.5**	**48.6**	**22.8**	**17.6**	**13.5**	40/60
Per capita	23	8	31	67	84	142	205	
Per household	149	66	172	289	342	549	777	
Transportation	**368.0**	**45.1**	**112.4**	**79.5**	**55.7**	**42.3**	**33.0**	51/49
Per capita	33	7	36	109	206	342	502	
Per household	211	51	196	473	837	1319	1901	
ICT	**57.6**	**3.4**	**9.6**	**11.6**	**12.3**	**11.0**	**9.6**	75/25
Per capita	5	0	3	16	45	89	145	
Per household	33	4	17	69	184	343	551	
Education	**93.9**	**16.7**	**28.5**	**17.1**	**15.1**	**8.8**	**7.7**	81/19
Per capita	8	2	9	24	56	71	117	
Per household	54	19	50	102	227	275	444	
Other	**508.9**	**204.2**	**177.2**	**60.4**	**31.7**	**22.0**	**13.3**	31/69
Per capita	45	29	56	83	118	178	202	
Per household	292	231	310	359	478	685	766	
Total	**6,530.6**	**2,311.5**	**2,306.4**	**932.8**	**494.9**	**294.2**	**190.8**	30/70

Note: All dollar amounts in 2005 PPP

Household expenditure by sector

	National ($ millions)	BOP (%)
Food	3,664.5	96.1
Housing	637.6	93.3
Water	95.1	90.9
Energy	483.7	93.5
Household goods	638.5	92.2
Health	285.2	90.8
Transportation	546.2	67.4
ICT	98.4	58.5
Education	105.7	88.8
Other	539.5	94.3
Total	7,094.5	92.1

Sector shares of household expenditure
(%)

	National	BOP
Food	51.7	53.9
Housing	9.0	9.1
Water	1.3	1.3
Energy	6.8	6.9
Household goods	9.0	9.0
Health	4.0	4.0
Transportation	7.7	5.6
ICT	1.4	0.9
Education	1.5	1.4
Other	7.6	7.8
Total	100.0	100.0

BURUNDI

Total national household market $5159.5 million
Population 6.0 million
Households 1.2 million

BOP segment	Population: Total (millions)	Population: Share (% of national)	Population: Urban (% of segment)	Annual expenditure: Total ($ millions)	Annual expenditure: Share (% of national)	Annual expenditure: Urban (% of segment)
BOP3000	0.0	0.7	56.1	124.6	2.4	56.8
BOP2500	0.1	1.4	31.6	211.4	4.1	31.8
BOP2000	0.2	4.0	15.2	458.9	8.9	15.3
BOP1500	0.8	12.5	5.3	1,010.9	19.6	5.5
BOP1000	2.2	36.8	2.0	1,764.4	34.2	2.1
BOP500	2.6	42.5	0.8	888.2	17.2	0.9
BOP total	5.9	97.9	3.2	4,458.5	86.4	6.9

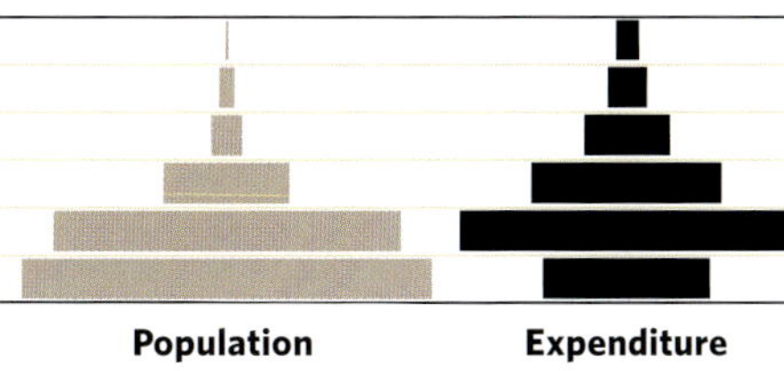

BOP expenditure by sector

$ (**Boldface** numbers are millions)	Total BOP	BOP 500	BOP 1000	BOP 1500	BOP 2000	BOP 2500	BOP 3000	Urban / rural (% of BOP)
Food	**3,424.2**	**635.5**	**1,364.9**	**809.0**	**369.5**	**160.2**	**85.0**	6/94
Per capita	580	248	615	1070	1538	1870	2058	
Per household	2859	1384	3006	4384	5633	6788	8048	
Housing	**182.9**	**61.9**	**65.1**	**28.8**	**12.4**	**7.7**	**7.0**	13/87
Per capita	31	24	29	38	51	90	171	
Per household	153	135	143	156	188	326	667	
Water	n.a.	n.a.	n.a.	n.a.	n.a.	n.a.	n.a.	n.a.
Per capita								
Per household								
Energy	**318.4**	**89.3**	**133.3**	**56.2**	**22.3**	**10.7**	**6.5**	7/93
Per capita	54	35	60	74	93	125	157	
Per household	266	195	294	305	340	453	614	
Household goods	**292.5**	**60.3**	**117.7**	**62.6**	**27.8**	**14.1**	**9.9**	9/91
Per capita	50	24	53	83	116	165	240	
Per household	244	131	259	339	424	598	939	
Health	**49.0**	**12.8**	**17.8**	**9.6**	**4.4**	**2.4**	**2.1**	16/84
Per capita	8	5	8	13	18	28	50	
Per household	41	28	39	52	67	102	196	
Transportation	**30.3**	**3.8**	**10.2**	**6.9**	**4.1**	**3.0**	**2.2**	27/73
Per capita	5	1	5	9	17	35	54	
Per household	25	8	23	38	63	128	211	
ICT	**1.3**	**0.0**	**0.1**	**0.1**	**0.5**	**0.3**	**0.3**	77/23
Per capita	0	0	0	0	2	3	7	
Per household	1	0	0	1	8	13	29	
Education	**10.0**	**2.2**	**2.6**	**1.5**	**1.3**	**1.0**	**1.4**	47/53
Per capita	2	1	1	2	5	11	35	
Per household	8	5	6	8	20	41	136	
Other	**150.0**	**22.3**	**52.7**	**36.2**	**16.6**	**12.1**	**10.1**	16/84
Per capita	25	9	24	48	69	141	246	
Per household	125	49	116	196	253	511	961	
Total	**4,458.5**	**888.2**	**1,764.4**	**1,010.9**	**458.9**	**211.4**	**124.6**	7/93

Note: All dollar amounts in 2005 PPP

Household expenditure by sector

	National ($ millions)	BOP (%)
Food	3,763.9	91.0
Housing	248.8	73.5
Water	n.a.	n.a.
Energy	358.0	88.9
Household goods	384.0	76.2
Health	60.1	81.4
Transportation	74.3	40.8
ICT	11.0	11.5
Education	21.3	47.0
Other	238.2	63.0
Total	5,159.5	86.4

Sector shares of household expenditure
(%)

	National	BOP
Food	73.0	76.8
Housing	4.8	4.1
Water	n.a.	n.a.
Energy	6.9	7.1
Household goods	7.4	6.6
Health	1.2	1.1
Transportation	1.4	0.7
ICT	0.2	0.0
Education	0.4	0.2
Other	4.6	3.4
Total	100.0	100.0

CAMBODIA

Total national household market $17006.1 million
Population 13.0 million
Households 2.4 million

BOP segment	Population: Total (millions)	Population: Share (% of national)	Population: Urban (% of segment)	Annual expenditure: Total ($ millions)	Annual expenditure: Share (% of national)	Annual expenditure: Urban (% of segment)
BOP3000	0.4	3.0	40.0	1,094.4	6.4	40.1
BOP2500	0.7	5.5	31.1	1,669.9	9.8	31.2
BOP2000	1.4	10.7	19.8	2,490.4	14.6	19.9
BOP1500	2.7	20.5	13.7	3,413.6	20.1	14.0
BOP1000	4.7	36.2	7.1	3,619.0	21.3	7.4
BOP500	2.3	18.0	4.2	828.9	4.9	4.3
BOP total	12.2	93.8	11.9	13,116.2	77.1	17.0

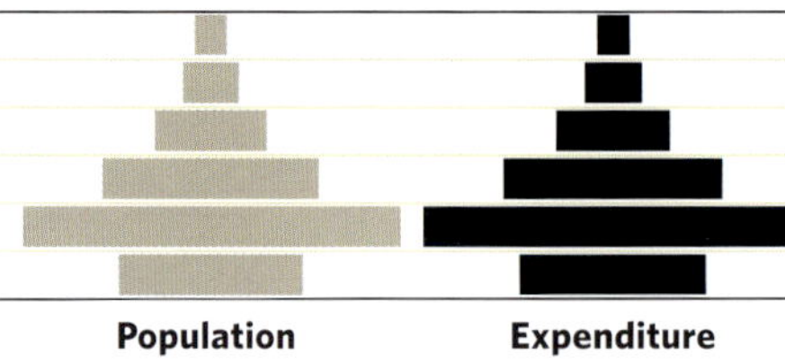

BOP expenditure by sector

$ (**Boldface** numbers are millions)	Total BOP	BOP 500	BOP 1000	BOP 1500	BOP 2000	BOP 2500	BOP 3000	Urban / rural (% of BOP)
Food	**8,320.1**	**468.3**	**2,350.3**	**2,235.7**	**1,608.7**	**1,020.0**	**637.2**	17/83
Per capita	683	200	500	838	1161	1424	1660	
Per household	3433	1159	2609	3969	5182	6439	7376	
Housing	**199.8**	**4.3**	**34.2**	**37.1**	**43.3**	**44.4**	**36.4**	12/88
Per capita	16	2	7	14	31	62	95	
Per household	82	11	38	66	140	280	421	
Water	n.a.	n.a.	n.a.	n.a.	n.a.	n.a.	n.a.	n.a.
Per capita								
Per household								
Energy	**1,205.1**	**134.5**	**372.0**	**290.6**	**191.0**	**130.6**	**86.5**	18/82
Per capita	99	58	79	109	138	182	225	
Per household	497	333	413	516	615	825	1001	
Household goods	**752.6**	**68.3**	**228.6**	**190.1**	**130.1**	**79.9**	**55.6**	16/84
Per capita	62	29	49	71	94	112	145	
Per household	311	169	254	337	419	505	644	
Health	**474.3**	**32.7**	**157.8**	**134.6**	**75.7**	**46.4**	**27.1**	15/85
Per capita	39	14	34	50	55	65	71	
Per household	196	81	175	239	244	293	313	
Transportation	**532.6**	**16.2**	**70.3**	**124.6**	**125.2**	**111.9**	**84.4**	15/85
Per capita	44	7	15	47	90	156	220	
Per household	220	40	78	221	403	706	977	
ICT	**129.9**	**5.6**	**24.8**	**31.2**	**28.6**	**21.3**	**18.5**	20/80
Per capita	11	2	5	12	21	30	48	
Per household	54	14	27	55	92	134	214	
Education	**212.3**	**5.6**	**33.6**	**49.0**	**43.2**	**47.2**	**33.6**	36/64
Per capita	17	2	7	18	31	66	88	
Per household	88	14	37	87	139	298	389	
Other	**1,289.4**	**93.3**	**347.5**	**320.9**	**244.6**	**168.1**	**115.0**	18/82
Per capita	106	40	74	120	177	235	300	
Per household	532	231	386	570	788	1061	1332	
Total	**13,116.2**	**828.9**	**3,619.0**	**3,413.6**	**2,490.4**	**1,669.9**	**1,094.4**	17/83

Note: All dollar amounts in 2005 PPP

Household expenditure by sector

	National ($ millions)	BOP (%)
Food	9,921.3	83.9
Housing	354.7	56.3
Water	n.a.	n.a.
Energy	1,478.1	81.5
Household goods	955.3	78.8
Health	539.4	87.9
Transportation	1,267.5	42.0
ICT	244.1	53.2
Education	435.2	48.8
Other	1,810.6	71.2
Total	17,006.1	77.1

Sector shares of household expenditure
(%)

	National	BOP
Food	58.3	63.4
Housing	2.1	1.5
Water	n.a.	n.a.
Energy	8.7	9.2
Household goods	5.6	5.7
Health	3.2	3.6
Transportation	7.5	4.1
ICT	1.4	1.0
Education	2.6	1.6
Other	10.6	9.8
Total	100.0	100.0

CAMEROON

Total national household market $17,873.5 million
Population 15.5 million
Households 2.9 million

BOP segment	Population: Total (millions)	Population: Share (% of national)	Population: Urban (% of segment)
BOP3000	0.4	2.6	80.6
BOP2500	0.6	4.2	84.4
BOP2000	1.3	8.3	68.2
BOP1500	2.8	18.1	50.0
BOP1000	5.7	36.9	23.8
BOP500	4.0	26.0	7.1
BOP total	14.9	96.0	32.2

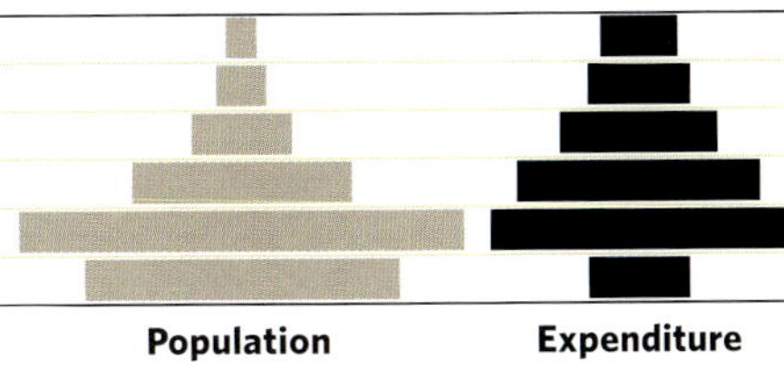

BOP segment	Annual expenditure: Total ($ millions)	Annual expenditure: Share (% of national)	Annual expenditure: Urban (% of segment)
BOP3000	1,154.0	6.5	80.7
BOP2500	1,535.2	8.6	84.6
BOP2000	2,364.6	13.2	68.4
BOP1500	3,624.4	20.3	50.7
BOP1000	4,413.3	24.7	25.7
BOP500	1,511.9	8.5	7.8
BOP total	14,603.4	81.7	47.5

BOP expenditure by sector

$ (**Boldface** numbers are millions)	**Total BOP**	BOP 500	BOP 1000	BOP 1500	BOP 2000	BOP 2500	BOP 3000	Urban / rural (% of BOP)
Food	**6,013.8**	**800.1**	**2,151.9**	**1,475.8**	**823.1**	**440.5**	**322.4**	36/64
Per capita	404	199	376	527	640	684	815	
Per household	2087	1332	2059	2397	2491	2671	2581	
Housing	**1,837.5**	**176.3**	**544.0**	**454.6**	**306.3**	**197.9**	**158.6**	53/47
Per capita	124	44	95	162	238	307	401	
Per household	638	294	521	738	927	1200	1269	
Water	**103.6**	**2.4**	**20.2**	**27.4**	**21.3**	**17.8**	**14.5**	85/15
Per capita	7	1	4	10	17	28	37	
Per household	36	4	19	44	64	108	116	
Energy	**689.3**	**66.5**	**197.8**	**181.6**	**120.8**	**71.4**	**51.2**	54/46
Per capita	46	17	35	65	94	111	129	
Per household	239	111	189	295	366	433	410	
Household goods	**1,836.2**	**204.6**	**554.2**	**448.8**	**288.2**	**193.0**	**147.3**	43/57
Per capita	123	51	97	160	224	299	372	
Per household	637	341	530	729	872	1170	1179	
Health	**756.7**	**64.5**	**199.7**	**183.8**	**140.3**	**103.2**	**65.2**	57/43
Per capita	51	16	35	66	109	160	165	
Per household	263	107	191	298	425	626	522	
Transportation	**1,223.8**	**66.6**	**277.2**	**305.8**	**239.3**	**189.0**	**145.9**	59/41
Per capita	82	17	48	109	186	293	369	
Per household	425	111	265	497	724	1146	1168	
ICT	**97.7**	**0.4**	**6.9**	**16.4**	**23.9**	**27.8**	**22.2**	89/11
Per capita	7	0	1	6	19	43	56	
Per household	34	1	7	27	72	169	178	
Education	**261.0**	**15.7**	**60.7**	**73.2**	**51.6**	**33.9**	**25.8**	74/26
Per capita	18	4	11	26	40	53	65	
Per household	91	26	58	119	156	206	207	
Other	**1,783.8**	**114.8**	**400.8**	**456.9**	**349.8**	**260.7**	**200.8**	61/39
Per capita	120	29	70	163	272	405	507	
Per household	619	191	384	742	1059	1581	1608	
Total	**14,603.4**	**1,511.9**	**4,413.3**	**3,624.4**	**2,364.6**	**1,535.2**	**1,154.0**	47/53

Note: All dollar amounts in 2005 PPP

Household expenditure by sector

	National ($ millions)	BOP (%)
Food	6,695.4	89.8
Housing	2,310.4	79.5
Water	138.1	75.0
Energy	806.6	85.5
Household goods	2,253.2	81.5
Health	915.2	82.7
Transportation	1,872.0	65.4
ICT	189.0	51.7
Education	339.5	76.9
Other	2,354.2	75.8
Total	17,873.5	81.7

Sector shares of household expenditure
(%)

	National	BOP
Food	37.5	41.2
Housing	12.9	12.6
Water	0.8	0.7
Energy	4.5	4.7
Household goods	12.6	12.6
Health	5.1	5.2
Transportation	10.5	8.4
ICT	1.1	0.7
Education	1.9	1.8
Other	13.2	12.2
Total	100.0	100.0

COLOMBIA

Total national household market $170,092.6 million
Population 43.7 million
Households 5.5 million

BOP segment	Population: Total (millions)	Population: Share (% of national)	Population: Urban (% of segment)	Annual expenditure: Total ($ millions)	Annual expenditure: Share (% of national)	Annual expenditure: Urban (% of segment)
BOP3000	4.1	9.5	91.9	12,108.8	7.1	91.8
BOP2500	4.6	10.6	86.7	11,093.1	6.5	86.9
BOP2000	5.2	11.8	82.1	9,598.8	5.6	82.4
BOP1500	5.2	11.9	69.2	6,955.3	4.1	69.4
BOP1000	4.5	10.3	54.6	3,688.9	2.2	56.4
BOP500	1.5	3.4	27.3	530.5	0.3	30.0
BOP total	25.2	57.6	73.8	43,975.4	25.9	81.3

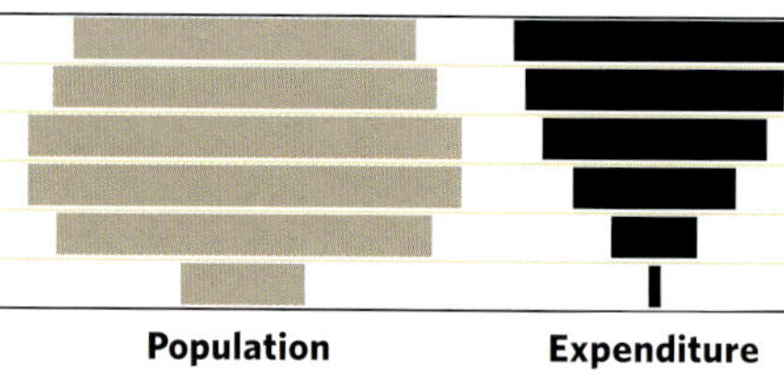

BOP expenditure by sector

$ (**Boldface** numbers are millions)	Total BOP	BOP 500	BOP 1000	BOP 1500	BOP 2000	BOP 2500	BOP 3000	Urban / rural (% of BOP)
Food	**18,154.5**	**257.5**	**1,809.9**	**3,170.8**	**3,916.2**	**4,416.8**	**4,583.4**	74/26
Per capita	722	174	403	607	757	951	1106	
Per household	3321	962	2155	2868	3420	4077	4471	
Housing	**9,352.5**	**117.9**	**710.9**	**1,423.7**	**2,070.6**	**2,377.2**	**2,652.2**	92/8
Per capita	372	80	158	273	400	512	640	
Per household	1711	441	847	1288	1808	2194	2587	
Water	**533.1**	**2.8**	**30.2**	**81.0**	**116.1**	**147.4**	**155.8**	93/7
Per capita	21	2	7	16	22	32	38	
Per household	98	10	36	73	101	136	152	
Energy	**2,278.7**	**22.3**	**210.1**	**380.3**	**522.1**	**578.2**	**565.6**	86/14
Per capita	91	15	47	73	101	125	137	
Per household	417	83	250	344	456	534	552	
Household goods	**3,768.5**	**43.5**	**288.7**	**576.1**	**845.3**	**938.5**	**1,076.3**	79/21
Per capita	150	29	64	110	163	202	260	
Per household	689	163	344	521	738	866	1050	
Health	**660.2**	**10.1**	**67.1**	**115.4**	**157.2**	**145.5**	**164.9**	73/27
Per capita	26	7	15	22	30	31	40	
Per household	121	38	80	104	137	134	161	
Transportation	**2,900.7**	**16.2**	**139.5**	**379.0**	**628.6**	**796.0**	**941.5**	81/19
Per capita	115	11	31	73	121	171	227	
Per household	531	60	166	343	549	735	918	
ICT	**802.2**	**0.9**	**19.4**	**65.5**	**151.6**	**258.1**	**306.7**	93/7
Per capita	32	1	4	13	29	56	74	
Per household	147	3	23	59	132	238	299	
Education	**593.9**	**3.8**	**28.9**	**63.0**	**122.0**	**178.2**	**197.9**	94/6
Per capita	24	3	6	12	24	38	48	
Per household	109	14	34	57	107	165	193	
Other	**4,931.1**	**55.5**	**384.2**	**700.4**	**1,069.3**	**1,257.1**	**1,464.6**	81/19
Per capita	196	38	85	134	207	271	354	
Per household	902	208	457	633	934	1160	1429	
Total	**43,975.4**	**530.5**	**3,688.9**	**6,955.3**	**9,598.8**	**11,093.1**	**12,108.8**	81/19

Note: All dollar amounts in 2005 PPP

Household expenditure by sector

	National ($ millions)	BOP (%)
Food	54,754.4	33.2
Housing	34,343.4	27.2
Water	2,105.2	25.3
Energy	6,512.2	35.0
Household goods	15,284.1	24.7
Health	2,098.2	31.5
Transportation	16,809.6	17.3
ICT	6,951.5	11.5
Education	4,014.0	14.8
Other	27,220.0	18.1
Total	170,092.6	25.9

Sector shares of household expenditure
(%)

	National	BOP
Food	32.2	41.3
Housing	20.2	21.3
Water	1.2	1.2
Energy	3.8	5.2
Household goods	9.0	8.6
Health	1.2	1.5
Transportation	9.9	6.6
ICT	4.1	1.8
Education	2.4	1.4
Other	16.0	11.2
Total	100.0	100.0

CÔTE D' IVOIRE

Total national household market $14,167.6 million
Population 17.1 million
Households 3.1 million

BOP segment	Population: Total (millions)	Population: Share (% of national)	Population: Urban (% of segment)	Annual expenditure: Total ($ millions)	Annual expenditure: Share (% of national)	Annual expenditure: Urban (% of segment)
BOP3000	0.2	1.2	99.8	585.9	4.1	99.8
BOP2500	0.3	1.8	94.0	742.7	5.2	94.0
BOP2000	0.9	5.1	86.8	1,637.1	11.6	87.4
BOP1500	2.0	11.4	65.5	2,553.3	18.0	65.8
BOP1000	6.0	35.4	45.0	4,621.0	32.6	46.3
BOP500	7.4	43.3	25.3	2,562.2	18.1	27.4
BOP total	16.8	98.2	42.4	12,702.3	89.7	57.0

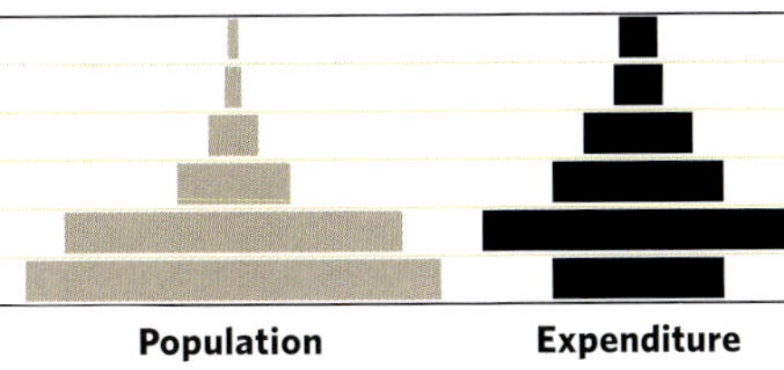

BOP expenditure by sector

$ (**Boldface** numbers are millions)	Total BOP	BOP 500	BOP 1000	BOP 1500	BOP 2000	BOP 2500	BOP 3000	Urban / rural (% of BOP)
Food	**6,285.5**	**1,561.1**	**2,515.0**	**1,186.7**	**616.5**	**238.7**	**167.5**	44/56
Per capita	374	211	416	608	704	776	847	
Per household	2031	1403	2240	2517	2600	2537	2962	
Housing	**621.6**	**51.2**	**169.8**	**153.5**	**124.4**	**69.4**	**53.4**	93/7
Per capita	37	7	28	79	142	225	270	
Per household	201	46	151	326	525	737	945	
Water	**167.7**	**29.8**	**61.8**	**33.7**	**23.7**	**10.7**	**7.9**	79/21
Per capita	10	4	10	17	27	35	40	
Per household	54	27	55	71	100	113	141	
Energy	**616.2**	**116.5**	**224.2**	**126.3**	**86.2**	**35.0**	**28.0**	78/22
Per capita	37	16	37	65	98	114	141	
Per household	199	105	200	268	364	372	494	
Household goods	**1,119.6**	**246.8**	**381.5**	**212.2**	**143.3**	**74.3**	**61.6**	58/42
Per capita	67	33	63	109	164	242	311	
Per household	362	222	340	450	604	790	1089	
Health	**858.0**	**154.5**	**321.5**	**178.6**	**118.9**	**49.3**	**35.1**	57/43
Per capita	51	21	53	91	136	160	177	
Per household	277	139	286	379	502	524	621	
Transportation	**957.4**	**87.5**	**270.6**	**195.2**	**201.2**	**110.0**	**92.9**	78/22
Per capita	57	12	45	100	230	357	470	
Per household	309	79	241	414	849	1169	1644	
ICT	**178.3**	**10.7**	**44.5**	**41.5**	**38.5**	**21.6**	**21.5**	88/12
Per capita	11	1	7	21	44	70	109	
Per household	58	10	40	88	162	230	380	
Education	**382.3**	**46.5**	**131.1**	**82.6**	**71.0**	**23.2**	**27.9**	77/23
Per capita	23	6	22	42	81	76	141	
Per household	124	42	117	175	299	247	493	
Other	**1,515.6**	**257.5**	**501.0**	**343.2**	**213.3**	**110.6**	**90.1**	63/37
Per capita	90	35	83	176	244	359	455	
Per household	490	231	446	728	900	1175	1593	
Total	**12,702.3**	**2,562.2**	**4,621.0**	**2,553.3**	**1,637.1**	**742.7**	**585.9**	57/43

Note: All dollar amounts in 2005 PPP

Household expenditure by sector

	National ($ millions)	BOP (%)
Food	6,661.8	94.4
Housing	723.6	85.9
Water	186.2	90.1
Energy	669.6	92.0
Household goods	1,266.2	88.4
Health	961.5	89.2
Transportation	1,288.2	74.3
ICT	225.7	79.0
Education	448.4	85.3
Other	1,736.4	87.3
Total	14,167.6	89.7

Sector shares of household expenditure
(%)

	National	BOP
Food	47.0	49.5
Housing	5.1	4.9
Water	1.3	1.3
Energy	4.7	4.9
Household goods	8.9	8.8
Health	6.8	6.8
Transportation	9.1	7.5
ICT	1.6	1.4
Education	3.2	3.0
Other	12.3	11.9
Total	100.0	100.0

DJIBOUTI

Total national household market $374.4 million
Population 260 thousand
Households 37 thousand

BOP segment	Population: Total (thousands)	Population: Share (% of national)	Population: Urban (% of segment)	Annual expenditure: Total ($ millions)	Annual expenditure: Share (% of national)	Annual expenditure: Urban (% of segment)
BOP3000	14	5.4	99.4	35.7	9.5	99.4
BOP2500	37	14.2	99.0	76.2	20.4	99.2
BOP2000	68	26.3	98.2	110.8	29.6	98.2
BOP1500	77	29.6	95.4	89.7	23.9	95.5
BOP1000	41	15.6	83.0	30.1	8.0	84.0
BOP500	14	5.5	79.4	4.2	1.1	76.6
BOP total	250	96.6	94.0	346.7	92.6	96.4

Population **Expenditure**

BOP expenditure by sector

$ (**Boldface** numbers are millions)	Total BOP	BOP 500	BOP 1000	BOP 1500	BOP 2000	BOP 2500	BOP 3000	Urban / rural (% of BOP)
Food	**192.7**	**1.4**	**17.8**	**49.9**	**59.9**	**43.2**	**20.4**	96/4
Per capita	768	100	440	650	878	1171	1452	
Per household	5281	512	3186	4901	6239	7516	7949	
Housing	**37.3**	**1.6**	**4.7**	**11.7**	**12.8**	**5.0**	**1.4**	95/5
Per capita	149	116	117	153	187	136	97	
Per household	1022	592	845	1152	1330	875	533	
Water	**14.5**	**0.2**	**1.0**	**3.1**	**4.7**	**3.9**	**1.6**	99/1
Per capita	58	14	25	40	68	106	115	
Per household	398	73	180	305	485	681	632	
Energy	**36.8**	**0.2**	**2.2**	**8.9**	**12.7**	**8.6**	**4.1**	98/2
Per capita	147	17	54	116	186	235	291	
Per household	1008	87	389	877	1321	1506	1595	
Household goods	**23.0**	**0.3**	**2.0**	**5.9**	**7.2**	**5.3**	**2.5**	96/4
Per capita	92	23	49	76	105	143	174	
Per household	632	116	351	575	747	917	956	
Health	**7.3**	**0.1**	**0.3**	**1.5**	**2.1**	**2.1**	**1.1**	99/1
Per capita	29	6	8	20	31	58	80	
Per household	201	31	59	150	221	373	440	
Transportation	**17.0**	**0.1**	**0.9**	**4.2**	**5.8**	**4.0**	**2.1**	98/2
Per capita	68	10	21	55	84	108	147	
Per household	466	50	154	413	599	694	802	
ICT	n.a.	n.a.	n.a.	n.a.	n.a.	n.a.	n.a.	n.a.
Per capita								
Per household								
Education	**0.9**	**0.0**	**0.1**	**0.2**	**0.2**	**0.3**	**0.2**	99/1
Per capita	4	0	2	3	4	7	11	
Per household	26	0	16	19	25	45	61	
Other	**17.1**	**0.1**	**1.1**	**4.2**	**5.4**	**3.9**	**2.4**	97/3
Per capita	68	8	28	55	80	104	171	
Per household	470	41	203	413	565	671	936	
Total	**346.7**	**4.2**	**30.1**	**89.7**	**110.8**	**76.2**	**35.7**	96/4

Note: All dollar amounts in 2005 PPP

Household expenditure by sector

	National ($ millions)	BOP (%)
Food	209.6	91.9
Housing	37.6	99.2
Water	16.0	90.9
Energy	39.2	93.9
Household goods	25.3	91.2
Health	8.6	85.6
Transportation	18.1	94.1
ICT	n.a	n.a
Education	1.1	88.9
Other	19.1	89.7
Total	374.4	92.6

Sector shares of household expenditure
(%)

	National	BOP
Food	56.0	55.6
Housing	10.0	10.8
Water	4.3	4.2
Energy	10.5	10.6
Household goods	6.8	6.6
Health	2.3	2.1
Transportation	4.8	4.9
ICT	n.a	n.a
Education	0.3	0.3
Other	5.1	4.9
Total	100.0	100.0

GABON

Total national household market $2,190.0 million
Population 1.3 million
Households 0.2 million

BOP segment	Population: Total (millions)	Population: Share (% of national)	Population: Urban (% of segment)	Annual expenditure: Total ($ millions)	Annual expenditure: Share (% of national)	Annual expenditure: Urban (% of segment)
BOP3000	0.1	5.3	90.8	200.7	9.2	90.7
BOP2500	0.1	9.0	89.2	282.5	12.9	89.1
BOP2000	0.2	14.0	88.9	341.4	15.6	89.1
BOP1500	0.3	21.0	83.8	363.2	16.6	84.2
BOP1000	0.3	21.7	78.7	229.1	10.5	79.4
BOP500	0.2	17.6	54.6	56.2	2.6	61.2
BOP total	1.2	88.7	78.5	1,473.2	67.3	85.5

BOP expenditure by sector

$ (**Boldface** numbers are millions)	Total BOP	BOP 500	BOP 1000	BOP 1500	BOP 2000	BOP 2500	BOP 3000	Urban / rural (% of BOP)
Food	**622.6**	**16.9**	**112.6**	**165.3**	**142.4**	**109.2**	**76.2**	81/19
Per capita	535	73	394	600	773	922	1104	
Per household	2774	430	2602	3375	3533	3544	3500	
Housing	**309.6**	**31.4**	**47.3**	**70.3**	**63.5**	**55.8**	**41.3**	87/13
Per capita	266	135	166	255	345	471	599	
Per household	1379	797	1094	1435	1576	1810	1899	
Water	**21.2**	**0.2**	**2.8**	**5.2**	**5.3**	**4.8**	**2.9**	97/3
Per capita	18	1	10	19	29	41	42	
Per household	95	4	64	106	133	157	135	
Energy	**78.7**	**1.3**	**12.4**	**19.6**	**19.4**	**15.8**	**10.2**	92/8
Per capita	68	5	44	71	105	134	148	
Per household	351	32	287	399	482	514	468	
Household goods	**115.9**	**1.9**	**14.8**	**27.0**	**28.8**	**24.9**	**18.6**	88/12
Per capita	100	8	52	98	156	210	269	
Per household	517	49	343	551	714	807	852	
Health	**37.7**	**1.0**	**6.1**	**9.3**	**7.6**	**10.0**	**3.6**	87/13
Per capita	32	5	21	34	41	84	53	
Per household	168	27	141	190	188	324	167	
Transportation	**116.1**	**1.4**	**13.0**	**27.3**	**29.4**	**24.9**	**20.2**	91/9
Per capita	100	6	46	99	159	210	292	
Per household	517	35	300	558	728	808	926	
ICT	**59.4**	**0.3**	**5.1**	**13.7**	**16.7**	**14.1**	**9.4**	93/7
Per capita	51	1	18	50	91	119	137	
Per household	265	7	119	279	415	459	433	
Education	n.a.	n.a.	n.a.	n.a.	n.a.	n.a.	n.a.	n.a.
Per capita								
Per household								
Other	**112.0**	**1.9**	**15.0**	**25.5**	**28.3**	**22.9**	**18.3**	85/15
Per capita	96	8	53	93	154	193	266	
Per household	499	48	347	522	702	743	843	
Total	**1,473.2**	**56.2**	**229.1**	**363.2**	**341.4**	**282.5**	**200.7**	86/14

Note: All dollar amounts in 2005 PPP

Household expenditure by sector

	National ($ millions)	BOP (%)
Food	834.5	74.6
Housing	446.2	69.4
Water	33.2	64.1
Energy	114.5	68.7
Household goods	187.8	61.7
Health	52.6	71.7
Transportation	218.9	53.1
ICT	109.9	54.0
Education	n.a.	n.a.
Other	192.5	58.2
Total	2,190.0	67.3

Sector shares of household expenditure
(%)

	National	BOP
Food	38.1	42.3
Housing	20.4	21.0
Water	1.5	1.4
Energy	5.2	5.3
Household goods	8.6	7.9
Health	2.4	2.6
Transportation	10.0	7.9
ICT	5.0	4.0
Education	n.a.	n.a.
Other	8.8	7.6
Total	100.0	100.0

GUATEMALA

Total national household market $23,549.0 million
Population 11.4 million
Households 1.8 million

BOP segment	Population: Total (millions)	Population: Share (% of national)	Population: Urban (% of segment)	Annual expenditure: Total ($ millions)	Annual expenditure: Share (% of national)	Annual expenditure: Urban (% of segment)
BOP3000	0.7	5.8	69.8	2,057.8	8.7	70.2
BOP2500	0.9	7.8	58.2	2,245.2	9.5	58.3
BOP2000	1.4	12.3	44.8	2,727.4	11.6	44.7
BOP1500	2.5	21.8	29.5	3,459.9	14.7	30.0
BOP1000	3.4	29.7	14.8	2,874.6	12.2	15.8
BOP500	0.9	7.9	6.9	401.5	1.7	7.1
BOP total	9.7	85.2	29.8	13,766.3	58.5	39.9

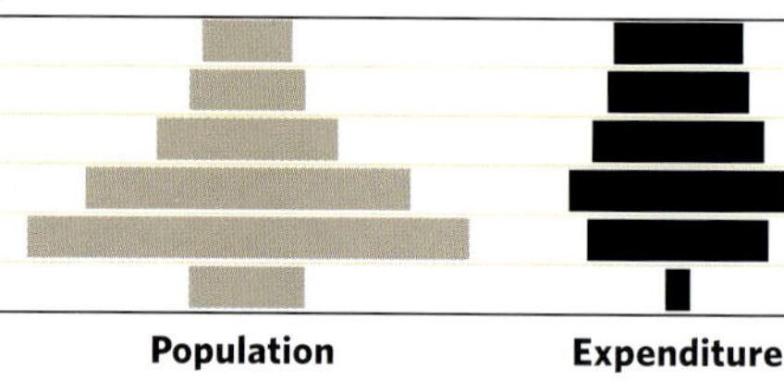

BOP expenditure by sector

$ (**Boldface** numbers are millions)	Total BOP	BOP 500	BOP 1000	BOP 1500	BOP 2000	BOP 2500	BOP 3000	Urban / rural (% of BOP)
Food	**6,414.8**	**224.4**	**1,571.8**	**1,700.7**	**1,217.7**	**929.1**	**771.2**	34/66
Per capita	660	251	464	685	872	1044	1166	
Per household	3646	1875	3005	3681	4150	4639	4791	
Housing	**1,602.2**	**42.3**	**297.0**	**387.0**	**330.1**	**273.6**	**272.1**	48/52
Per capita	165	47	88	156	236	307	412	
Per household	911	353	568	838	1125	1366	1691	
Water	**43.4**	**0.5**	**4.0**	**9.4**	**8.9**	**11.6**	**9.0**	60/40
Per capita	4	1	1	4	6	13	14	
Per household	25	5	8	20	30	58	56	
Energy	**943.3**	**34.9**	**227.1**	**250.9**	**174.5**	**144.7**	**111.2**	40/60
Per capita	97	39	67	101	125	163	168	
Per household	536	292	434	543	595	722	691	
Household goods	**1,110.5**	**42.8**	**253.1**	**289.8**	**205.9**	**167.5**	**151.3**	36/64
Per capita	114	48	75	117	147	188	229	
Per household	631	358	484	627	702	837	940	
Health	**698.3**	**11.7**	**105.6**	**165.3**	**164.8**	**130.1**	**120.7**	36/64
Per capita	72	13	31	67	118	146	182	
Per household	397	98	202	358	562	650	750	
Transportation	**477.1**	**4.4**	**50.5**	**92.2**	**96.0**	**105.3**	**128.8**	44/56
Per capita	49	5	15	37	69	118	195	
Per household	271	37	97	200	327	526	800	
ICT	**129.2**	**0.0**	**7.2**	**20.0**	**24.2**	**39.5**	**38.2**	57/43
Per capita	13	0	2	8	17	44	58	
Per household	73	0	14	43	83	197	237	
Education	**118.7**	**0.7**	**8.9**	**21.9**	**27.7**	**31.4**	**28.3**	63/37
Per capita	12	1	3	9	20	35	43	
Per household	67	6	17	47	94	157	176	
Other	**2,228.7**	**39.7**	**349.4**	**522.5**	**477.6**	**412.5**	**427.1**	49/51
Per capita	229	44	103	210	342	463	646	
Per household	1267	332	668	1131	1628	2060	2654	
Total	**13,766.3**	**401.5**	**2,874.6**	**3,459.9**	**2,727.4**	**2,245.2**	**2,057.8**	40/60

Note: All dollar amounts in 2005 PPP

Household expenditure by sector

	National ($ millions)	BOP (%)
Food	8,991.6	71.3
Housing	2,479.5	64.6
Water	107.1	40.6
Energy	1,303.9	72.3
Household goods	1,953.7	56.8
Health	1,365.7	51.1
Transportation	1,753.4	27.2
ICT	462.8	27.9
Education	439.1	27.0
Other	4,692.2	47.5
Total	23,549.0	58.5

Sector shares of household expenditure
(%)

	National	BOP
Food	38.2	46.6
Housing	10.5	11.6
Water	0.5	0.3
Energy	5.5	6.9
Household goods	8.3	8.1
Health	5.8	5.1
Transportation	7.4	3.5
ICT	2.0	0.9
Education	1.9	0.9
Other	19.9	16.2
Total	100.0	100.0

HONDURAS

Total national household market $12,057.6 million
Population 7.1 million
Households 1.2 million

BOP segment	Population: Total (millions)	Population: Share (% of national)	Population: Urban (% of segment)	Annual expenditure: Total ($ millions)	Annual expenditure: Share (% of national)	Annual expenditure: Urban (% of segment)
BOP3000	0.3	4.8	75.9	981.9	8.1	76.3
BOP2500	0.5	6.9	73.8	1,152.0	9.6	73.7
BOP2000	0.9	12.5	64.7	1,607.4	13.3	65.3
BOP1500	1.2	17.5	55.9	1,560.7	12.9	56.8
BOP1000	1.7	24.4	36.2	1,272.8	10.6	37.8
BOP500	1.5	21.8	15.5	528.2	4.4	15.5
BOP total	6.2	87.9	44.2	7,102.9	58.9	57.7

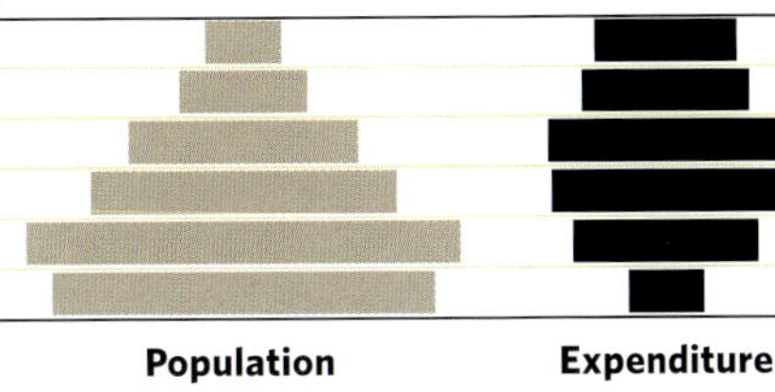

BOP expenditure by sector

$ (**Boldface** numbers are millions)	Total BOP	BOP 500	BOP 1000	BOP 1500	BOP 2000	BOP 2500	BOP 3000	Urban / rural (% of BOP)
Food	**4,844.0**	**434.7**	**972.5**	**1,118.6**	**1,100.5**	**707.5**	**510.0**	57/43
Per capita	779	282	563	905	1244	1444	1516	
Per household	4033	1704	3082	4530	5817	6184	6373	
Housing	**184.4**	**19.0**	**31.7**	**36.9**	**39.4**	**30.3**	**27.1**	61/39
Per capita	30	12	18	30	45	62	80	
Per household	154	75	100	149	208	265	338	
Water	n.a.	n.a.	n.a.	n.a.	n.a.	n.a.	n.a.	n.a.
Per capita								
Per household								
Energy	n.a.	n.a.	n.a.	n.a.	n.a.	n.a.	n.a.	n.a.
Per capita								
Per household								
Household goods	**502.2**	**31.0**	**76.7**	**104.0**	**113.8**	**92.5**	**84.2**	56/44
Per capita	81	20	44	84	129	189	250	
Per household	418	122	243	421	601	809	1052	
Health	**3.1**	**0.1**	**0.3**	**0.7**	**0.8**	**0.8**	**0.5**	69/31
Per capita	0	0	0	1	1	2	1	
Per household	3	0	1	3	4	7	6	
Transportation	**865.2**	**20.0**	**91.8**	**154.2**	**190.1**	**181.1**	**228.0**	57/43
Per capita	139	13	53	125	215	370	678	
Per household	720	78	291	624	1005	1583	2850	
ICT	**33.6**	**0.6**	**3.2**	**4.6**	**8.6**	**8.1**	**8.5**	59/41
Per capita	5	0	2	4	10	16	25	
Per household	28	2	10	19	45	71	107	
Education	n.a.	n.a.	n.a.	n.a.	n.a.	n.a.	n.a.	n.a.
Per capita								
Per household								
Other	**670.4**	**22.7**	**96.5**	**141.7**	**154.2**	**131.7**	**123.6**	64/36
Per capita	108	15	56	115	174	269	367	
Per household	558	89	306	574	815	1151	1544	
Total	**7,102.9**	**528.2**	**1,272.8**	**1,560.7**	**1,607.4**	**1,152.0**	**981.9**	58/42

Note: All dollar amounts in 2005 PPP

Household expenditure by sector

	National ($ millions)	BOP (%)
Food	6,295.8	76.9
Housing	379.2	48.6
Water	n.a.	n.a.
Energy	n.a.	n.a.
Household goods	1,012.0	49.6
Health	9.2	33.6
Transportation	2,854.3	30.3
ICT	83.0	40.5
Education	n.a.	n.a.
Other	1,424.0	47.1
Total	12,057.6	58.9

Sector shares of household expenditure
(%)

	National	BOP
Food	52.2	68.2
Housing	3.1	2.6
Water	n.a.	n.a.
Energy	n.a.	n.a.
Household goods	8.4	7.1
Health	0.1	0.0
Transportation	23.7	12.2
ICT	0.7	0.5
Education	n.a.	n.a.
Other	11.8	9.4
Total	100.0	100.0

INDIA

Total national household market $1,421,921.7 million
Population 973.0 million
Households 183.3 million

BOP segment	Population: Total (millions)	Population: Share (% of national)	Population: Urban (% of segment)	Annual expenditure: Total ($ millions)	Annual expenditure: Share (% of national)	Annual expenditure: Urban (% of segment)
BOP3000	31.5	3.2	67.6	89,836.0	6.3	72.4
BOP2500	68.3	7.0	53.4	159,043.6	11.2	62.4
BOP2000	147.0	15.1	37.4	264,285.7	18.6	45.4
BOP1500	309.0	31.8	19.8	394,937.0	27.8	28.2
BOP1000	349.0	35.9	8.2	288,957.9	20.3	13.8
BOP500	19.3	2.0	5.6	8,608.2	0.6	8.8
BOP total	924.1	95.0	22.0	1,205,668.5	84.8	31.1

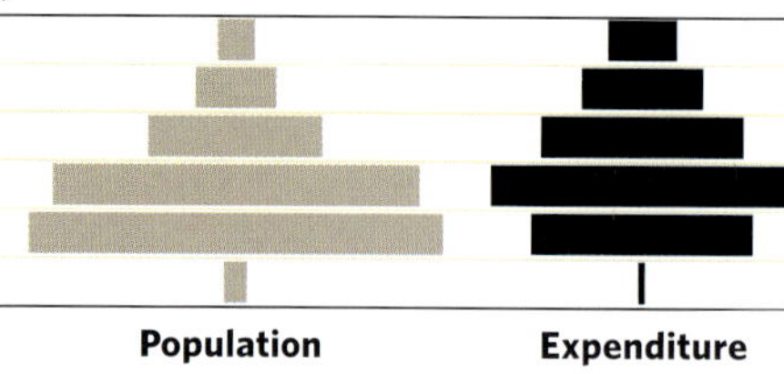

BOP expenditure by sector

$ (**Boldface** numbers are millions)	Total BOP	BOP 500	BOP 1000	BOP 1500	BOP 2000	BOP 2500	BOP 3000	Urban / rural (% of BOP)
Food	**850,246.0**	**6,335.2**	**216,214.1**	**286,721.4**	**182,228.3**	**103,399.5**	**55,347.5**	26/74
Per capita	920	328	620	928	1240	1514	1757	
Per household	4640	1772	3616	4610	5607	6229	6448	
Housing	**30,125.1**	**27.1**	**1,383.0**	**5,588.8**	**8,479.6**	**8,230.2**	**6,416.4**	100/0
Per capita	33	1	4	18	58	121	204	
Per household	164	8	23	90	261	496	748	
Water	**1,213.2**	**2.5**	**117.9**	**268.7**	**350.3**	**294.7**	**179.1**	69/31
Per capita	1	0	0	1	2	4	6	
Per household	7	1	2	4	11	18	21	
Energy	**142,046.4**	**1,223.8**	**36,244.6**	**46,683.1**	**30,438.1**	**17,718.7**	**9,737.9**	30/70
Per capita	154	63	104	151	207	259	309	
Per household	775	342	606	751	937	1067	1135	
Household goods	**21,028.6**	**151.9**	**4,762.4**	**6,696.3**	**4,571.1**	**3,013.6**	**1,833.1**	29/71
Per capita	23	8	14	22	31	44	58	
Per household	115	43	80	108	141	182	214	
Health	**35,112.5**	**145.2**	**6,664.4**	**11,395.3**	**8,580.7**	**5,403.0**	**2,923.9**	27/73
Per capita	38	8	19	37	58	79	93	
Per household	192	41	111	183	264	325	341	
Transportation	**24,844.2**	**85.2**	**3,250.2**	**6,600.6**	**6,256.7**	**5,162.7**	**3,488.8**	36/64
Per capita	27	4	9	21	43	76	111	
Per household	136	24	54	106	193	311	406	
ICT	**7,767.5**	**9.4**	**355.3**	**1,283.9**	**2,042.9**	**2,396.1**	**1,679.9**	51/49
Per capita	8	0	1	4	14	35	53	
Per household	42	3	6	21	63	144	196	
Education	**14,117.3**	**26.2**	**1,575.8**	**3,605.0**	**3,820.4**	**2,958.8**	**2,131.2**	50/50
Per capita	15	1	5	12	26	43	68	
Per household	77	7	26	58	118	178	248	
Other	**79,167.6**	**601.7**	**18,390.2**	**26,093.9**	**17,517.7**	**10,466.1**	**6,098.0**	29/71
Per capita	86	31	53	84	119	153	194	
Per household	432	168	308	420	539	630	710	
Total	**1,205,668.5**	**8,608.2**	**288,957.9**	**394,937.0**	**264,285.7**	**159,043.6**	**89,836.0**	29/71

Note: All dollar amounts in 2005 PPP

Household expenditure by sector

	National ($ millions)	BOP (%)
Food	965,108.6	88.1
Housing	62,123.3	48.5
Water	1,723.1	70.4
Energy	162,903.5	87.2
Household goods	26,692.0	78.8
Health	41,178.1	85.3
Transportation	35,022.0	70.9
ICT	14,758.8	52.6
Education	19,838.6	71.2
Other	92,573.7	85.5
Total	1,421,921.7	84.8

Sector shares of household expenditure (%)

	National	BOP
Food	67.9	70.5
Housing	4.4	2.5
Water	0.1	0.1
Energy	11.5	11.8
Household goods	1.9	1.7
Health	2.9	2.9
Transportation	2.5	2.1
ICT	1.0	0.6
Education	1.4	1.2
Other	6.5	6.6
Total	100.0	100.0

INDONESIA

Total national household market $214,912.1 million
Population 208.6 million
Households 52.1 million

BOP segment	Population: Total (millions)	Population: Share (% of national)	Population: Urban (% of segment)	Annual expenditure: Total ($ millions)	Annual expenditure: Share (% of national)	Annual expenditure: Urban (% of segment)
BOP3000	2.1	1.0	98.3	8,256.1	3.8	100.0
BOP2500	5.0	2.4	96.2	14,000.5	6.5	98.7
BOP2000	12.8	6.1	86.8	26,213.5	12.2	93.9
BOP1500	35.6	17.1	70.0	49,854.1	23.2	80.1
BOP1000	108.3	51.9	39.5	86,833.7	40.4	57.8
BOP500	42.9	20.6	17.4	19,481.6	9.1	32.8
BOP total	206.8	99.1	45.1	204,639.4	95.2	53.8

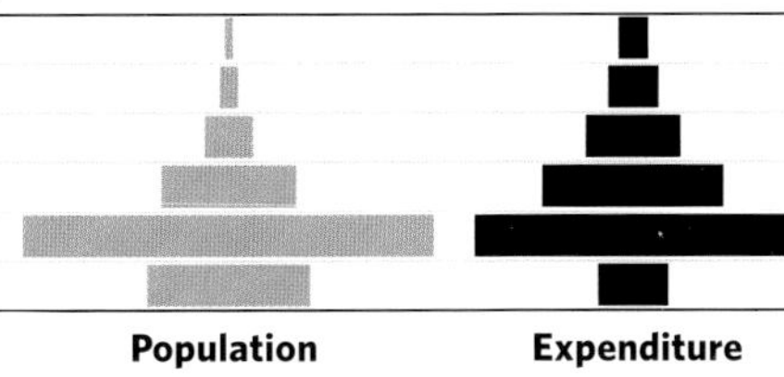

BOP expenditure by sector

$ (**Boldface** numbers are millions)	Total BOP	BOP 500	BOP 1000	BOP 1500	BOP 2000	BOP 2500	BOP 3000	Urban / rural (% of BOP)
Food	**107,515.5**	**12,355.1**	**49,255.3**	**25,286.9**	**11,985.0**	**5,735.9**	**2,897.2**	53/47
Per capita	520	288	455	710	937	1141	1351	
Per household	2064	1353	1803	2575	3226	3879	4586	
Housing	**20,082.6**	**1,194.7**	**6,628.2**	**4,984.2**	**3,281.5**	**2,197.1**	**1,797.0**	73/27
Per capita	97	28	61	140	257	437	838	
Per household	386	131	243	508	883	1486	2844	
Water	**739.4**	**13.2**	**182.8**	**225.0**	**155.6**	**98.7**	**64.0**	90/10
Per capita	4	0	2	6	12	20	30	
Per household	14	1	7	23	42	67	101	
Energy	**12,683.0**	**1,244.4**	**5,427.0**	**3,015.4**	**1,586.7**	**872.0**	**537.5**	57/43
Per capita	61	29	50	85	124	173	251	
Per household	243	136	199	307	427	590	851	
Household goods	**15,722.0**	**1,470.0**	**6,735.3**	**3,768.0**	**2,030.8**	**1,075.9**	**642.0**	55/45
Per capita	76	34	62	106	159	214	299	
Per household	302	161	247	384	547	728	1016	
Health	**4,074.8**	**294.4**	**1,612.4**	**1,044.5**	**578.7**	**364.5**	**180.2**	62/38
Per capita	20	7	15	29	45	72	84	
Per household	78	32	59	106	156	247	285	
Transportation	**8,395.7**	**252.8**	**2,685.8**	**2,577.8**	**1,563.8**	**833.1**	**482.3**	67/33
Per capita	41	6	25	72	122	166	225	
Per household	161	28	98	263	421	563	763	
ICT	**2,139.2**	**4.5**	**173.7**	**491.2**	**598.8**	**497.4**	**373.6**	93/7
Per capita	10	0	2	14	47	99	174	
Per household	41	0	6	50	161	336	591	
Education	**3,740.3**	**207.6**	**1,184.1**	**1,014.4**	**678.9**	**406.5**	**248.8**	79/21
Per capita	18	5	11	28	53	81	116	
Per household	72	23	43	103	183	275	394	
Other	**29,547.2**	**2,444.8**	**12,949.1**	**7,446.6**	**3,753.7**	**1,919.4**	**1,033.5**	55/45
Per capita	143	57	120	209	293	382	482	
Per household	567	268	474	758	1010	1298	1636	
Total	**204,639.4**	**19,481.6**	**86,833.7**	**49,854.1**	**26,213.5**	**14,000.5**	**8,256.1**	58/42

Note: All dollar amounts in 2005 PPP

Household expenditure by sector

	National ($ millions)	BOP (%)
Food	110,619.9	97.2
Housing	22,410.6	89.6
Water	813.1	90.9
Energy	13,391.9	94.7
Household goods	16,688.3	94.2
Health	4,330.1	94.1
Transportation	8,924.0	94.1
ICT	2,711.5	78.9
Education	4,065.3	92.0
Other	30,957.4	95.4
Total	214,912.1	95.2

Sector shares of household expenditure
(%)

	National	BOP
Food	51.5	52.5
Housing	10.4	9.8
Water	0.4	0.4
Energy	6.2	6.2
Household goods	7.8	7.7
Health	2.0	2.0
Transportation	4.2	4.1
ICT	1.3	1.0
Education	1.9	1.8
Other	14.4	14.4
Total	100.0	100.0

JAMAICA

Total national household market $4,930.9 million
Population 2.6 million
Households 0.6 million

BOP segment	Population: Total (millions)	Population: Share (% of national)	Population: Urban (% of segment)	Annual expenditure: Total ($ millions)	Annual expenditure: Share (% of national)	Annual expenditure: Urban (% of segment)
BOP3000	0.1	3.6	58.5	305.5	6.2	58.7
BOP2500	0.1	5.6	48.3	392.3	8.0	48.4
BOP2000	0.3	10.8	47.8	583.0	11.8	48.1
BOP1500	0.5	18.4	44.2	710.5	14.4	44.5
BOP1000	0.8	29.5	43.0	680.0	13.8	42.1
BOP500	0.6	23.8	46.0	204.6	4.1	43.9
BOP total	2.4	91.7	45.5	2,875.8	58.3	46.7

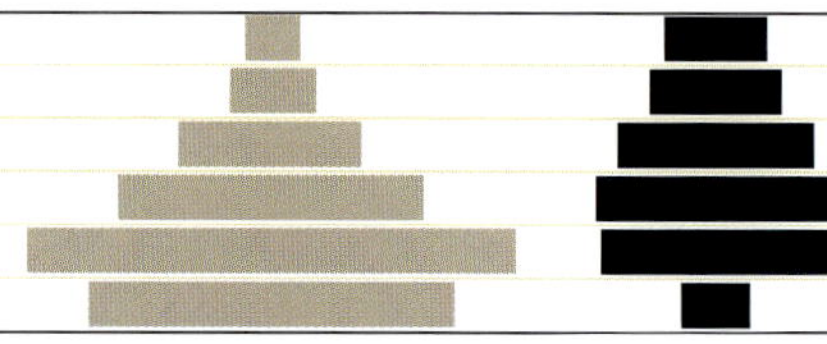

BOP expenditure by sector

$ (**Boldface** numbers are millions)	Total BOP	BOP 500	BOP 1000	BOP 1500	BOP 2000	BOP 2500	BOP 3000	Urban / rural (% of BOP)
Food	**934.1**	**28.0**	**210.4**	**253.2**	**204.3**	**145.1**	**93.1**	31/69
Per capita	391	45	274	527	724	989	1000	
Per household	1451	191	1151	1901	2257	2624	2639	
Housing	**92.5**	**2.2**	**20.0**	**20.5**	**25.3**	**13.3**	**11.1**	81/19
Per capita	39	3	26	43	90	91	120	
Per household	144	15	110	154	280	241	315	
Water	**67.3**	**5.0**	**17.2**	**16.1**	**13.4**	**9.7**	**5.9**	66/34
Per capita	28	8	22	34	47	66	64	
Per household	105	34	94	121	148	175	168	
Energy	**224.5**	**25.2**	**66.2**	**58.0**	**38.4**	**23.2**	**13.4**	52/48
Per capita	94	41	86	121	136	158	144	
Per household	349	172	362	436	425	420	380	
Household goods	**204.8**	**19.9**	**57.8**	**49.8**	**40.6**	**21.6**	**15.1**	49/51
Per capita	86	32	75	104	144	147	162	
Per household	318	136	316	374	448	391	427	
Health	**56.9**	**5.3**	**17.5**	**13.3**	**11.1**	**6.0**	**3.7**	43/57
Per capita	24	9	23	28	39	41	40	
Per household	88	36	96	100	122	109	106	
Transportation	**213.4**	**14.6**	**51.6**	**56.0**	**41.3**	**28.8**	**21.1**	55/45
Per capita	89	24	67	117	146	196	227	
Per household	331	99	282	420	456	521	598	
ICT	**32.4**	**0.8**	**8.0**	**7.6**	**7.4**	**4.9**	**3.7**	67/33
Per capita	14	1	10	16	26	33	40	
Per household	50	6	44	57	81	88	106	
Education	n.a.	n.a.	n.a.	n.a.	n.a.	n.a.	n.a.	n.a.
Per capita								
Per household								
Other	**1,049.9**	**103.6**	**231.3**	**235.9**	**201.2**	**139.7**	**138.2**	53/47
Per capita	439	167	301	491	714	953	1484	
Per household	1631	707	1265	1771	2223	2527	3915	
Total	**2,875.8**	**204.6**	**680.0**	**710.5**	**583.0**	**392.3**	**305.5**	47/53

Note: All dollar amounts in 2005 PPP

Household expenditure by sector

	National ($ millions)	BOP (%)
Food	1,136.7	82.2
Housing	105.0	88.1
Water	82.1	81.9
Energy	245.7	91.3
Household goods	228.6	89.6
Health	63.3	89.9
Transportation	264.7	80.6
ICT	45.7	70.9
Education	n.a.	n.a.
Other	2,759.1	38.1
Total	4,930.9	58.3

Sector shares of household expenditure
(%)

	National	BOP
Food	23.1	32.5
Housing	2.1	3.2
Water	1.7	2.3
Energy	5.0	7.8
Household goods	4.6	7.1
Health	1.3	2.0
Transportation	5.4	7.4
ICT	0.9	1.1
Education	n.a.	n.a.
Other	56.0	36.5
Total	100.0	100.0

KAZAKHSTAN

Total national household market $28,447.8 million
Population 15.4 million
Households 3.7 million

BOP segment	Population: Total (millions)	Population: Share (% of national)	Population: Urban (% of segment)	Annual expenditure: Total ($ millions)	Annual expenditure: Share (% of national)	Annual expenditure: Urban (% of segment)
BOP3000	1.2	7.5	80.3	3,473.4	12.2	80.4
BOP2500	2.1	13.3	73.7	5,048.6	17.7	73.9
BOP2000	3.1	20.0	62.3	5,921.5	20.8	62.6
BOP1500	4.3	27.8	47.0	5,867.6	20.6	47.7
BOP1000	3.4	21.7	33.0	2,939.9	10.3	33.1
BOP500	0.2	1.5	35.6	105.2	0.4	34.9
BOP total	14.2	91.8	53.4	23,356.2	82.1	60.1

BOP expenditure by sector

$ (**Boldface** numbers are millions)	Total BOP	BOP 500	BOP 1000	BOP 1500	BOP 2000	BOP 2500	BOP 3000	Urban / rural (% of BOP)
Food	**13,641.2**	**71.8**	**1,897.0**	**3,570.2**	**3,391.3**	**2,799.2**	**1,911.8**	56/44
Per capita	959	306	564	829	1092	1358	1649	
Per household	3687	1737	3147	3590	3746	4026	4154	
Housing	**95.3**	**0.2**	**5.8**	**19.5**	**27.9**	**25.0**	**17.0**	98/2
Per capita	7	1	2	5	9	12	15	
Per household	26	5	10	20	31	36	37	
Water	**178.4**	**1.2**	**21.6**	**47.0**	**46.5**	**38.3**	**23.8**	79/21
Per capita	13	5	6	11	15	19	21	
Per household	48	28	36	47	51	55	52	
Energy	**2,149.7**	**9.4**	**260.7**	**521.4**	**548.3**	**479.4**	**330.6**	63/37
Per capita	151	40	78	121	176	233	285	
Per household	581	227	433	524	606	689	718	
Household goods	**2,699.3**	**9.3**	**324.3**	**683.0**	**691.8**	**594.4**	**396.5**	62/38
Per capita	190	40	96	159	223	288	342	
Per household	730	226	538	687	764	855	862	
Health	**480.5**	**1.4**	**46.7**	**102.6**	**128.1**	**112.9**	**88.7**	69/31
Per capita	34	6	14	24	41	55	77	
Per household	130	33	78	103	142	162	193	
Transportation	**833.7**	**2.9**	**82.6**	**190.1**	**215.9**	**200.1**	**142.1**	72/28
Per capita	59	12	25	44	70	97	123	
Per household	225	70	137	191	239	288	309	
ICT	**321.8**	**0.5**	**19.5**	**59.3**	**90.4**	**86.0**	**66.1**	78/22
Per capita	23	2	6	14	29	42	57	
Per household	87	13	32	60	100	124	144	
Education	**397.3**	**0.8**	**30.7**	**96.1**	**115.2**	**94.9**	**59.5**	75/25
Per capita	28	4	9	22	37	46	51	
Per household	107	20	51	97	127	137	129	
Other	**2,558.9**	**7.7**	**251.0**	**578.5**	**666.0**	**618.5**	**437.2**	64/36
Per capita	180	33	75	134	214	300	377	
Per household	692	186	416	582	736	890	950	
Total	**23,356.2**	**105.2**	**2,939.9**	**5,867.6**	**5,921.5**	**5,048.6**	**3,473.4**	60/40

Note: All dollar amounts in 2005 PPP

Household expenditure by sector

	National ($ millions)	BOP (%)
Food	16,324.5	83.6
Housing	118.8	80.2
Water	215.4	82.8
Energy	2,616.4	82.2
Household goods	3,304.3	81.7
Health	622.0	77.3
Transportation	1,076.5	77.4
ICT	436.9	73.7
Education	469.9	84.6
Other	3,263.2	78.4
Total	28,447.8	82.1

Sector shares of household expenditure (%)

	National	BOP
Food	57.4	58.4
Housing	0.4	0.4
Water	0.8	0.8
Energy	9.2	9.2
Household goods	11.6	11.6
Health	2.2	2.1
Transportation	3.8	3.6
ICT	1.5	1.4
Education	1.7	1.7
Other	11.5	11.0
Total	100.0	100.0

FYR MACEDONIA

Total national household market $6,903.7 million
Population 2.0 million
Households 0.3 million

BOP segment	Population: Total (millions)	Population: Share (% of national)	Population: Urban (% of segment)	Annual expenditure: Total ($ millions)	Annual expenditure: Share (% of national)	Annual expenditure: Urban (% of segment)
BOP3000	0.2	10.7	51.6	636.4	9.2	51.9
BOP2500	0.3	13.6	58.8	663.3	9.6	58.9
BOP2000	0.3	13.6	52.7	518.9	7.5	52.7
BOP1500	0.3	12.7	54.2	346.3	5.0	53.9
BOP1000	0.1	6.8	51.2	118.6	1.7	51.1
BOP500	0.0	0.8	55.2	7.0	0.1	54.2
BOP total	1.2	58.2	54.1	2,290.4	33.2	54.4

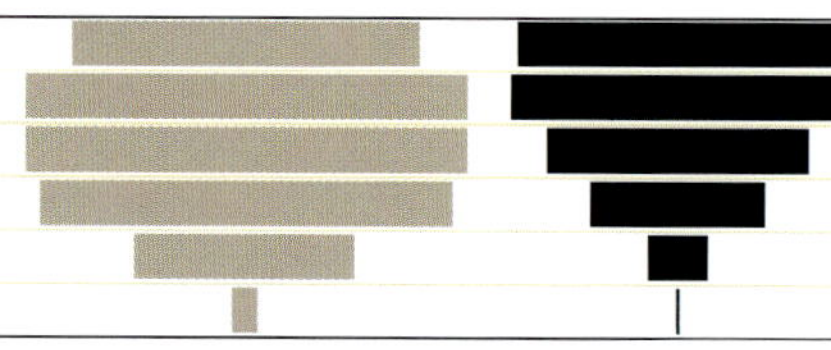

BOP expenditure by sector

$ (**Boldface** numbers are millions)	Total BOP	BOP 500	BOP 1000	BOP 1500	BOP 2000	BOP 2500	BOP 3000	Urban / rural (% of BOP)
Food	**1,332.0**	**5.5**	**87.1**	**236.5**	**308.2**	**361.7**	**333.1**	56/44
Per capita	1132	349	633	922	1121	1316	1536	
Per household	5145	2025	3487	4453	5172	5519	6286	
Housing	**3.2**	**0.0**	**0.0**	**0.1**	**0.9**	**1.0**	**1.2**	69/31
Per capita	3	1	0	0	3	4	6	
Per household	12	9	1	1	15	16	23	
Water	**0.9**	**0.0**	**0.0**	**0.1**	**0.2**	**0.3**	**0.3**	82/18
Per capita	1	0	0	0	1	1	1	
Per household	4	0	1	2	4	4	6	
Energy	**140.0**	**0.0**	**1.2**	**12.7**	**26.6**	**47.7**	**51.8**	54/46
Per capita	119	2	8	50	97	174	239	
Per household	541	11	46	239	446	728	978	
Household goods	**221.4**	**0.3**	**8.2**	**25.9**	**49.7**	**67.1**	**70.2**	49/51
Per capita	188	18	60	101	181	244	324	
Per household	855	106	329	488	835	1024	1324	
Health	**64.9**	**0.1**	**3.3**	**8.6**	**16.6**	**17.8**	**18.5**	57/43
Per capita	55	8	24	33	60	65	85	
Per household	251	44	133	161	278	272	349	
Transportation	**111.4**	**0.1**	**1.9**	**8.1**	**24.2**	**38.1**	**39.0**	46/54
Per capita	95	7	13	32	88	139	180	
Per household	430	40	74	153	406	581	737	
ICT	**86.7**	**0.0**	**0.7**	**7.1**	**17.0**	**30.3**	**31.5**	53/47
Per capita	74	0	5	28	62	110	145	
Per household	335	0	27	133	286	463	595	
Education	**1.6**	**0.0**	**0.0**	**0.1**	**0.4**	**0.5**	**0.6**	84/16
Per capita	1	0	0	0	1	2	3	
Per household	6	0	2	2	6	7	12	
Other	**328.2**	**0.9**	**16.1**	**47.2**	**75.2**	**98.7**	**90.2**	53/47
Per capita	279	58	117	184	274	359	416	
Per household	1268	338	645	889	1262	1506	1701	
Total	**2,290.4**	**7.0**	**118.6**	**346.3**	**518.9**	**663.3**	**636.4**	54/46

Note: All dollar amounts in 2005 PPP

Household expenditure by sector

	National ($ millions)	BOP (%)
Food	3,201.4	41.6
Housing	24.4	13.1
Water	3.9	24.4
Energy	711.1	19.7
Household goods	858.3	25.8
Health	171.2	37.9
Transportation	494.7	22.5
ICT	406.1	21.3
Education	15.1	10.3
Other	1,017.5	32.3
Total	6,903.7	33.2

Sector shares of household expenditure
(%)

	National	BOP
Food	46.4	58.2
Housing	0.4	0.1
Water	0.1	0.0
Energy	10.3	6.1
Household goods	12.4	9.7
Health	2.5	2.8
Transportation	7.2	4.9
ICT	5.9	3.8
Education	0.2	0.1
Other	14.7	14.3
Total	100.0	100.0

MALAWI

Total national household market $7,560.0 million
Population 12.2 million
Households 2.7 million

BOP segment	Population: Total (millions)	Population: Share (% of national)	Population: Urban (% of segment)	Annual expenditure: Total ($ millions)	Annual expenditure: Share (% of national)	Annual expenditure: Urban (% of segment)
BOP3000	0.1	0.6	68.5	191.5	2.5	68.4
BOP2500	0.1	0.8	61.1	219.9	2.9	61.2
BOP2000	0.3	2.1	54.0	445.1	5.9	54.1
BOP1500	0.8	6.6	30.5	1,005.2	13.3	31.0
BOP1000	3.7	30.0	13.8	2,600.7	34.4	14.9
BOP500	7.1	58.6	3.5	2,315.1	30.6	4.1
BOP total	12.0	98.6	10.3	6,777.4	89.6	19.2

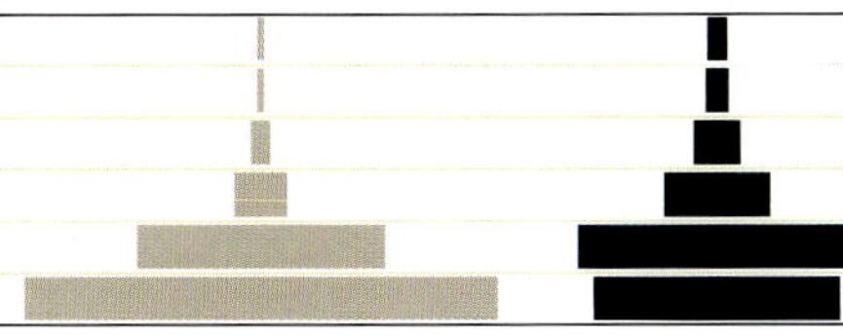

Population **Expenditure**

BOP expenditure by sector

$ (**Boldface** numbers are millions)	Total BOP	BOP 500	BOP 1000	BOP 1500	BOP 2000	BOP 2500	BOP 3000	Urban / rural (% of BOP)
Food	**4,527.1**	**1,681.3**	**1,777.6**	**619.0**	**243.6**	**119.4**	**86.3**	16/84
Per capita	376	235	486	765	968	1239	1272	
Per household	1706	1220	1950	2605	3164	3959	4273	
Housing	**546.5**	**204.4**	**197.1**	**75.2**	**38.8**	**16.2**	**14.8**	25/75
Per capita	45	29	54	93	154	169	219	
Per household	206	148	216	316	504	539	735	
Water	**29.9**	**3.5**	**9.4**	**6.7**	**5.1**	**2.5**	**2.7**	86/14
Per capita	2	0	3	8	20	26	40	
Per household	11	3	10	28	66	83	135	
Energy	**228.8**	**49.6**	**80.6**	**46.9**	**26.9**	**13.1**	**11.8**	45/55
Per capita	19	7	22	58	107	136	173	
Per household	86	36	88	197	349	434	582	
Household goods	**762.6**	**217.6**	**290.1**	**129.4**	**66.8**	**29.5**	**29.0**	21/79
Per capita	63	30	79	160	265	306	428	
Per household	287	158	318	545	868	979	1438	
Health	**52.1**	**24.5**	**18.9**	**5.9**	**1.6**	**0.8**	**0.5**	14/86
Per capita	4	3	5	7	6	8	7	
Per household	20	18	21	25	21	25	24	
Transportation	**333.4**	**47.3**	**114.8**	**73.2**	**37.5**	**26.7**	**34.0**	24/76
Per capita	28	7	31	90	149	277	501	
Per household	126	34	126	308	487	885	1682	
ICT	**4.8**	**0.0**	**0.4**	**1.4**	**0.7**	**1.1**	**1.1**	55/45
Per capita	0	0	0	2	3	12	16	
Per household	2	0	0	6	9	38	54	
Education	**48.8**	**14.5**	**13.5**	**7.1**	**7.6**	**3.1**	**3.0**	55/45
Per capita	4	2	4	9	30	32	44	
Per household	18	11	15	30	99	102	149	
Other	**243.5**	**72.4**	**98.4**	**40.5**	**16.4**	**7.5**	**8.3**	15/85
Per capita	20	10	27	50	65	77	123	
Per household	92	53	108	171	213	247	412	
Total	**6,777.4**	**2,315.1**	**2,600.7**	**1,005.2**	**445.1**	**219.9**	**191.5**	19/81

Note: All dollar amounts in 2005 PPP

Household expenditure by sector

	National ($ millions)	BOP (%)
Food	4,795.1	94.4
Housing	580.2	94.2
Water	37.6	79.5
Energy	264.5	86.5
Household goods	890.0	85.7
Health	54.0	96.5
Transportation	568.5	58.6
ICT	17.6	27.0
Education	58.0	84.1
Other	294.5	82.7
Total	7,560.0	89.6

Sector shares of household expenditure
(%)

	National	BOP
Food	63.4	66.8
Housing	7.7	8.1
Water	0.5	0.4
Energy	3.5	3.4
Household goods	11.8	11.3
Health	0.7	0.8
Transportation	7.5	4.9
ICT	0.2	0.1
Education	0.8	0.7
Other	3.9	3.6
Total	100.0	100.0

MEXICO

Total national household market $318,603.8 million
Population 104.0 million
Households 15.6 million

BOP segment	Population: Total (millions)	Population: Share (% of national)	Population: Urban (% of segment)	Annual expenditure: Total ($ millions)	Annual expenditure: Share (% of national)	Annual expenditure: Urban (% of segment)
BOP3000	9.7	9.3	85.1	28,896.1	9.1	85.0
BOP2500	13.2	12.7	83.3	32,204.2	10.1	83.4
BOP2000	17.3	16.6	75.1	32,785.3	10.3	75.2
BOP1500	16.9	16.3	65.7	23,044.6	7.2	66.0
BOP1000	12.4	11.9	47.9	10,387.8	3.3	49.1
BOP500	2.8	2.7	14.0	1,192.3	0.4	14.8
BOP total	72.4	69.6	68.7	128,510.4	40.3	75.1

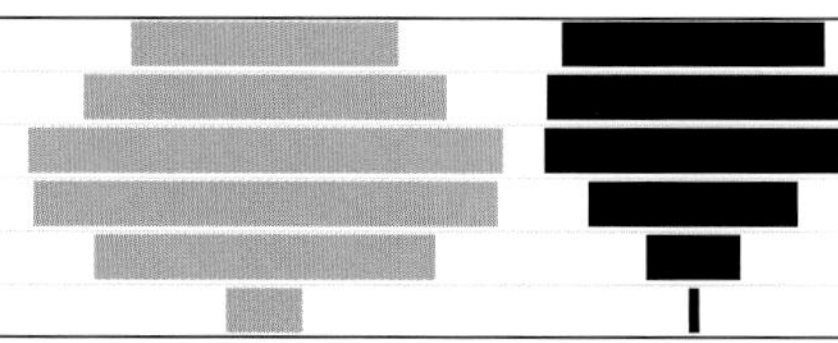

BOP expenditure by sector

$ (**Boldface** numbers are millions)	Total BOP	BOP 500	BOP 1000	BOP 1500	BOP 2000	BOP 2500	BOP 3000	Urban / rural (% of BOP)
Food	**41,912.8**	**559.7**	**4,215.9**	**8,299.9**	**10,751.4**	**9,866.2**	**8,219.6**	72/28
Per capita	579	198	340	491	621	747	845	
Per household	2684	1397	1871	2435	2756	3137	3281	
Housing	**19,995.7**	**225.3**	**1,780.8**	**3,600.0**	**5,063.4**	**4,936.0**	**4,390.3**	79/21
Per capita	276	80	144	213	293	374	452	
Per household	1281	562	790	1056	1298	1570	1753	
Water	**1,042.0**	**4.3**	**92.5**	**189.6**	**253.3**	**276.5**	**225.8**	86/14
Per capita	14	2	7	11	15	21	23	
Per household	67	11	41	56	65	88	90	
Energy	**7,011.5**	**44.2**	**605.8**	**1,416.0**	**1,894.9**	**1,619.0**	**1,431.6**	76/24
Per capita	97	16	49	84	110	123	147	
Per household	449	110	269	415	486	515	571	
Household goods	**12,426.0**	**139.8**	**1,105.9**	**2,216.6**	**3,172.6**	**2,988.1**	**2,803.1**	72/28
Per capita	172	49	89	131	183	226	288	
Per household	796	349	491	650	813	950	1119	
Health	**4,064.2**	**33.4**	**278.8**	**720.5**	**916.8**	**1,127.7**	**987.1**	69/31
Per capita	56	12	22	43	53	85	102	
Per household	260	83	124	211	235	359	394	
Transportation	**12,638.2**	**42.6**	**660.1**	**1,973.2**	**3,241.7**	**3,515.0**	**3,205.7**	77/23
Per capita	175	15	53	117	187	266	330	
Per household	809	106	293	579	831	1118	1280	
ICT	**3,798.9**	**5.4**	**144.7**	**525.6**	**910.2**	**1,093.7**	**1,119.4**	80/20
Per capita	53	2	12	31	53	83	115	
Per household	243	13	64	154	233	348	447	
Education	**5,869.8**	**36.3**	**431.4**	**1,100.1**	**1,412.8**	**1,577.8**	**1,311.4**	80/20
Per capita	81	13	35	65	82	120	135	
Per household	376	91	191	323	362	502	524	
Other	**19,751.2**	**101.4**	**1,072.1**	**3,003.2**	**5,168.2**	**5,204.2**	**5,202.2**	75/25
Per capita	273	36	86	178	299	394	535	
Per household	1265	253	476	881	1325	1655	2077	
Total	**128,510.4**	**1,192.3**	**10,387.8**	**23,044.6**	**32,785.3**	**32,204.2**	**28,896.1**	75/25

Note: All dollar amounts in 2005 PPP

Household expenditure by sector

	National ($ millions)	BOP (%)
Food	74,842.7	56.0
Housing	45,603.8	43.8
Water	2,156.8	48.3
Energy	14,511.3	48.3
Household goods	32,872.9	37.8
Health	10,582.0	38.4
Transportation	39,960.6	31.6
ICT	12,861.1	29.5
Education	17,370.1	33.8
Other	67,842.4	29.1
Total	318,603.8	40.3

Sector shares of household expenditure
(%)

	National	BOP
Food	23.5	32.6
Housing	14.3	15.6
Water	0.7	0.8
Energy	4.6	5.5
Household goods	10.3	9.7
Health	3.3	3.2
Transportation	12.5	9.8
ICT	4.0	3.0
Education	5.5	4.6
Other	21.3	15.4
Total	100.0	100.0

NEPAL

Total national household market $21,915.9 million
Population 23.6 million
Households 4.3 million

BOP segment	Population: Total (millions)	Population: Share (% of national)	Population: Urban (% of segment)	Annual expenditure: Total ($ millions)	Annual expenditure: Share (% of national)	Annual expenditure: Urban (% of segment)
BOP3000	0.2	0.9	100.0	608.2	2.8	100.0
BOP2500	0.5	2.0	74.8	1,131.3	5.2	75.4
BOP2000	1.0	4.1	43.0	1,728.0	7.9	43.6
BOP1500	3.4	14.6	17.9	4,347.9	19.8	18.7
BOP1000	10.8	45.8	6.3	8,042.4	36.7	6.6
BOP500	7.1	29.9	3.0	2,854.3	13.0	3.1
BOP total	23.0	97.3	10.9	18,712.2	85.4	19.5

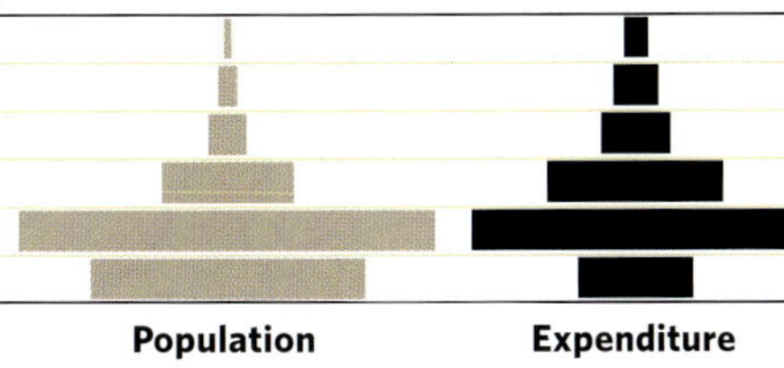

BOP expenditure by sector

$ (**Boldface** numbers are millions)	Total BOP	BOP 500	BOP 1000	BOP 1500	BOP 2000	BOP 2500	BOP 3000	Urban / rural (% of BOP)
Food	**11,012.0**	**1,993.2**	**5,151.4**	**2,431.8**	**806.5**	**439.6**	**189.5**	13/87
Per capita	480	283	477	706	838	910	895	
Per household	2544	1802	2500	3147	3577	3791	3894	
Housing	**2,193.9**	**169.9**	**714.6**	**564.1**	**293.8**	**268.7**	**182.9**	39/61
Per capita	96	24	66	164	305	556	864	
Per household	507	154	347	730	1303	2317	3759	
Water	**22.1**	**1.0**	**4.2**	**4.8**	**3.9**	**4.3**	**3.9**	74/26
Per capita	1	0	0	1	4	9	18	
Per household	5	1	2	6	17	37	81	
Energy	**551.8**	**50.9**	**167.1**	**147.4**	**87.2**	**61.8**	**37.3**	38/62
Per capita	24	7	15	43	91	128	176	
Per household	127	46	81	191	387	533	767	
Household goods	**1,491.0**	**241.1**	**672.9**	**343.3**	**125.5**	**72.1**	**36.1**	16/84
Per capita	65	34	62	100	130	149	171	
Per household	344	218	327	444	557	621	743	
Health	**634.0**	**91.7**	**310.0**	**134.9**	**51.0**	**31.9**	**14.6**	17/83
Per capita	28	13	29	39	53	66	69	
Per household	146	83	150	175	226	275	299	
Transportation	**436.8**	**31.4**	**129.6**	**112.0**	**87.5**	**54.8**	**21.4**	23/77
Per capita	19	4	12	33	91	113	101	
Per household	101	28	63	145	388	472	440	
ICT	**274.1**	**6.8**	**44.1**	**76.8**	**60.0**	**54.2**	**32.2**	48/52
Per capita	12	1	4	22	62	112	152	
Per household	63	6	21	99	266	467	661	
Education	**771.7**	**52.0**	**245.2**	**235.5**	**101.2**	**80.0**	**57.9**	36/64
Per capita	34	7	23	68	105	166	273	
Per household	178	47	119	305	449	690	1189	
Other	**1,324.7**	**216.3**	**603.2**	**297.3**	**111.5**	**63.8**	**32.5**	18/82
Per capita	58	31	56	86	116	132	153	
Per household	306	196	293	385	495	550	668	
Total	**18,712.2**	**2,854.3**	**8,042.4**	**4,347.9**	**1,728.0**	**1,131.3**	**608.2**	20/80

Note: All dollar amounts in 2005 PPP

Household expenditure by sector

	National ($ millions)	BOP (%)
Food	11,704.4	94.1
Housing	3,431.3	63.9
Water	42.6	51.9
Energy	719.4	76.7
Household goods	1,665.8	89.5
Health	675.5	93.9
Transportation	697.7	62.6
ICT	480.5	57.0
Education	1,044.0	73.9
Other	1,454.7	91.1
Total	21,915.9	85.4

Sector shares of household expenditure
(%)

	National	BOP
Food	53.4	58.8
Housing	15.7	11.7
Water	0.2	0.1
Energy	3.3	2.9
Household goods	7.6	8.0
Health	3.1	3.4
Transportation	3.2	2.3
ICT	2.2	1.5
Education	4.8	4.1
Other	6.6	7.1
Total	100.0	100.0

NIGERIA

Total national household market $72,373.0 million
Population 126.0 million
Households 26.5 million

BOP segment	Population: Total (millions)	Population: Share (% of national)	Population: Urban (% of segment)	Annual expenditure: Total ($ millions)	Annual expenditure: Share (% of national)	Annual expenditure: Urban (% of segment)
BOP3000	0.3	0.2	88.7	743.1	1.0	88.7
BOP2500	0.6	0.5	74.5	1,374.0	1.9	74.8
BOP2000	2.3	1.8	74.7	4,223.8	5.8	74.8
BOP1500	9.4	7.4	65.4	12,215.3	16.9	65.7
BOP1000	39.2	31.1	53.1	29,617.9	40.9	53.7
BOP500	74.4	59.0	35.3	23,682.8	32.7	37.1
BOP total	126.1	100.1	44.1	71,857.0	99.3	52.3

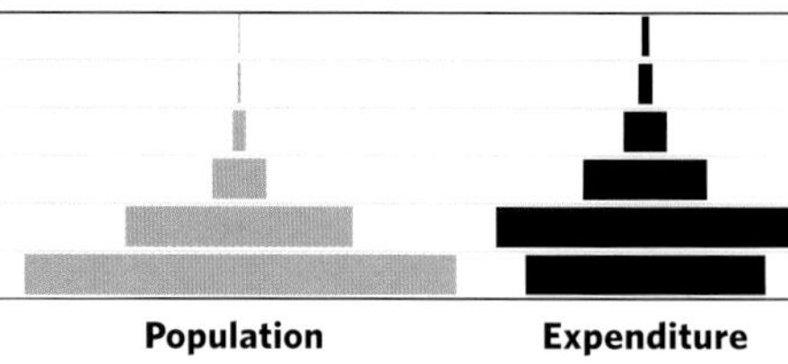

BOP expenditure by sector

$ (**Boldface** numbers are millions)	Total BOP	BOP 500	BOP 1000	BOP 1500	BOP 2000	BOP 2500	BOP 3000	Urban / rural (% of BOP)
Food	**37,336.3**	**12,620.6**	**15,863.8**	**6,097.5**	**1,899.7**	**594.3**	**260.4**	46/54
Per capita	296	170	405	651	829	1030	1015	
Per household	1407	971	1707	1990	2239	2337	3287	
Housing	**8,070.2**	**3,401.9**	**3,062.7**	**1,097.0**	**342.6**	**104.1**	**61.9**	57/43
Per capita	64	46	78	117	150	180	241	
Per household	304	262	330	358	404	409	781	
Water	**591.5**	**185.4**	**259.2**	**101.0**	**33.7**	**7.7**	**4.5**	76/24
Per capita	5	2	7	11	15	13	17	
Per household	22	14	28	33	40	30	56	
Energy	**5,091.2**	**1,823.7**	**2,063.5**	**808.8**	**264.4**	**85.1**	**45.7**	63/37
Per capita	40	25	53	86	115	148	178	
Per household	192	140	222	264	312	335	577	
Household goods	**6,767.4**	**2,170.6**	**2,716.1**	**1,182.1**	**451.5**	**158.4**	**88.7**	54/46
Per capita	54	29	69	126	197	275	346	
Per household	255	167	292	386	532	623	1120	
Health	**4,099.7**	**1,178.5**	**1,691.5**	**759.2**	**288.7**	**124.7**	**57.1**	48/52
Per capita	33	16	43	81	126	216	222	
Per household	154	91	182	248	340	491	721	
Transportation	**4,159.6**	**717.5**	**1,558.4**	**1,035.4**	**536.5**	**173.5**	**138.3**	68/32
Per capita	33	10	40	111	234	301	539	
Per household	157	55	168	338	632	682	1746	
ICT	**477.4**	**72.5**	**182.5**	**115.4**	**62.1**	**18.1**	**26.9**	77/23
Per capita	4	1	5	12	27	31	105	
Per household	18	6	20	38	73	71	339	
Education	**1,423.0**	**499.6**	**599.9**	**227.9**	**81.5**	**7.1**	**7.0**	75/25
Per capita	11	7	15	24	36	12	27	
Per household	54	38	65	74	96	28	88	
Other	**3,840.6**	**1,012.4**	**1,620.2**	**791.1**	**263.2**	**101.0**	**52.6**	60/40
Per capita	30	14	41	84	115	175	205	
Per household	145	78	174	258	310	397	664	
Total	**71,857.0**	**23,682.8**	**29,617.9**	**12,215.3**	**4,223.8**	**1,374.0**	**743.1**	52/48

Note: All dollar amounts in 2005 PPP

Household expenditure by sector

	National ($ millions)	BOP (%)
Food	37,489.9	99.6
Housing	8,108.7	99.5
Water	593.7	99.6
Energy	5,123.6	99.4
Household goods	6,832.0	99.1
Health	4,182.6	98.0
Transportation	4,240.9	98.1
ICT	488.7	97.7
Education	1,427.8	99.7
Other	3,885.1	98.9
Total	72,373.0	99.3

Sector shares of household expenditure
(%)

	National	BOP
Food	51.8	52.0
Housing	11.2	11.2
Water	0.8	0.8
Energy	7.1	7.1
Household goods	9.4	9.4
Health	5.8	5.7
Transportation	5.9	5.8
ICT	0.7	0.7
Education	2.0	2.0
Other	5.4	5.3
Total	100.0	100.0

PAKISTAN

Total national household market $98,997.8 million
Population 129.0 million
Households 18.5 million

BOP segment	Population: Total (millions)	Population: Share (% of national)	Population: Urban (% of segment)	Annual expenditure: Total ($ millions)	Annual expenditure: Share (% of national)	Annual expenditure: Urban (% of segment)
BOP3000	0.4	0.3	98.0	1,287.0	1.3	98.1
BOP2500	1.1	0.9	90.8	2,824.8	2.9	91.0
BOP2000	3.0	2.3	74.8	5,705.7	5.8	75.0
BOP1500	12.6	9.8	50.0	16,634.0	16.8	50.6
BOP1000	67.5	52.3	28.7	52,092.4	52.6	29.9
BOP500	44.4	34.4	16.6	19,318.1	19.5	16.7
BOP total	129.1	100.0	28.5	97,862.1	98.9	36.1

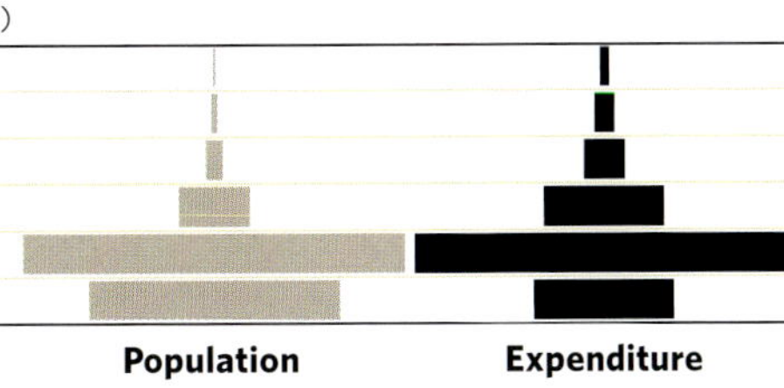

BOP expenditure by sector

$ (**Boldface** numbers are millions)	Total BOP	BOP 500	BOP 1000	BOP 1500	BOP 2000	BOP 2500	BOP 3000	Urban / rural (% of BOP)
Food	**48,987.5**	**10,530.0**	**27,096.9**	**7,672.5**	**2,280.8**	**968.0**	**439.2**	30/70
Per capita	380	237	401	609	763	847	1032	
Per household	2643	1996	2737	3175	3661	4397	4515	
Housing	**8,612.2**	**1,435.1**	**4,066.8**	**1,735.2**	**758.1**	**426.2**	**190.9**	64/36
Per capita	67	32	60	138	254	373	449	
Per household	465	272	411	718	1217	1936	1962	
Water	**223.7**	**23.0**	**99.9**	**51.0**	**27.7**	**14.0**	**8.1**	84/16
Per capita	2	1	1	4	9	12	19	
Per household	12	4	10	21	44	64	84	
Energy	**7,954.6**	**1,660.4**	**4,342.1**	**1,298.8**	**406.6**	**172.2**	**74.6**	35/65
Per capita	62	37	64	103	136	151	175	
Per household	429	315	439	537	653	782	767	
Household goods	**11,792.7**	**2,434.3**	**6,274.4**	**1,955.3**	**648.7**	**346.2**	**133.7**	33/67
Per capita	91	55	93	155	217	303	314	
Per household	636	461	634	809	1041	1573	1375	
Health	**3,655.2**	**769.3**	**2,043.8**	**564.8**	**186.5**	**65.7**	**25.1**	30/70
Per capita	28	17	30	45	62	58	59	
Per household	197	146	206	234	299	299	258	
Transportation	**4,039.3**	**473.2**	**1,914.8**	**899.7**	**379.1**	**230.2**	**142.3**	42/58
Per capita	31	11	28	71	127	201	334	
Per household	218	90	193	372	609	1046	1463	
ICT	**1,030.3**	**17.7**	**306.4**	**300.9**	**201.0**	**129.7**	**74.7**	69/31
Per capita	8	0	5	24	67	113	175	
Per household	56	3	31	124	323	589	768	
Education	**2,091.6**	**255.7**	**1,014.0**	**487.6**	**193.1**	**105.1**	**36.1**	61/39
Per capita	16	6	15	39	65	92	85	
Per household	113	48	102	202	310	478	371	
Other	**9,475.0**	**1,719.4**	**4,933.4**	**1,668.3**	**624.1**	**367.5**	**162.2**	36/64
Per capita	73	39	73	132	209	322	381	
Per household	511	326	498	690	1002	1669	1668	
Total	**97,862.1**	**19,318.1**	**52,092.4**	**16,634.0**	**5,705.7**	**2,824.8**	**1,287.0**	36/64

Note: All dollar amounts in 2005 PPP

Household expenditure by sector

	National ($ millions)	BOP (%)
Food	49,363.6	99.2
Housing	8,745.1	98.5
Water	229.6	97.4
Energy	8,022.2	99.2
Household goods	11,908.8	99.0
Health	3,671.2	99.6
Transportation	4,172.1	96.8
ICT	1,116.5	92.3
Education	2,124.8	98.4
Other	9,643.9	98.2
Total	98,997.8	98.9

Sector shares of household expenditure
(%)

	National	BOP
Food	49.9	50.1
Housing	8.8	8.8
Water	0.2	0.2
Energy	8.1	8.1
Household goods	12.0	12.1
Health	3.7	3.7
Transportation	4.2	4.1
ICT	1.1	1.1
Education	2.1	2.1
Other	9.7	9.7
Total	100.0	100.0

PARAGUAY

Total national household market $19,301.6 million
Population 5.8 million
Households 0.7 million

BOP segment	Population: Total (millions)	Population: Share (% of national)	Population: Urban (% of segment)	Annual expenditure: Total ($ millions)	Annual expenditure: Share (% of national)	Annual expenditure: Urban (% of segment)
BOP3000	0.6	9.5	75.4	1,719.4	8.9	75.5
BOP2500	0.4	6.9	58.7	1,023.3	5.3	59.2
BOP2000	0.7	11.7	44.9	1,329.6	6.9	45.5
BOP1500	0.7	12.0	25.4	980.3	5.1	26.2
BOP1000	0.9	16.4	9.7	795.3	4.1	10.7
BOP500	0.4	7.1	2.6	170.0	0.9	2.6
BOP total	3.7	63.7	33.5	6,018.0	31.2	47.5

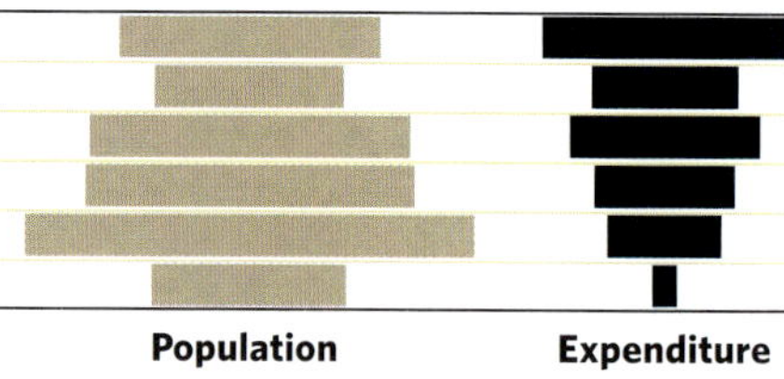

BOP expenditure by sector

$ (**Boldface** numbers are millions)	Total BOP	BOP 500	BOP 1000	BOP 1500	BOP 2000	BOP 2500	BOP 3000	Urban / rural (% of BOP)
Food	**2,729.9**	**87.3**	**416.3**	**478.1**	**607.1**	**435.1**	**706.0**	44/56
Per capita	742	213	440	687	897	1089	1279	
Per household	3948	1576	2733	3409	4724	4342	6148	
Housing	**1,113.0**	**39.2**	**154.9**	**191.1**	**247.8**	**178.4**	**301.5**	49/51
Per capita	302	96	164	275	366	446	546	
Per household	1610	709	1017	1363	1928	1780	2626	
Water	**38.5**	**0.2**	**1.3**	**3.8**	**9.4**	**8.1**	**15.6**	89/11
Per capita	10	0	1	5	14	20	28	
Per household	56	3	9	27	74	81	136	
Energy	**179.3**	**2.1**	**13.3**	**30.2**	**43.3**	**38.9**	**51.5**	57/43
Per capita	49	5	14	43	64	97	93	
Per household	259	38	87	216	337	389	448	
Household goods	**492.2**	**19.5**	**77.6**	**81.1**	**99.8**	**74.7**	**139.5**	41/59
Per capita	134	47	82	116	148	187	253	
Per household	712	352	510	578	777	746	1215	
Health	**236.9**	**5.7**	**32.8**	**31.3**	**54.4**	**44.5**	**68.2**	42/58
Per capita	64	14	35	45	80	111	124	
Per household	343	103	216	223	423	444	594	
Transportation	**360.5**	**3.9**	**28.9**	**45.3**	**97.6**	**64.1**	**120.7**	46/54
Per capita	98	10	31	65	144	160	219	
Per household	521	71	190	323	760	639	1051	
ICT	**153.5**	**1.2**	**9.0**	**23.4**	**39.3**	**34.2**	**46.4**	61/39
Per capita	42	3	10	34	58	86	84	
Per household	222	22	59	167	306	342	404	
Education	**21.9**	**0.2**	**1.6**	**2.3**	**4.5**	**3.7**	**9.6**	76/24
Per capita	6	1	2	3	7	9	17	
Per household	32	4	11	16	35	37	83	
Other	**692.3**	**10.7**	**59.5**	**93.7**	**126.5**	**141.4**	**260.4**	55/45
Per capita	188	26	63	135	187	354	472	
Per household	1001	194	391	668	984	1411	2268	
Total	**6,018.0**	**170.0**	**795.3**	**980.3**	**1,329.6**	**1,023.3**	**1,719.4**	47/53

Note: All dollar amounts in 2005 PPP

Household expenditure by sector

	National ($ millions)	BOP (%)
Food	6,980.4	39.1
Housing	3,140.8	35.4
Water	176.1	21.9
Energy	601.8	29.8
Household goods	2,006.6	24.5
Health	569.3	41.6
Transportation	1,856.6	19.4
ICT	618.8	24.8
Education	81.8	26.8
Other	3,269.3	21.2
Total	19,301.6	31.2

Sector shares of household expenditure
(%)

	National	BOP
Food	36.2	45.4
Housing	16.3	18.5
Water	0.9	0.6
Energy	3.1	3.0
Household goods	10.4	8.2
Health	2.9	3.9
Transportation	9.6	6.0
ICT	3.2	2.6
Education	0.4	0.4
Other	16.9	11.5
Total	100.0	100.0

PERU

Total national household market $45,365.0 million
Population 27.3 million
Households 5.4 million

BOP segment	Population: Total (millions)	Population: Share (% of national)	Population: Urban (% of segment)	Annual expenditure: Total ($ millions)	Annual expenditure: Share (% of national)	Annual expenditure: Urban (% of segment)
BOP3000	1.4	5.0	95.4	3,971.5	8.8	95.4
BOP2500	2.4	9.0	92.9	5,760.8	12.7	93.0
BOP2000	4.1	14.9	84.4	7,444.2	16.4	84.6
BOP1500	6.7	24.4	67.8	8,676.3	19.1	68.7
BOP1000	8.0	29.1	39.9	6,356.3	14.0	42.3
BOP500	2.2	8.0	22.1	887.6	2.0	22.2
BOP total	24.7	90.4	61.5	33,096.6	73.0	73.4

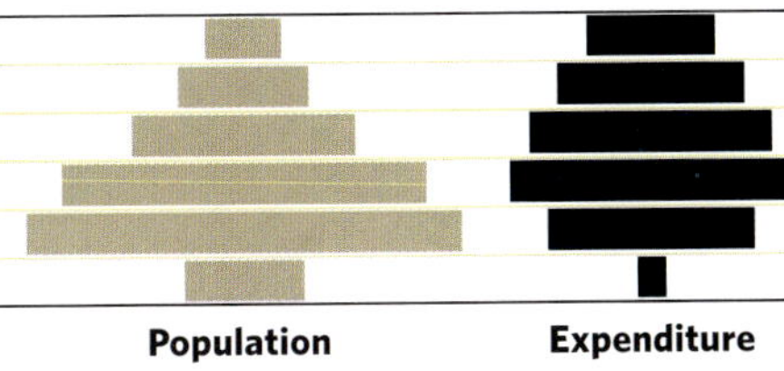

BOP expenditure by sector

$ (**Boldface** numbers are millions)	Total BOP	BOP 500	BOP 1000	BOP 1500	BOP 2000	BOP 2500	BOP 3000	Urban / rural (% of BOP)
Food	**16,403.0**	**522.9**	**3,771.4**	**4,560.4**	**3,494.8**	**2,480.6**	**1,572.9**	66/34
Per capita	665	240	474	685	861	1013	1145	
Per household	3050	1406	2467	3086	3534	3928	4155	
Housing	**4,834.8**	**109.3**	**672.5**	**1,178.0**	**1,189.7**	**986.5**	**698.9**	85/15
Per capita	196	50	85	177	293	403	509	
Per household	899	294	440	797	1203	1562	1846	
Water	**487.6**	**5.4**	**59.5**	**126.1**	**125.4**	**101.0**	**70.2**	97/3
Per capita	20	2	7	19	31	41	51	
Per household	91	14	39	85	127	160	185	
Energy	**1,989.0**	**37.3**	**297.0**	**530.3**	**493.0**	**382.4**	**249.1**	87/13
Per capita	81	17	37	80	121	156	181	
Per household	370	100	194	359	499	605	658	
Household goods	**3,403.2**	**112.0**	**716.3**	**883.0**	**731.8**	**554.1**	**405.9**	69/31
Per capita	138	51	90	133	180	226	295	
Per household	633	301	469	598	740	877	1072	
Health	**1,745.3**	**37.4**	**288.0**	**439.7**	**411.5**	**330.4**	**238.3**	81/19
Per capita	71	17	36	66	101	135	173	
Per household	325	101	188	298	416	523	630	
Transportation	**971.6**	**18.3**	**137.7**	**224.5**	**232.7**	**190.8**	**167.6**	66/34
Per capita	39	8	17	34	57	78	122	
Per household	181	49	90	152	235	302	443	
ICT	**577.5**	**1.2**	**18.1**	**86.7**	**147.6**	**179.1**	**144.8**	98/2
Per capita	23	1	2	13	36	73	105	
Per household	107	3	12	59	149	284	382	
Education	**440.0**	**9.9**	**73.1**	**107.5**	**101.0**	**91.7**	**56.8**	86/14
Per capita	18	5	9	16	25	37	41	
Per household	82	27	48	73	102	145	150	
Other	**2,244.6**	**34.0**	**322.8**	**540.0**	**516.6**	**464.2**	**367.1**	80/20
Per capita	91	16	41	81	127	190	267	
Per household	417	91	211	365	522	735	970	
Total	**33,096.6**	**887.6**	**6,356.3**	**8,676.3**	**7,444.2**	**5,760.8**	**3,971.5**	73/27

Note: All dollar amounts in 2005 PPP

Household expenditure by sector

	National ($ millions)	BOP (%)
Food	20,958.8	78.3
Housing	6,646.3	72.7
Water	682.9	71.4
Energy	2,613.4	76.1
Household goods	4,413.5	77.1
Health	2,273.9	76.8
Transportation	1,921.6	50.6
ICT	1,254.0	46.1
Education	562.5	78.2
Other	4,038.0	55.6
Total	45,365.0	73.0

Sector shares of household expenditure
(%)

	National	BOP
Food	46.2	49.6
Housing	14.7	14.6
Water	1.5	1.5
Energy	5.8	6.0
Household goods	9.7	10.3
Health	5.0	5.3
Transportation	4.2	2.9
ICT	2.8	1.7
Education	1.2	1.3
Other	8.9	6.8
Total	100.0	100.0

RUSSIA

Total national household market $349,168.9 million
Population 117.0 million
Households 25.4 million

BOP segment	Population: Total (millions)	Population: Share (% of national)	Population: Urban (% of segment)	Annual expenditure: Total ($ millions)	Annual expenditure: Share (% of national)	Annual expenditure: Urban (% of segment)
BOP3000	14.2	12.1	81.0	40,212.5	11.5	81.5
BOP2500	16.3	13.9	75.5	38,037.6	10.9	75.3
BOP2000	16.3	13.9	62.6	29,522.2	8.5	63.1
BOP1500	14.2	12.1	45.9	18,409.5	5.3	46.6
BOP1000	9.1	7.8	25.9	7,423.9	2.1	27.2
BOP500	1.7	1.5	12.4	679.6	0.2	12.3
BOP total	71.9	61.4	60.0	134,285.3	38.5	67.6

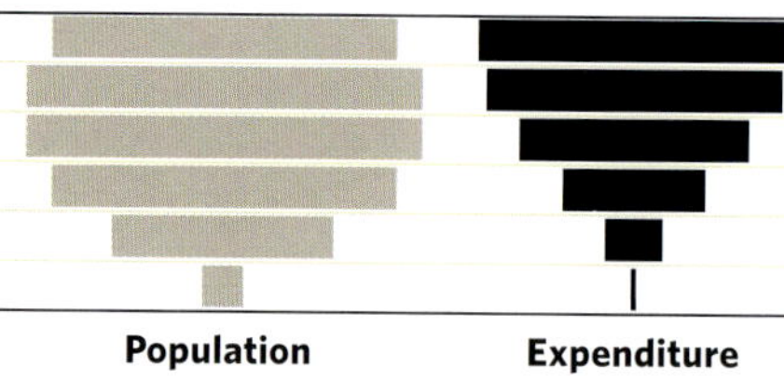

BOP expenditure by sector

$ (**Boldface** numbers are millions)	Total BOP	BOP 500	BOP 1000	BOP 1500	BOP 2000	BOP 2500	BOP 3000	Urban / rural (% of BOP)
Food	**56,052.5**	**303.8**	**3,417.1**	**8,166.1**	**12,435.2**	**15,846.0**	**15,884.3**	63/37
Per capita	780	175	375	575	763	972	1119	
Per household	2209	647	1275	1741	2093	2592	2901	
Housing	**32,171.0**	**137.8**	**1,345.2**	**3,790.6**	**6,863.3**	**9,419.2**	**10,614.9**	81/19
Per capita	448	79	148	267	421	578	748	
Per household	1268	294	502	808	1155	1541	1939	
Water	**967.8**	**4.1**	**41.3**	**116.8**	**199.1**	**284.4**	**322.0**	81/19
Per capita	13	2	5	8	12	17	23	
Per household	38	9	15	25	34	47	59	
Energy	**6,399.7**	**56.6**	**434.8**	**945.8**	**1,402.9**	**1,695.5**	**1,864.1**	66/34
Per capita	89	33	48	67	86	104	131	
Per household	252	121	162	202	236	277	340	
Household goods	**13,019.9**	**57.7**	**763.1**	**1,855.2**	**2,840.2**	**3,627.7**	**3,876.0**	63/37
Per capita	181	33	84	131	174	223	273	
Per household	513	123	285	396	478	593	708	
Health	**9,134.2**	**48.7**	**524.2**	**1,322.4**	**2,207.7**	**2,560.8**	**2,470.4**	61/39
Per capita	127	28	57	93	135	157	174	
Per household	360	104	196	282	372	419	451	
Transportation	**3,567.8**	**15.8**	**254.6**	**563.1**	**795.5**	**936.1**	**1,002.8**	45/55
Per capita	50	9	28	40	49	57	71	
Per household	141	34	95	120	134	153	183	
ICT	**1,356.6**	**4.7**	**58.0**	**158.5**	**281.5**	**403.8**	**450.1**	71/29
Per capita	19	3	6	11	17	25	32	
Per household	53	10	22	34	47	66	82	
Education	**1,273.6**	**2.3**	**26.8**	**114.8**	**283.4**	**365.7**	**480.5**	91/9
Per capita	18	1	3	8	17	22	34	
Per household	50	5	10	24	48	60	88	
Other	**10,342.2**	**48.2**	**558.8**	**1,376.2**	**2,213.3**	**2,898.3**	**3,247.4**	66/34
Per capita	144	28	61	97	136	178	229	
Per household	408	103	209	293	373	474	593	
Total	**134,285.3**	**679.6**	**7,423.9**	**18,409.5**	**29,522.2**	**38,037.6**	**40,212.5**	68/32

Note: All dollar amounts in 2005 PPP

Household expenditure by sector

	National ($ millions)	BOP (%)
Food	135,248.6	41.4
Housing	94,699.9	34.0
Water	2,488.9	38.9
Energy	14,537.2	44.0
Household goods	34,546.9	37.7
Health	20,214.9	45.2
Transportation	8,318.7	42.9
ICT	3,891.8	34.9
Education	3,647.0	34.9
Other	31,575.0	32.8
Total	349,168.9	38.5

Sector shares of household expenditure (%)

	National	BOP
Food	38.7	41.7
Housing	27.1	24.0
Water	0.7	0.7
Energy	4.2	4.8
Household goods	9.9	9.7
Health	5.8	6.8
Transportation	2.4	2.7
ICT	1.1	1.0
Education	1.0	0.9
Other	9.0	7.7
Total	100.0	100.0

RWANDA

Total national household market $6,961.2 million
Population 8.0 million
Households 1.6 million

BOP segment	Population: Total (millions)	Population: Share (% of national)	Population: Urban (% of segment)	Annual expenditure: Total ($ millions)	Annual expenditure: Share (% of national)	Annual expenditure: Urban (% of segment)
BOP3000	0.1	0.9	86.1	222.6	3.2	85.9
BOP2500	0.1	1.5	70.2	305.8	4.4	70.7
BOP2000	0.2	3.1	47.2	488.0	7.0	47.7
BOP1500	0.6	7.3	19.1	820.4	11.8	19.8
BOP1000	2.2	27.7	7.3	1,789.6	25.7	8.0
BOP500	4.5	56.1	1.3	1,451.3	20.8	1.8
BOP total	7.7	96.5	7.6	5,077.7	72.9	19.1

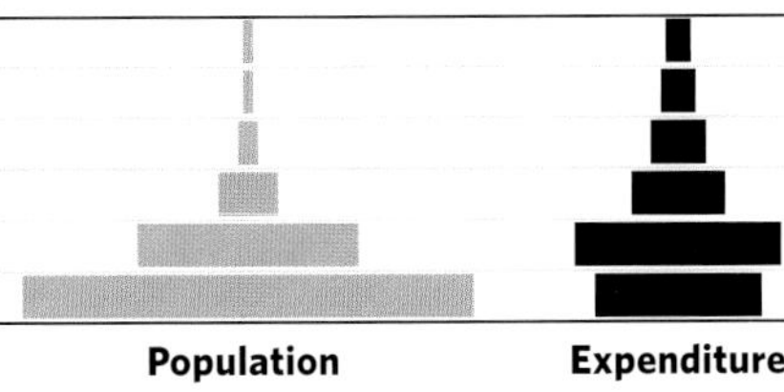

BOP expenditure by sector

$ (**Boldface** numbers are millions)	Total BOP	BOP 500	BOP 1000	BOP 1500	BOP 2000	BOP 2500	BOP 3000	Urban / rural (% of BOP)
Food	**2,961.1**	**941.3**	**1,147.6**	**447.8**	**220.8**	**125.3**	**78.2**	13/87
Per capita	385	211	520	773	902	1074	1116	
Per household	1906	1097	2426	3387	4262	5340	5203	
Housing	**706.0**	**234.8**	**222.2**	**102.4**	**64.7**	**44.7**	**37.1**	26/74
Per capita	92	53	101	177	264	383	530	
Per household	454	274	470	774	1249	1905	2470	
Water	**36.3**	**0.0**	**0.4**	**1.0**	**7.1**	**12.1**	**15.7**	100/0
Per capita	5	0	0	2	29	103	224	
Per household	23	0	1	7	138	514	1044	
Energy	**94.3**	**14.3**	**25.6**	**17.7**	**15.9**	**12.2**	**8.7**	49/51
Per capita	12	3	12	30	65	104	125	
Per household	61	17	54	134	307	518	581	
Household goods	**449.0**	**117.2**	**151.7**	**74.8**	**51.2**	**31.1**	**23.0**	23/77
Per capita	58	26	69	129	209	266	328	
Per household	289	137	321	566	988	1325	1528	
Health	**156.2**	**11.2**	**30.4**	**46.6**	**35.4**	**16.8**	**15.7**	9/91
Per capita	20	3	14	80	145	144	224	
Per household	101	13	64	353	683	718	1045	
Transportation	**114.5**	**11.8**	**26.2**	**24.4**	**23.0**	**17.8**	**11.2**	49/51
Per capita	15	3	12	42	94	153	160	
Per household	74	14	55	185	445	760	746	
ICT	**9.9**	**0.2**	**0.6**	**0.8**	**4.0**	**2.6**	**1.7**	74/26
Per capita	1	0	0	1	16	23	24	
Per household	6	0	1	6	78	113	111	
Education	**22.2**	**4.9**	**4.6**	**3.3**	**5.4**	**2.4**	**1.5**	57/43
Per capita	3	1	2	6	22	21	22	
Per household	14	6	10	25	105	104	103	
Other	**528.3**	**115.4**	**180.4**	**101.6**	**60.4**	**40.8**	**29.7**	23/77
Per capita	69	26	82	175	247	350	424	
Per household	340	135	381	768	1165	1739	1978	
Total	**5,077.7**	**1,451.3**	**1,789.6**	**820.4**	**488.0**	**305.8**	**222.6**	19/81

Note: All dollar amounts in 2005 PPP

Household expenditure by sector

	National ($ millions)	BOP (%)
Food	3,367.7	87.9
Housing	969.4	72.8
Water	265.8	13.6
Energy	148.3	63.6
Household goods	583.2	77.0
Health	497.6	31.4
Transportation	303.8	37.7
ICT	35.6	27.9
Education	32.1	69.2
Other	757.5	69.7
Total	6,961.2	72.9

Sector shares of household expenditure
(%)

	National	BOP
Food	48.4	58.3
Housing	13.9	13.9
Water	3.8	0.7
Energy	2.1	1.9
Household goods	8.4	8.8
Health	7.1	3.1
Transportation	4.4	2.3
ICT	0.5	0.2
Education	0.5	0.4
Other	10.9	10.4
Total	100.0	100.0

SIERRA LEONE

Total national household market $4,940.4 million
Population 5.1 million
Households 0.8 million

BOP segment	Population: Total (millions)	Population: Share (% of national)	Population: Urban (% of segment)	Annual expenditure: Total ($ millions)	Annual expenditure: Share (% of national)	Annual expenditure: Urban (% of segment)
BOP3000	0.1	1.6	100.0	246.4	5.0	100.0
BOP2500	0.2	3.8	94.2	449.6	9.1	94.2
BOP2000	0.4	7.3	76.4	679.9	13.8	76.7
BOP1500	0.8	16.1	52.9	1,059.0	21.4	54.0
BOP1000	2.2	44.5	37.6	1,734.1	35.1	38.8
BOP500	1.3	25.5	21.7	502.7	10.2	22.1
BOP total	5.0	98.8	42.1	4,671.8	94.6	54.5

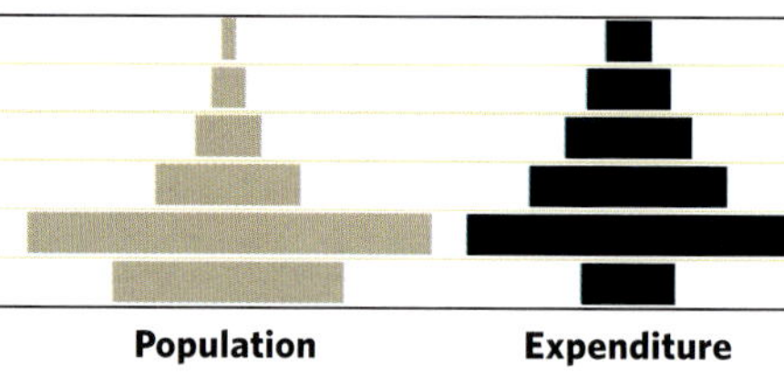

BOP expenditure by sector

$ (**Boldface** numbers are millions)	Total BOP	BOP 500	BOP 1000	BOP 1500	BOP 2000	BOP 2500	BOP 3000	Urban / rural (% of BOP)
Food	**2,489.7**	**303.0**	**1,016.8**	**585.0**	**315.6**	**175.6**	**93.8**	45/55
Per capita	499	235	453	718	854	922	1135	
Per household	3102	1633	2861	3926	4958	4963	6790	
Housing	**227.7**	**33.5**	**86.2**	**46.7**	**28.1**	**21.8**	**11.4**	62/38
Per capita	46	26	38	57	76	115	138	
Per household	284	180	243	313	441	617	827	
Water	**10.2**	**0.3**	**1.6**	**2.4**	**2.4**	**2.5**	**1.0**	94/6
Per capita	2	0	1	3	6	13	13	
Per household	13	2	4	16	38	70	76	
Energy	**220.1**	**21.1**	**68.8**	**48.6**	**38.2**	**29.9**	**13.5**	69/31
Per capita	44	16	31	60	103	157	163	
Per household	274	114	194	326	600	844	977	
Household goods	**658.0**	**65.0**	**232.9**	**146.4**	**107.5**	**70.6**	**35.5**	62/38
Per capita	132	51	104	180	291	371	430	
Per household	820	351	655	983	1688	1996	2572	
Health	**348.3**	**32.2**	**117.1**	**75.9**	**56.8**	**36.6**	**29.8**	66/34
Per capita	70	25	52	93	154	192	360	
Per household	434	173	330	509	892	1035	2154	
Transportation	**160.5**	**7.2**	**37.3**	**33.6**	**31.4**	**33.7**	**17.3**	75/25
Per capita	32	6	17	41	85	177	209	
Per household	200	39	105	226	493	953	1251	
ICT	**37.3**	**1.0**	**4.2**	**6.1**	**7.6**	**9.4**	**8.9**	80/20
Per capita	7	1	2	8	21	49	108	
Per household	46	6	12	41	119	265	643	
Education	**83.8**	**6.8**	**25.8**	**18.5**	**16.3**	**10.7**	**5.7**	81/19
Per capita	17	5	11	23	44	56	70	
Per household	104	37	73	124	255	303	416	
Other	**436.2**	**32.7**	**143.4**	**95.8**	**76.1**	**58.8**	**29.4**	62/38
Per capita	87	25	64	118	206	309	356	
Per household	543	176	404	643	1196	1662	2128	
Total	**4,671.8**	**502.7**	**1,734.1**	**1,059.0**	**679.9**	**449.6**	**246.4**	55/45

Note: All dollar amounts in 2005 PPP

Household expenditure by sector

	National ($ millions)	BOP (%)
Food	2,576.3	96.6
Housing	235.6	96.6
Water	11.9	85.3
Energy	233.0	94.5
Household goods	690.7	95.3
Health	365.8	95.2
Transportation	236.2	68.0
ICT	43.9	84.9
Education	87.7	95.5
Other	459.4	94.9
Total	4,940.4	94.6

Sector shares of household expenditure
(%)

	National	BOP
Food	52.1	53.3
Housing	4.8	4.9
Water	0.2	0.2
Energy	4.7	4.7
Household goods	14.0	14.1
Health	7.4	7.5
Transportation	4.8	3.4
ICT	0.9	0.8
Education	1.8	1.8
Other	9.3	9.3
Total	100.0	100.0

SOUTH AFRICA

Total national household market $135,825.8 million
Population 42.6 million
Households 6.8 million

BOP segment	Population: Total (millions)	Population: Share (% of national)	Population: Urban (% of segment)	Annual expenditure: Total ($ millions)	Annual expenditure: Share (% of national)	Annual expenditure: Urban (% of segment)
BOP3000	2.0	4.8	77.6	6,172.5	4.5	77.7
BOP2500	2.9	6.7	70.6	7,057.8	5.2	70.8
BOP2000	4.2	9.8	66.1	7,924.5	5.8	66.3
BOP1500	6.4	15.1	54.1	8,675.1	6.4	54.6
BOP1000	10.0	23.5	37.8	8,140.7	6.0	38.9
BOP500	6.2	14.5	20.1	2,364.3	1.7	20.6
BOP total	31.7	74.4	46.9	40,334.9	29.7	58.1

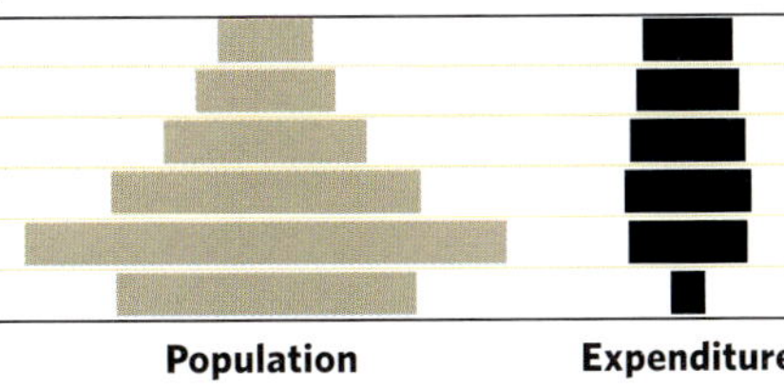

BOP expenditure by sector

$ (**Boldface** numbers are millions)	Total BOP	BOP 500	BOP 1000	BOP 1500	BOP 2000	BOP 2500	BOP 3000	Urban / rural (% of BOP)
Food	**17,358.5**	**1,265.6**	**4,036.8**	**3,891.2**	**3,245.4**	**2,705.4**	**2,214.1**	54/46
Per capita	548	205	404	606	779	944	1080	
Per household	2548	1426	2222	2684	2909	3091	3315	
Housing	**4,440.4**	**305.7**	**867.5**	**922.9**	**845.3**	**771.2**	**727.8**	66/34
Per capita	140	49	87	144	203	269	355	
Per household	652	344	477	637	758	881	1090	
Water	**543.8**	**17.0**	**85.6**	**113.5**	**122.5**	**116.5**	**88.6**	86/14
Per capita	17	3	9	18	29	41	43	
Per household	80	19	47	78	110	133	133	
Energy	**2,582.9**	**147.5**	**572.7**	**593.4**	**514.2**	**418.7**	**336.4**	61/39
Per capita	82	24	57	92	123	146	164	
Per household	379	166	315	409	461	478	504	
Household goods	**4,509.6**	**193.4**	**810.2**	**979.3**	**925.5**	**836.6**	**764.6**	56/44
Per capita	142	31	81	153	222	292	373	
Per household	662	218	446	676	830	956	1145	
Health	**576.9**	**20.8**	**91.3**	**97.7**	**108.5**	**125.2**	**133.3**	58/42
Per capita	18	3	9	15	26	44	65	
Per household	85	23	50	67	97	143	200	
Transportation	**2,267.3**	**60.9**	**300.6**	**408.5**	**509.6**	**511.0**	**476.6**	64/36
Per capita	72	10	30	64	122	178	233	
Per household	333	69	165	282	457	584	714	
ICT	**744.9**	**13.6**	**88.4**	**151.2**	**162.7**	**165.8**	**163.2**	68/32
Per capita	24	2	9	24	39	58	80	
Per household	109	15	49	104	146	189	244	
Education	**895.2**	**53.8**	**152.4**	**166.3**	**174.3**	**183.7**	**164.8**	64/36
Per capita	28	9	15	26	42	64	80	
Per household	131	61	84	115	156	210	247	
Other	**6,415.4**	**285.9**	**1,135.2**	**1,351.0**	**1,316.5**	**1,223.6**	**1,103.2**	59/41
Per capita	203	46	114	210	316	427	538	
Per household	942	322	625	932	1180	1398	1652	
Total	**40,334.9**	**2,364.3**	**8,140.7**	**8,675.1**	**7,924.5**	**7,057.8**	**6,172.5**	58/42

Note: All dollar amounts in 2005 PPP

Household expenditure by sector

	National ($ millions)	BOP (%)
Food	37,888.4	45.8
Housing	14,359.7	30.9
Water	1,847.2	29.4
Energy	6,366.3	40.6
Household goods	12,909.6	34.9
Health	6,749.8	8.5
Transportation	16,663.5	13.6
ICT	5,412.3	13.8
Education	4,067.9	22.0
Other	29,561.1	21.7
Total	135,825.8	29.7

Sector shares of household expenditure (%)

	National	BOP
Food	27.9	43.0
Housing	10.6	11.0
Water	1.4	1.3
Energy	4.7	6.4
Household goods	9.5	11.2
Health	5.0	1.4
Transportation	12.3	5.6
ICT	4.0	1.8
Education	3.0	2.2
Other	21.8	15.9
Total	100.0	100.0

SRI LANKA

Total national household market $23,519.9 million
Population 16.9 million
Households 3.8 million

BOP segment	Population: Total (millions)	Population: Share (% of national)	Population: Urban (% of segment)	Annual expenditure: Total ($ millions)	Annual expenditure: Share (% of national)	Annual expenditure: Urban (% of segment)
BOP3000	0.6	3.5	29.6	1,783.6	7.6	29.7
BOP2500	1.1	6.5	23.0	2,630.3	11.2	23.3
BOP2000	2.1	12.5	19.1	3,932.7	16.7	19.2
BOP1500	4.3	25.7	13.4	5,752.7	24.5	13.6
BOP1000	6.8	40.3	6.1	5,601.4	23.8	6.4
BOP500	1.2	7.0	3.6	541.1	2.3	3.7
BOP total	16.1	95.5	11.6	20,241.8	86.1	15.1

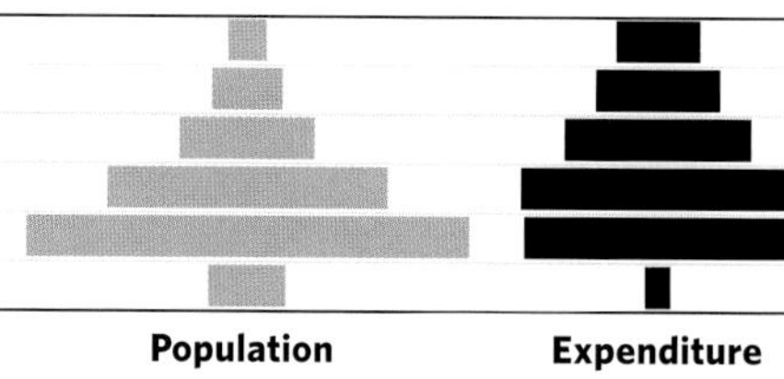

BOP expenditure by sector

$ (**Boldface** numbers are millions)	Total BOP	BOP 500	BOP 1000	BOP 1500	BOP 2000	BOP 2500	BOP 3000	Urban / rural (% of BOP)
Food	**11,817.4**	**389.3**	**3,763.9**	**3,478.2**	**2,118.1**	**1,272.7**	**795.2**	13/87
Per capita	732	329	552	801	1005	1165	1326	
Per household	3096	1720	2533	3220	3786	4263	4775	
Housing	**2,437.9**	**40.2**	**486.4**	**642.1**	**549.9**	**409.7**	**309.6**	23/77
Per capita	151	34	71	148	261	375	516	
Per household	639	178	327	595	983	1372	1859	
Water	**43.2**	**0.3**	**5.2**	**11.1**	**10.1**	**9.0**	**7.4**	54/46
Per capita	3	0	1	3	5	8	12	
Per household	11	1	4	10	18	30	45	
Energy	**945.1**	**29.2**	**261.5**	**263.9**	**184.6**	**124.0**	**81.8**	19/81
Per capita	59	25	38	61	88	114	136	
Per household	248	129	176	244	330	415	491	
Household goods	**1,278.4**	**27.5**	**314.9**	**356.3**	**261.0**	**187.8**	**130.9**	13/87
Per capita	79	23	46	82	124	172	218	
Per household	335	121	212	330	467	629	786	
Health	**499.3**	**6.6**	**115.3**	**154.5**	**104.2**	**72.6**	**46.1**	14/86
Per capita	31	6	17	36	49	66	77	
Per household	131	29	78	143	186	243	277	
Transportation	**1,004.1**	**9.6**	**163.9**	**255.8**	**235.2**	**191.6**	**148.0**	13/87
Per capita	62	8	24	59	112	175	247	
Per household	263	42	110	237	420	642	889	
ICT	**262.5**	**0.0**	**9.3**	**40.8**	**69.5**	**77.3**	**65.6**	24/76
Per capita	16	0	1	9	33	71	109	
Per household	69	0	6	38	124	259	394	
Education	**230.4**	**1.7**	**36.1**	**60.4**	**57.6**	**41.5**	**33.1**	20/80
Per capita	14	1	5	14	27	38	55	
Per household	60	8	24	56	103	139	199	
Other	**1,723.5**	**36.6**	**444.8**	**489.6**	**342.5**	**244.2**	**165.7**	13/87
Per capita	107	31	65	113	163	224	276	
Per household	452	162	299	453	612	818	995	
Total	**20,241.8**	**541.1**	**5,601.4**	**5,752.7**	**3,932.7**	**2,630.3**	**1,783.6**	15/85

Note: All dollar amounts in 2005 PPP

Household expenditure by sector

	National ($ millions)	BOP (%)
Food	12,993.8	90.9
Housing	3,042.1	80.1
Water	58.5	73.8
Energy	1,079.1	87.6
Household goods	1,559.2	82.0
Health	588.5	84.8
Transportation	1,453.8	69.1
ICT	408.1	64.3
Education	293.1	78.6
Other	2,043.7	84.3
Total	23,519.9	86.1

Sector shares of household expenditure
(%)

	National	BOP
Food	55.2	58.4
Housing	12.9	12.0
Water	0.2	0.2
Energy	4.6	4.7
Household goods	6.6	6.3
Health	2.5	2.5
Transportation	6.2	5.0
ICT	1.7	1.3
Education	1.2	1.1
Other	8.7	8.5
Total	100.0	100.0

TAJIKISTAN

Total national household market $7,569.9 million
Population 6.7 million
Households 1.0 million

BOP segment	Population: Total (millions)	Population: Share (% of national)	Population: Urban (% of segment)	Annual expenditure: Total ($ millions)	Annual expenditure: Share (% of national)	Annual expenditure: Urban (% of segment)
BOP3000	0.0	0.5	70.9	123.8	1.6	71.6
BOP2500	0.1	1.5	56.3	306.5	4.0	56.5
BOP2000	0.4	6.1	41.1	939.4	12.4	41.5
BOP1500	1.3	19.1	31.8	2,074.8	27.4	31.9
BOP1000	3.3	49.9	24.8	3,251.1	42.9	25.1
BOP500	1.5	22.6	20.5	787.0	10.4	19.4
BOP total	6.7	99.7	26.9	7,482.6	98.8	30.5

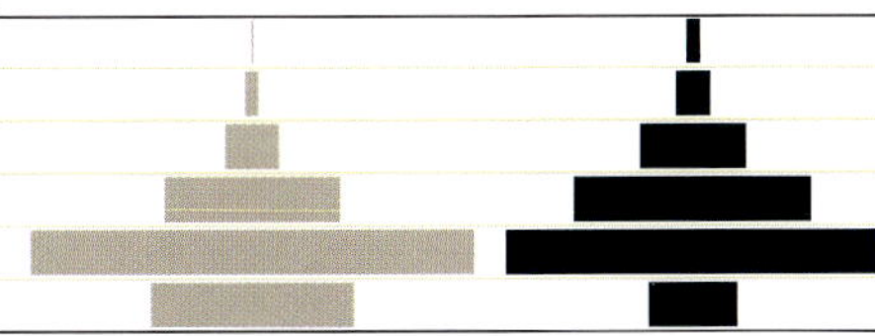

Population **Expenditure**

BOP expenditure by sector

$ (**Boldface** numbers are millions)	Total BOP	BOP 500	BOP 1000	BOP 1500	BOP 2000	BOP 2500	BOP 3000	Urban / rural (% of BOP)
Food	**4,409.5**	**478.4**	**1,953.6**	**1,200.8**	**534.8**	**171.4**	**70.4**	30/70
Per capita	663	318	587	941	1311	1661	2072	
Per household	4241	2587	3894	5292	6293	5791	6074	
Housing	**830.0**	**101.5**	**380.8**	**209.8**	**89.2**	**34.3**	**14.3**	38/62
Per capita	125	67	114	164	219	332	422	
Per household	798	549	759	925	1050	1159	1237	
Water	**26.2**	**3.1**	**12.0**	**7.1**	**2.8**	**0.8**	**0.3**	58/42
Per capita	4	2	4	6	7	8	9	
Per household	25	17	24	31	33	28	25	
Energy	**838.0**	**81.4**	**361.5**	**244.2**	**110.4**	**32.0**	**8.4**	19/81
Per capita	126	54	109	191	271	310	248	
Per household	806	440	720	1076	1300	1082	727	
Household goods	**645.2**	**74.4**	**272.5**	**183.3**	**79.5**	**24.4**	**11.1**	32/68
Per capita	97	49	82	144	195	236	327	
Per household	621	402	543	808	935	824	960	
Health	**118.1**	**12.6**	**54.5**	**34.0**	**11.8**	**3.6**	**1.6**	32/68
Per capita	18	8	16	27	29	35	49	
Per household	114	68	109	150	139	123	142	
Transportation	**218.9**	**6.8**	**70.8**	**75.7**	**43.3**	**15.5**	**6.7**	35/65
Per capita	33	5	21	59	106	151	199	
Per household	211	37	141	334	509	525	582	
ICT	**20.4**	**1.0**	**5.9**	**6.1**	**4.6**	**1.4**	**1.4**	46/54
Per capita	3	1	2	5	11	13	40	
Per household	20	5	12	27	55	47	118	
Education	**37.3**	**2.6**	**14.4**	**11.5**	**5.4**	**2.7**	**0.6**	51/49
Per capita	6	2	4	9	13	27	19	
Per household	36	14	29	51	64	93	54	
Other	**339.0**	**25.2**	**125.1**	**102.1**	**57.5**	**20.2**	**8.8**	35/65
Per capita	51	17	38	80	141	196	260	
Per household	326	137	249	450	676	682	761	
Total	**7,482.6**	**787.0**	**3,251.1**	**2,074.8**	**939.4**	**306.5**	**123.8**	30/70

Note: All dollar amounts in 2005 PPP

Household expenditure by sector

	National ($ millions)	BOP (%)
Food	4,464.5	98.8
Housing	838.2	99.0
Water	26.6	98.8
Energy	841.0	99.6
Household goods	651.1	99.1
Health	119.5	98.8
Transportation	222.5	98.4
ICT	22.5	90.5
Education	37.8	98.7
Other	346.1	97.9
Total	7,569.9	98.8

Sector shares of household expenditure
(%)

	National	BOP
Food	59.0	58.9
Housing	11.1	11.1
Water	0.4	0.4
Energy	11.1	11.2
Household goods	8.6	8.6
Health	1.6	1.6
Transportation	2.9	2.9
ICT	0.3	0.3
Education	0.5	0.5
Other	4.6	4.5
Total	100.0	100.0

THAILAND

Total national household market $163,832.5 million
Population 57.4 million
Households 11.4 million

BOP segment	Population: Total (millions)	Population: Share (% of national)	Population: Urban (% of segment)	Annual expenditure: Total ($ millions)	Annual expenditure: Share (% of national)	Annual expenditure: Urban (% of segment)
BOP3000	4.8	8.4	42.7	15,223.7	9.3	42.9
BOP2500	6.8	11.8	30.9	17,504.8	10.7	31.1
BOP2000	9.7	16.8	18.6	19,404.4	11.8	18.9
BOP1500	12.9	22.5	11.4	18,547.1	11.3	11.6
BOP1000	8.7	15.1	6.6	8,120.8	5.0	6.8
BOP500	0.4	0.7	2.4	198.6	0.1	2.6
BOP total	43.3	75.4	18.5	78,999.3	48.2	23.2

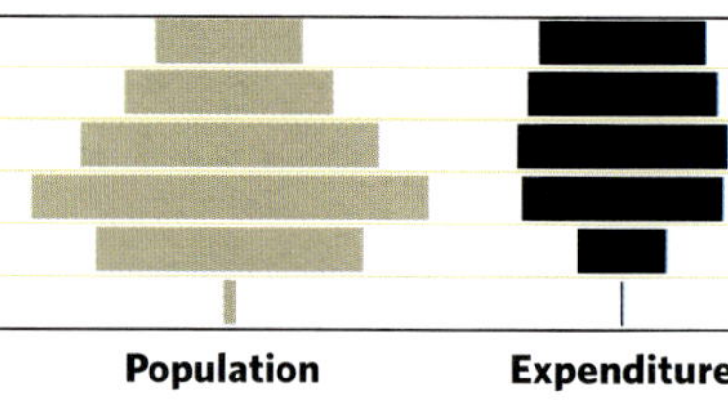

BOP expenditure by sector

$ (**Boldface** numbers are millions)	Total BOP	BOP 500	BOP 1000	BOP 1500	BOP 2000	BOP 2500	BOP 3000	Urban / rural (% of BOP)
Food	**29,241.1**	**112.4**	**3,920.9**	**7,988.7**	**7,286.2**	**5,652.0**	**4,281.0**	19/81
Per capita	676	265	453	619	754	833	886	
Per household	2571	1424	2092	2456	2711	2864	2842	
Housing	**12,565.7**	**28.1**	**1,288.6**	**2,871.9**	**3,076.1**	**2,734.5**	**2,566.6**	25/75
Per capita	290	66	149	223	318	403	531	
Per household	1105	356	687	883	1145	1385	1704	
Water	**850.4**	**2.7**	**86.5**	**185.7**	**199.5**	**192.1**	**183.9**	34/66
Per capita	20	6	10	14	21	28	38	
Per household	75	34	46	57	74	97	122	
Energy	**3,391.8**	**7.8**	**369.0**	**834.5**	**834.5**	**733.9**	**612.1**	24/76
Per capita	78	18	43	65	86	108	127	
Per household	298	99	197	257	310	372	406	
Household goods	**4,347.5**	**8.8**	**376.1**	**1,020.0**	**1,145.9**	**958.0**	**838.7**	18/82
Per capita	100	21	43	79	119	141	174	
Per household	382	111	201	314	426	485	557	
Health	**1,435.6**	**2.2**	**111.7**	**288.1**	**380.4**	**346.2**	**306.9**	22/78
Per capita	33	5	13	22	39	51	64	
Per household	126	28	60	89	142	175	204	
Transportation	**6,838.7**	**9.3**	**414.8**	**1,271.7**	**1,700.7**	**1,825.4**	**1,616.8**	21/79
Per capita	158	22	48	99	176	269	335	
Per household	601	118	221	391	633	925	1073	
ICT	**2,225.4**	**0.2**	**42.5**	**230.2**	**485.4**	**700.9**	**766.3**	33/67
Per capita	51	1	5	18	50	103	159	
Per household	196	3	23	71	181	355	509	
Education	**780.3**	**0.5**	**23.1**	**108.0**	**157.4**	**245.2**	**246.1**	35/65
Per capita	18	1	3	8	16	36	51	
Per household	69	6	12	33	59	124	163	
Other	**17,322.8**	**26.6**	**1,487.7**	**3,748.2**	**4,138.5**	**4,116.6**	**3,805.2**	29/71
Per capita	400	63	172	291	428	607	787	
Per household	1523	337	794	1152	1540	2086	2526	
Total	**78,999.3**	**198.6**	**8,120.8**	**18,547.1**	**19,404.4**	**17,504.8**	**15,223.7**	23/77

Note: All dollar amounts in 2005 PPP

Household expenditure by sector

	National ($ millions)	BOP (%)
Food	43,615.4	67.0
Housing	26,618.7	47.2
Water	1,692.7	50.2
Energy	6,107.5	55.5
Household goods	10,093.6	43.1
Health	3,252.1	44.1
Transportation	22,861.4	29.9
ICT	7,790.4	28.6
Education	3,028.6	25.8
Other	38,772.2	44.7
Total	163,832.5	48.2

Sector shares of household expenditure
(%)

	National	BOP
Food	26.6	37.0
Housing	16.2	15.9
Water	1.0	1.1
Energy	3.7	4.3
Household goods	6.2	5.5
Health	2.0	1.8
Transportation	14.0	8.7
ICT	4.8	2.8
Education	1.8	1.0
Other	23.7	21.9
Total	100.0	100.0

UGANDA

Total national household market $28,475.4 million
Population 26.1 million
Households 4.7 million

BOP segment	Population: Total (millions)	Population: Share (% of national)	Population: Urban (% of segment)	Annual expenditure: Total ($ millions)	Annual expenditure: Share (% of national)	Annual expenditure: Urban (% of segment)
BOP3000	0.5	1.9	56.6	1,463.0	5.1	56.8
BOP2500	1.0	3.8	49.5	2,391.7	8.4	49.2
BOP2000	2.0	7.5	32.2	3,658.0	12.8	32.7
BOP1500	4.3	16.6	16.5	5,651.5	19.8	17.0
BOP1000	11.2	42.9	6.8	8,798.8	30.9	7.2
BOP500	6.4	24.4	2.8	2,545.6	8.9	2.9
BOP total	25.3	97.1	12.1	24,508.7	86.1	19.9

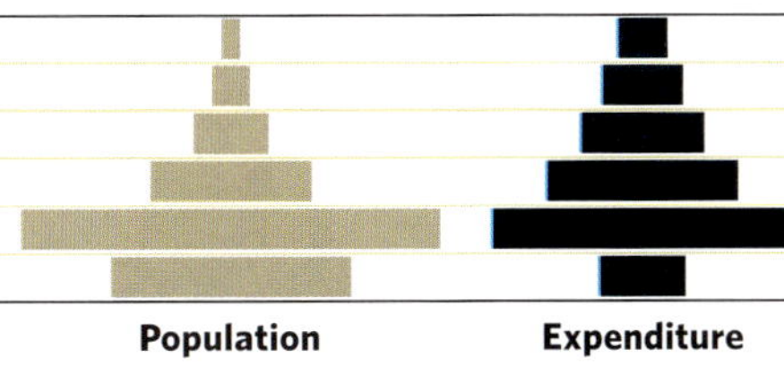

BOP expenditure by sector

$ (**Boldface** numbers are millions)	Total BOP	BOP 500	BOP 1000	BOP 1500	BOP 2000	BOP 2500	BOP 3000	Urban / rural (% of BOP)
Food	**12,229.3**	**1,424.4**	**4,788.0**	**2,839.9**	**1,608.4**	**997.1**	**571.5**	16/84
Per capita	483	224	427	657	824	1000	1150	
Per household	2611	1414	2439	3191	3599	4296	3943	
Housing	**1,737.8**	**229.7**	**607.8**	**363.7**	**258.8**	**170.3**	**107.4**	29/71
Per capita	69	36	54	84	133	171	216	
Per household	371	228	310	409	579	734	741	
Water	**917.2**	**131.0**	**388.6**	**195.1**	**109.2**	**56.6**	**36.7**	15/85
Per capita	36	21	35	45	56	57	74	
Per household	196	130	198	219	244	244	253	
Energy	**1,599.2**	**220.4**	**615.1**	**342.6**	**204.4**	**132.6**	**84.1**	21/79
Per capita	63	35	55	79	105	133	169	
Per household	341	219	313	385	457	571	580	
Household goods	**2,459.5**	**228.2**	**868.5**	**600.9**	**378.2**	**244.5**	**139.2**	18/82
Per capita	97	36	78	139	194	245	280	
Per household	525	227	442	675	846	1054	960	
Health	**898.0**	**95.3**	**344.1**	**231.7**	**123.2**	**60.2**	**43.5**	18/82
Per capita	35	15	31	54	63	60	87	
Per household	192	95	175	260	276	259	300	
Transportation	**1,289.5**	**54.5**	**338.7**	**314.4**	**286.3**	**158.0**	**137.6**	19/81
Per capita	51	9	30	73	147	159	277	
Per household	275	54	173	353	641	681	949	
ICT	**328.2**	**3.8**	**31.2**	**53.7**	**74.3**	**100.3**	**64.8**	45/55
Per capita	13	1	3	12	38	101	130	
Per household	70	4	16	60	166	432	447	
Education	**1,165.9**	**41.5**	**347.6**	**295.7**	**242.4**	**165.8**	**72.9**	32/68
Per capita	46	7	31	68	124	166	147	
Per household	249	41	177	332	543	714	503	
Other	**1,884.1**	**116.8**	**469.2**	**413.8**	**372.7**	**306.2**	**205.4**	29/71
Per capita	74	18	42	96	191	307	413	
Per household	402	116	239	465	834	1319	1417	
Total	**24,508.7**	**2,545.6**	**8,798.8**	**5,651.5**	**3,658.0**	**2,391.7**	**1,463.0**	20/80

Note: All dollar amounts in 2005 PPP

Household expenditure by sector

	National ($ millions)	BOP (%)
Food	13,363.7	91.5
Housing	2,011.6	86.4
Water	992.0	92.5
Energy	1,779.6	89.9
Household goods	2,814.6	87.4
Health	976.9	91.9
Transportation	1,935.1	66.6
ICT	636.3	51.6
Education	1,373.2	84.9
Other	2,592.5	72.7
Total	28,475.4	86.1

Sector shares of household expenditure
(%)

	National	BOP
Food	46.9	49.9
Housing	7.1	7.1
Water	3.5	3.7
Energy	6.2	6.5
Household goods	9.9	10.0
Health	3.4	3.7
Transportation	6.8	5.3
ICT	2.2	1.3
Education	4.8	4.8
Other	9.1	7.7
Total	100.0	100.0

UKRAINE

Total national household market $151,346.1 million
Population 46.2 million
Households 9.4 million

BOP segment	Population: Total (millions)	Population: Share (% of national)	Population: Urban (% of segment)	Annual expenditure: Total ($ millions)	Annual expenditure: Share (% of national)	Annual expenditure: Urban (% of segment)
BOP3000	7.4	16.0	68.3	22,241.1	14.7	68.4
BOP2500	8.6	18.6	60.9	21,172.0	14.0	61.0
BOP2000	7.3	15.7	58.2	14,006.3	9.3	58.3
BOP1500	3.9	8.4	52.3	5,524.6	3.7	51.9
BOP1000	0.8	1.7	48.3	719.8	0.5	47.8
BOP500	0.1	0.1	54.3	23.9	0.0	44.4
BOP total	27.9	60.5	60.6	63,687.5	42.1	62.0

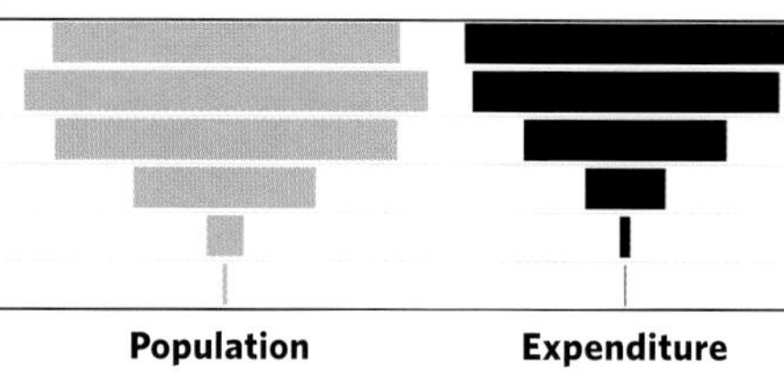

BOP expenditure by sector

$ (**Boldface** numbers are millions)	Total BOP	BOP 500	BOP 1000	BOP 1500	BOP 2000	BOP 2500	BOP 3000	Urban / rural (% of BOP)
Food	**44,792.5**	**18.8**	**549.8**	**4,107.1**	**10,092.1**	**14,819.6**	**15,205.1**	58/42
Per capita	1603	340	709	1062	1392	1723	2059	
Per household	4749	1302	2703	3804	4342	5023	5318	
Housing	**1,246.0**	**0.0**	**12.8**	**89.0**	**251.0**	**437.6**	**455.6**	85/15
Per capita	45	1	16	23	35	51	62	
Per household	132	2	63	82	108	148	159	
Water	**557.7**	**0.6**	**6.2**	**53.8**	**119.9**	**197.3**	**179.8**	87/13
Per capita	20	11	8	14	17	23	24	
Per household	59	44	31	50	52	67	63	
Energy	**4,794.0**	**1.2**	**55.1**	**442.5**	**1,072.4**	**1,586.9**	**1,635.9**	67/33
Per capita	172	22	71	114	148	185	221	
Per household	508	84	271	410	461	538	572	
Household goods	**4,206.3**	**0.9**	**36.0**	**297.0**	**886.8**	**1,435.9**	**1,549.7**	63/37
Per capita	151	17	46	77	122	167	210	
Per household	446	66	177	275	382	487	542	
Health	**1,437.3**	**0.8**	**14.2**	**112.6**	**314.9**	**475.7**	**519.2**	66/34
Per capita	51	15	18	29	43	55	70	
Per household	152	58	70	104	135	161	182	
Transportation	**1,334.1**	**0.1**	**7.4**	**77.3**	**253.3**	**440.1**	**555.9**	69/31
Per capita	48	1	10	20	35	51	75	
Per household	141	4	37	72	109	149	194	
ICT	**998.3**	**0.0**	**6.5**	**64.7**	**182.8**	**336.6**	**407.8**	79/21
Per capita	36	0	8	17	25	39	55	
Per household	106	0	32	60	79	114	143	
Education	**510.0**	**0.0**	**4.2**	**29.5**	**83.9**	**179.8**	**212.5**	76/24
Per capita	18	0	5	8	12	21	29	
Per household	54	0	21	27	36	61	74	
Other	**3,811.3**	**1.3**	**27.5**	**251.0**	**749.2**	**1,262.6**	**1,519.7**	75/25
Per capita	136	24	35	65	103	147	206	
Per household	404	91	135	232	322	428	532	
Total	**63,687.5**	**23.9**	**719.8**	**5,524.6**	**14,006.3**	**21,172.0**	**22,241.1**	62/38

Note: All dollar amounts in 2005 PPP

Household expenditure by sector

	National ($ millions)	BOP (%)
Food	101,138.9	44.3
Housing	3,270.7	38.1
Water	1,133.5	49.2
Energy	10,212.1	46.9
Household goods	11,200.6	37.6
Health	3,612.4	39.8
Transportation	4,551.6	29.3
ICT	3,299.0	30.3
Education	1,602.1	31.8
Other	11,325.2	33.7
Total	151,346.1	42.1

Sector shares of household expenditure
(%)

	National	BOP
Food	66.8	70.3
Housing	2.2	2.0
Water	0.7	0.9
Energy	6.7	7.5
Household goods	7.4	6.6
Health	2.4	2.3
Transportation	3.0	2.1
ICT	2.2	1.6
Education	1.1	0.8
Other	7.5	6.0
Total	100.0	100.0

UZBEKISTAN

Total national household market $23,150.9 million
Population 23.8 million
Households 4.7 million

BOP segment	Population: Total (millions)	Population: Share (% of national)	Population: Urban (% of segment)	Annual expenditure: Total ($ millions)	Annual expenditure: Share (% of national)	Annual expenditure: Urban (% of segment)
BOP3000	0.1	0.5	88.9	444.7	1.9	88.9
BOP2500	0.3	1.2	90.5	876.7	3.8	90.6
BOP2000	0.7	3.1	76.5	1,707.4	7.4	76.8
BOP1500	2.7	11.4	66.9	4,419.8	19.1	67.1
BOP1000	11.6	48.7	32.6	10,891.6	47.0	33.6
BOP500	8.2	34.5	25.6	4,043.1	17.5	25.1
BOP total	23.7	99.5	36.5	22,383.4	96.7	45.3

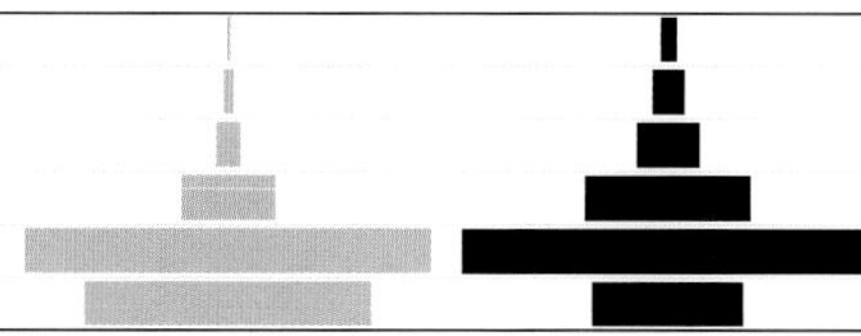

Population **Expenditure**

BOP expenditure by sector

$ (**Boldface** numbers are millions)	Total BOP	BOP 500	BOP 1000	BOP 1500	BOP 2000	BOP 2500	BOP 3000	Urban / rural (% of BOP)
Food	**17,432.6**	**3,553.2**	**9,042.2**	**3,161.6**	**1,030.4**	**438.9**	**206.4**	42/58
Per capita	736	433	779	1167	1387	1508	1722	
Per household	3744	2683	3972	4545	4584	4658	5141	
Housing	**188.0**	**28.7**	**68.4**	**47.3**	**23.5**	**10.1**	**10.0**	59/41
Per capita	8	3	6	17	32	35	83	
Per household	40	22	30	68	104	107	248	
Water	**21.4**	**2.3**	**8.0**	**6.9**	**2.8**	**1.1**	**0.3**	89/11
Per capita	1	0	1	3	4	4	2	
Per household	5	2	4	10	12	12	7	
Energy	**184.4**	**26.3**	**76.0**	**50.0**	**19.1**	**9.3**	**3.7**	66/34
Per capita	8	3	7	18	26	32	31	
Per household	40	20	33	72	85	98	92	
Household goods	**2,287.5**	**220.4**	**851.3**	**568.7**	**309.7**	**214.4**	**123.0**	45/55
Per capita	97	27	73	210	417	737	1026	
Per household	491	166	374	817	1378	2276	3063	
Health	n.a.	n.a.	n.a.	n.a.	n.a.	n.a.	n.a.	n.a.
Per capita								
Per household								
Transportation	**0.5**	**0.0**	**0.1**	**0.3**	**0.1**	**0.0**	**0.0**	100/0
Per capita	0	0	0	0	0	0	0	
Per household	0	0	0	0	0	0	0	
ICT	**35.6**	**2.8**	**6.0**	**6.4**	**8.3**	**10.0**	**2.1**	59/41
Per capita	2	0	1	2	11	34	18	
Per household	8	2	3	9	37	106	53	
Education	**32.6**	**3.4**	**11.8**	**11.7**	**3.3**	**1.6**	**0.8**	86/14
Per capita	1	0	1	4	4	5	7	
Per household	7	3	5	17	15	17	21	
Other	**2,200.7**	**205.8**	**827.8**	**567.1**	**310.3**	**191.3**	**98.5**	64/36
Per capita	93	25	71	209	418	657	822	
Per household	473	155	364	815	1380	2030	2453	
Total	**22,383.4**	**4,043.1**	**10,891.6**	**4,419.8**	**1,707.4**	**876.7**	**444.7**	45/55

Note: All dollar amounts in 2005 PPP

Household expenditure by sector

	National ($ millions)	BOP (%)
Food	17,667.8	98.7
Housing	205.1	91.6
Water	21.8	98.1
Energy	193.7	95.2
Household goods	2,623.6	87.2
Health	n.a.	n.a.
Transportation	0.6	91.7
ICT	57.0	62.5
Education	33.2	98.3
Other	2,348.1	93.7
Total	23,150.9	96.7

Sector shares of household expenditure
(%)

	National	BOP
Food	76.3	77.9
Housing	0.9	0.8
Water	0.1	0.1
Energy	0.8	0.8
Household goods	11.3	10.2
Health	n.a.	n.a.
Transportation	0.0	0.0
ICT	0.2	0.2
Education	0.1	0.1
Other	10.1	9.8
Total	100.0	100.0

THE INTERNATIONAL FINANCE CORPORATION, the private sector arm of the World Bank Group, promotes open and competitive markets in developing countries. IFC supports sustainable private sector companies and other partners in generating productive jobs and delivering basic services, so that people have opportunities to escape poverty and improve their lives. Through FY06, IFC Financial Products has committed more than $56 billion in funding for private sector investments and mobilized an additional $25 billion in syndications for 3,531 companies in 140 developing countries. IFC Advisory Services and donor partners have provided more than $1 billion in program support to build small enterprises, to accelerate private participation in infrastructure, to improve the business enabling environment, to increase access to finance, and to strengthen environmental and social sustainability. For more information, please visit www.ifc.org.

THE WORLD RESOURCES INSTITUTE is an environmental and international development think tank that goes beyond research to create practical ways to protect the Earth and improve people's lives.

WRI is the first environmental organization to engage the business sector in a new way of thinking about poverty alleviation. Our work is influencing the way business leaders think about markets, profit, poverty and the environment.

Development Through Enterprise (DTE) is a project within WRI's broader Enterprise and Innovation objective. Other projects within this objective include New Ventures (www.new-ventures.org), which supports sustainable enterprises by accelerating the transfer of capital to outstanding companies that deliver social and environmental benefits.

The Next 4 Billion, a part of the Tomorrow's Markets series, is a publication authored by the DTE team at WRI. DTE catalyzes sustainable economic growth by identifying market opportunities and business models that meet the needs of underserved communities in emerging economies. Through direct engagements with corporations, aid agencies, business schools, and other partners, DTE transforms its intellectual capital into on-the-ground initiatives.

Find more information and opportunities to engage in discussion about DTE's subject expertise at http://www.NextBillion.net.

Ordering publications

Hopkins Fulfillment Service
P.O. Box 50370
Baltimore, MD 21211-4370
Phone: (410) 516-6956 or (1-800) 537-5487
Fax: (410) 516-6998
Email: hfscustserv@press.jhu.edu

Visit WRI's online bookstore: www.wristore.com

Eurospan Group, c/o Turpin Distribution
Phone: +44 (0) 1767 604972
Fax: +44 (0)1767 601640
Email: eurospan@turpin-distribution.com

Visit Eurospan's online bookstore: www.eurospangroup.com/bookstore

To view the report online, visit www.wri.org/thenext4billion.